Aquinas and Empowerment

MORAL TRADITIONS & MORAL ARGUMENTS
A SERIES EDITED BY JAMES F. KEENAN, S.J.

The Evolution of Altruism and the Ordering of Love
  STEPHEN J. POPE

Love, Human and Divine: The Heart of Christian Ethics
  EDWARD COLLINS VACEK, S.J.

Bridging the Sacred and the Secular:
Selected Writings of John Courtney Murray, S.J.
  J. LEON HOOPER, S.J., editor

The Context of Casuistry
  Edited by
  JAMES F. KEENAN, S.J. and THOMAS A. SHANNON

Aquinas and Empowerment: Classical Ethics for Ordinary Lives

EDITED BY
G. SIMON HARAK, S.J.

GEORGETOWN UNIVERSITY PRESS / WASHINGTON, D.C.

Georgetown University Press, Washington, D.C.
© 1996 by Georgetown University Press. All rights reserved.
Printed in the United States of America

10   9   8   7   6   5   4   3   2   1   1996

THIS VOLUME IS PRINTED ON ACID-FREE OFFSET BOOK PAPER

Library of Congress Cataloging-in-Publication Data

Aquinas and empowerment : classical ethics for ordinary lives / G.
  Simon Harak, editor.
     p.   cm.
  Includes bibliographical references and and index.
    1. Ethics.   2. Ethics, Modern—20th century.   3. Thomas, Aquinas,
Saint, 1225?–1274—Ethics.   4. Thomas, Aquinas, Saint, 1225?–1274—
Influence.   I. Harak, G. Simon, 1948–
BJ1031.A73   1996
170—dc20
  ISBN: 978-0-87840-614-2   95-42743

*To all from whom we have learned.
And, of course, to the One Teacher.*

Contents

Introduction   ix

JUDITH W. KAY
Getting Egypt out of the People: Aquinas's Contributions to Liberation   1

DIANA FRITZ CATES
Taking Women's Experience Seriously: Thomas Aquinas and Audre Lorde on Anger   47

G. SIMON HARAK, S. J.
Child Abuse and Embodiment from a Thomistic Perspective   89

PAUL J. WADELL, C.P.
Growing Together in the Divine Love: The Role of Charity in the Moral Theology of Thomas Aquinas   134

ROMANUS CESSARIO, O.P.
Epieikeia *and the Accomplishment of the Just*   170

Index   207

Introduction

This book draws together essays by scholars who are struggling to address specific areas of need in our modern world and who have found themselves relying on Thomas Aquinas to help them in their efforts. Judith Kay first approached me with the idea for such a volume two years ago. She observed that many "new scholars" were using Thomas Aquinas as a primary resource for structuring their ethical reflections. What if we offered those new scholars an opportunity to grapple with specific issues in current ethical discourse? And what if we asked them to make their reliance on Thomas explicit? The result would be a unique perspective on these current issues, together with a deeper appreciation, and perhaps even a clarification, of the writings of Thomas.

I believe we have been faithful to Dr. Kay's academic vision in *Aquinas and Empowerment: Classical Ethics for Ordinary Lives*. We take the term "ordinary lives" from Charles Taylor, whose work remarks on "the continuation in modern culture of a trend that is now centuries old and places the centre of gravity not in some higher sphere but in what I want to call 'ordinary life,' that is, the life of production and the family, of work and love."[1] It is to that specific, ordinary dimension of modern life that we address our Thomistic ethics.

The book begins with Dr. Kay's essay, "Getting Egypt out of the People: Aquinas's Contributions to Liberation." In that essay, Kay brings together several important notions in Taylor's philosophy. Taylor observes that although our modern identities are supposed to be "inwardly generated," the nature of our ordinary lives requires that "I negotiate [my identity] through dialogue, partly overt, partly internalized, with others."[2] Taylor is also aware of "how identity can be formed or malformed in our contact with significant others."[3] In her essay, Kay examines that inward deformation of our identities through exchange with significant others. Specifically, she sees Thomas as providing a framework for understanding the phenomenon of internalized oppression, classically expressed in Paulo Freire's *Pedagogy of the Oppressed*. Thomas teaches that anger arises from unmerited slights to our excellences. By focusing on the ordinary lives of white working-class men, Kay suggests that those unmerited slights are offenses to our very nature, and therefore hurtful regardless of whether or not they are socially constructed as slights. Kay examines the habits of internalized oppression under the rubric of *vice* and suggests that we add *oppression* to the Thomistic list of ways that vices are involuntarily acquired. And she uses Thomas's distinction between nature and the "second nature" of virtues and vices to show that, no matter how profound the inflicted violations, oppressed people "can never become their internalized oppression essentially." Internalized oppression, as acquired habit or habits, can therefore be dismantled. She finds echoes of that Thomistic position, for example, in the work of Katie Cannon, who praises as a virtue the African American woman's refusal "to become inwardly brutalized," and in the resistance of African American womanists to being treated as inherent victims, as though internalized oppression exhaustively defines the character of the oppressed. Kay closes her essay by presenting ways in which Thomistic thinking critiques and reconstructs our understanding and treatment of the oppressed as well as of the oppressors. Kay employs Thomistic categories to show us the uses of appeals to nature in liberation ethics and to expose the oppressive dynamics of ascribing to inherent nature what are in fact culturally imposed habits. Her work reminds us that dismantling internalized oppression is a moral practice in its own right, showing that this dialogue between Thomas and the liberationists can be both provocative and fruitful.

The essay by Diana Fritz Cates that follows Kay's describes one way in which "Egypt" is in the oppressed, namely in certain ways of feeling anger. Taylor remarks that "On a social plane, we have a continuing politics of equal recognition . . . On an intimate level, we can see how much an original identity needs and is vulnerable to the recognition given or withheld by others."[4] In her "Taking Women's Experience Seriously: Thomas Aquinas and Audre Lorde on Anger," Cates boldly invites us to use Thomas's analysis of anger to "shed light on certain aspects of Audre Lorde's moral experience" of anger. Cates carefully and thoroughly reconstructs Thomas's rich account of the passion of anger, paying particular attention to the complexity of its physical and intellectual dimensions, its combination of sorrow and hopefulness. In her discussion of Thomas's *causes* for anger (a slight to our excellences), however, she reveals how socially constructed Thomas's account of anger is—how identified those excellences are with the economic, political, and social privileges of a member of a broader social hierarchy. When Cates introduces Audre Lorde into the dialogue, she shows that it is precisely those assumed privileges, with their implied right to dominance, that cause Lorde's anger in the first place. In Lorde, Thomas's "'unmerited slight' takes the form of the racist and sexist presumption that white men—and women—have the right to dominate black women's minds and bodies by depriving them, ignoring them, stereotyping and ridiculing them, loathing them, and silencing them through thoughtlessness, intimidation, and violence." Cates uses Thomas's analysis to describe Lorde's causes for anger. On the one hand, much of that anger reflects the internalization of a racist and sexist "social yardstick" against which the oppressed could never measure up. To use Kay's image, Egypt continues surreptitiously to enslave "the People" by controlling the way in which they think and feel about themselves and their value. On the other hand, much of the anger of the oppressed reflects a powerful resistance to this distorted measure. In examining the second, Cates presents us with an anger that empowers victims to challenge and subvert any system that abuses, violates, and in so many ways degrades others and their unique experience and perspective on life. And again, the Thomistic goal of such anger is to establish "perhaps for the first time, a relationship that is truly respectful of human equality in difference." This essay is an insightful, liberating, and even exhilarating study of the anger of marginalized people.

We follow with my discussion of "Child Abuse and Embodiment from a Thomistic Perspective." Taylor observes that recognition, so crucial to the formation of identity, was formerly "inbuilt" through established social roles. Now, however, recognition is "won through exchange, and it can fail."[5] My essay considers a specific type of failure: child abuse. I continue the themes from the previous two essays by showing how forms of oppression can be inscribed into our very bodies. My research has led me to a great appreciation of the importance of the body (we might say, of the incarnation) in Thomas's ethical thinking. I believe that Thomas's hylomorphic anthropology helps us understand how physical abuse can create or alter noncorporeal states, such as dispositions, intentions, and choice, and that, in turn, allows us to grasp more fully the terrible impact of child abuse on the whole person—that it "deforms the soul as it disfigures the body." The chapter begins with current empirical research on the effects of child abuse and uses literature to indicate the profound emotional impact of this practice. It then adduces the writings of Thomas, and especially his *Treatise on the Passions*, to give a theological construct to these physical and emotional wounds. Finally, it uses Thomistic theology to suggest a path toward healing of the survivor's suffering by the remaking of her embodied habits. I believe that Thomas would present to those suffering from abuse an empowerment that is therapeutically sound and that leads toward the most liberating and joyful of healings: reconciliation.

Paul Wadell's essay then discusses the locus for that liberation and empowerment. Picking up on Taylor's observation that "this culture puts a great emphasis on relationships in the intimate sphere, especially love relationships,"[6] Wadell's "Growing Together in the Divine Love: The Role of Charity in the Moral Theology of Thomas Aquinas" teaches us that the proper moral fashioning (and refashioning) of our thoughts, passions, and bodies can only occur in the context of friendship "first with God and then with all those loved by God." Continuing this volume's perhaps surprising use of Thomas to undergird countercultural claims, Wadell alerts us to dynamisms in our culture that trivialize friendship and notes that misunderstandings of friendship's crucial role in the moral life extend even to Christian attitudes toward friendship. He challenges modern society's consumerism, where "friends are just another commodity to pick up or dispose of as we see fit . . . ," its "understanding of the self which sees us not as social and relational beings, but as essentially solitary and autonomous," and its understanding that the self gains identity by *dominium*, or dominance over others. In such a view, the truth of the self would be discovered only through a kind of private introspection, and the other is seen as an intrusion upon the self—at best superfluous, and at worst as one whose domination is the price necessary for establishment of the self. "No wonder," he observes with a poetic clarity we have come to expect from Wadell's ethical reflections, "so many people live shoulder-to-shoulder, but their lives hardly touch." For contrast, Wadell turns to the Aristotelian notion of friendship, the ground of Thomas's own reflections. There he discovers "intensity, commitment, availability, and permanence." He then accurately indicates how Thomas goes beyond Aristotle, inviting us to *charity*: a friendship with God that "explodes the boundaries Aristotle put on what the best of friendship might be." The essay comes full circle as he discusses the shared life that friendship with God in Christ entails and the kind of sacramental faith community the Church must be to encourage and even to embody that saving friendship. He teaches us that the life of charity, of friendship with God, means "a summons to cross over to a new kind of life," one that entails "a metamorphosis so complete that those who enter charity go from being sinners to saints." Wadell's chapter is methodology realized: it encourages and fosters for the reader the very friendship of which it speaks.

In his current bestseller, Philip K. Howard argues that the multiplicity of laws is suffocating our ordinary lives. "Today," he laments, "we have lost our joy, and much more, because modern law tells us our duty is only to comply, not to accomplish. Understanding of the situation has been replaced by legal absolutism."[7] Worse, with so much stress on proper procedure,

> Compassion is nonexistent, because compassion is basically unlawful. Why should one person get special help? Who is to decide? The specter of favoritism drives the social reformer back to the volume of rules. All must be the same. Rights, as Professor Joel Handler has noted, only get in the way of a "cooperative, continuing relationship . . . The situation calls for a community. . . . Instead of sensitive, individualized exploration of needs, nonfinancial as well, there is mindless application of harsh rules, people treated as objects, and a proletarianized staff.[8]

Romanus Cessario responds to this modern difficulty that increasingly encroaches upon our ordinary lives in his "*Epieikeia* and the Accomplishment of the Just." Of course, Cessario goes far beyond mere legal-procedural concerns to provide a vision of how a healed and rightly ordered ethical person responds to the obligations and claims of the moral life. Cessario notes with concern the evanescence of the concept of *epieikeia*—a notion until recently considered crucial in Christian moral reasoning, where it denoted "a benign and equitable interpretation not of the law itself, but of the mind of the lawgiver." He undertakes to redress this deficiency by carefully tracing the development of the concept through Aristotle, Albertus Magnus, and finally Thomas. With the exceptional breadth of his scholarship, Cessario shows us how each thinker synthesized and furthered the received reflection on *epieikeia*. In his remarkable in-depth study of Thomas, however, Cessario presents *epieikeia* clearly as a *virtue*, which "operates on the basis of clear and certain practical conviction of the truly *(simpliciter)* just in a given case." This "truly just" is the innate sense of the common good, which the person with *epieikeia* "lives and breathes." Cessario's account is even more attractive because he insists, with Thomas, that such a sense comes from a knowledge not of the law, but of the law*giver*. That allows him to present *epieikeia* as a supremely Christian virtue, since it "displays a special filial attitude toward God . . . one that manifests itself in a heightened reverence for accomplishing the Father's plan of salvation." In Cessario's recounting of Thomas's virtue of *epieikeia*, we hear the echo of Paul's description of life in the Spirit: "we have the mind of Christ." Cessario's scholarly essay provides our volume with a satisfyingly robust academic conclusion and provides us with a hopeful and practical future for our ordinary lives.

We believe, then, that Thomas has much to offer our current ethical discussions. As we bring Thomas's teleology to these modern questions, we hope to respond to Taylor's observation that the "eclipse of ends" has led to a "narrowing and flattening of our lives," to a "loss of resonance, depth, richness."[9] And Taylor suggests that, even though we now may no longer subscribe to Thomas's Chain of Being, "We may still need to see ourselves as part of a larger order that can make claims on us"[10] to make sense of our lives.

I believe also, however, that these new voices will give to the community of ethicists not only a new perspective on current ethical discourse, but a new view of Thomas as well. Kay's contribution shows how Thomas can give us a theological "purchase point" from which to evict internalized oppression, and as she does, she presents us with a Thomas whose concern is for liberation. Cates's chapter uses Thomas's analysis of anger to understand Lorde's anger. But then she draws Thomas beyond himself, as it were, into a more revolutionary posture—a position in which (because of his appropriation of the suspect Aristotle) I do not think he would find himself uncomfortable. My essay finds in Thomas a theological structure for understanding and healing child abuse, but it also reveals a Thomas who is truly sensitive to the terrible pain of victims of abuse. Wadell's work shows how Thomas challenges the modern self's isolation and its sterile, even destructive relationships, and so presents us with a Thomas whom we would very much like to befriend. Cessario's observation of the disappearance of *epieikeia* in modern ethical discourse compels him to return to Thomas's account of this virtue, and leads us to appreciate a Thomas whose love of justice was rooted in his friendship with Christ and filial devotion to God. Each time our authors place Thomas's theology in dialogue with a different aspect of modern suffering, they reveal an ethical theory that is deeply concerned with relationship and embodiment. Those aspects of Thomistic theology are often overlooked, and their rediscovery here will, we believe, present Thomas as an even richer resource in our common struggle for justice.

In the end we find that as Thomas suggests fruitful ways of considering modern ethical questions, so the modern discussion suggests fresh insights into Thomas's own character and work. This mutual transformation is not so unusual. I think Thomas himself would say that the best exchange between friends leads them to transcend themselves and so, paradoxically, to become more authentically who they are. I hope this volume invites all its readers to that same exchange, transcendence, and authenticity.

NOTES

My thanks to Diana Fritz Cates who helped so much with this Introduction.

1. Charles Taylor, *The Ethics of Authenticity* (Cambridge, Mass.: Harvard University Press, 1992), p. 45.
2. Taylor, *Ethics of Authenticity*, p. 47.
3. Taylor, *Ethics of Authenticity*, p. 49.
4. Taylor, *Ethics of Authenticity*, p. 49.
5. Taylor, *Ethics of Authenticity*, p. 48.
6. Taylor, *Ethics of Authenticity*, p. 45.
7. Philip K. Howard, *The Death of Common Sense: How Law is Suffocating America* (New York: Random House, 1995), p. 174.
8. Howard, *Death of Common Sense*, p. 147.
9. Taylor, *Ethics of Authenticity*, p. 10.
10. Taylor, *Ethics of Authenticity*, p. 89.

Getting Egypt out of the People: Aquinas's Contributions to Liberation

JUDITH W. KAY

INTRODUCTION.

"We got the people out of Egypt," my minister exclaimed to me not long ago, summarizing an engrossing afternoon conversation about African American liberation struggles. "But," he inquired, "how do we get Egypt out of the people?" If the Israelite Exodus from slavery remains a paradigmatic vision of liberation for some Christians, then the Israelites' subsequent divisiveness and longing for the fleshpots of Egypt remains a cautionary tale. Former slaves may carry the vices of their masters into the promised land. How should we understand that people carry the habits of Egypt within them long after having left Egypt?[1]

In spite of the fact that Thomas does not explicitly address the problem of internalized oppression, I believe that he offers a framework for understanding this phenomenon. By internalized oppression I mean the behavioral and affective habits acquired from oppressive mistreatment in which oppressed peoples incorporate and accept the perspective of the oppressor toward themselves and their group.[2] I propose to show how Thomas's analysis of habit can yield the view that internalized oppression consists of one or more habits acquired in response to oppressive mistreatment. His recognition that some habits are "contrary to nature" can provide us with the normative judgment that internalized oppression is "contrary to nature" and the insight that people can never become their internalized oppression essentially. His distinction between nature and second nature can help explain both collusion and rebellion on the part of the oppressed. Furthermore, this distinction can provide the theoretical basis for distinguishing fully human functioning from the distorted habits of internalized oppression. Thomas's theological framework can remind us that it is possible for the oppressed to rid themselves of internalized oppression in contradistinction to some perspectives that posit internalized oppression as a permanent feature of the psyche. Thomas recognizes the depth of affective allegiance to habits, which requires an analysis of the role of passions in the moral life. And his framework suggests that the elimination of internalized oppression is an urgent moral task, a demanding moral practice of acquiring virtues and abandoning destructive habits.

By studying only the internal aspects of oppression, I do not deny the necessity of combating external causes of oppression. I also cannot explore in this essay the nature of the habits that oppressors acquire. Furthermore, I wish neither to lay the responsibility for liberation entirely at the feet of the oppressed nor to blame the oppressed for having acquired habits of internalized oppression.

Although the label *internalized oppression* is somewhat new (and other labels exist, such as *horizontal violence*[3]), the phenomenon is as old as oppression itself. It is helpful to remember that some of the psychological and moral difficulties that Thomas observed in ordinary life were due to internalized oppression. He was grappling with similar phenomena that liberationists grapple with today. Although many aspects of medieval thought have been soundly criticized by feminists and others,[4] Aquinas's careful thinking on the passions,[5] virtue and vice,[6] and natural law[7] provides useful insights that can help us look at internalized oppression freshly.

Internalized oppression and strategies for eliminating it have been conceptualized differently by liberal and radical feminists,[8] Marxists, Freudians, and poststructuralists. This essay does not undertake a review and critique of these efforts, yet some appreciation of them is important in order to evaluate the strengths and weaknesses of the perspective I will derive from Aquinas. I briefly highlight their major differences from the perspective to be developed here.

Liberal feminists have discussed internalized sexism in terms of socialization into sex-roles and have placed their hopes for change in education and the pursuit of civil liberties.[9] The perspective to be presented here, in contrast, emphasizes the depth of our emotional allegiance to habits, rendering their dissolution more complicated and demanding than simply being exposed to new information. Nor does the attainment of civil liberties inevitably empower the formerly disenfranchised to free themselves from their internalized oppression. Barrington Moore describes the Untouchables of India who have been emancipated *de jure*, but who remain untouchable not only *de facto* but also in their own self-understanding. They live, in the words of a high Untouchable politician, in "psychological cages."[10] Internalized oppression persists because the effects of oppressive mistreatment are much more far-reaching than the inequalities emphasized by political liberalism. Its pernicious patterns penetrate into the person herself, leaving her with habits of being that become obstacles to her efforts to utilize newfound equalities to the fullest.

Radical feminists have emphasized the differences between women's and men's inherent natures.[11] They argue that women acquire "false" selves as a result of living under patriarchy. Women's "true female nature," once freed from patriarchy, should blossom forth with relatively little effort.[12] Presumably men have a different (bestial) nature and are not susceptible to the acquisition of false selves. In contrast, the framework to be developed here speaks to the common humanity of all people. Both sexes will be presumed to possess the *imago dei* and be inherently intelligent, social, inclined to the good, and motivated by love. This perspective will assume that both men and women can acquire habits that become like a second nature. This second nature distorts but does not obliterate basic humanity. This perspective will highlight the effort required to develop new habits and the need for a commitment to gain ever clearer perceptions of reality.

Marxists have tended to think of internalized oppression in terms of false consciousness. Some Marxists think that ending false consciousness will be an inevitable (and secondary) by-product of the elimination of fundamental economic exploitation. The expectation that changes in the economic relations of production would inevitably transform consciousness has not borne out, as recent events in Eastern Europe suggest. The perspective to be presented appreciates the persistence of habits and therefore suggests that the elimination of internalized oppression is a project in its own right. A person's character cannot be presumed to change automatically following political or economic change. This project of transforming our character cannot be neglected until after fundamental economic change, but is necessary to guide the liberation struggle itself.[13]

Other Marxists suggest that since we can create our own nature through our own activity, humans have no given nature except this malleability.[14] Unfortunately, by making illicit all substantive claims about human nature, these Marxists make it hard to argue that certain lines of development are dehumanizing or undesirable. In contrast, the perspective to be provided makes claims about humans' inherent nature. These claims empower us to identify our false consciousness and suggest in which directions we might develop ourselves.

Freudians discuss internalized oppression as fixed character structures to which the individual adapts.[15] In contrast, this essay suggests that internalized oppression can never be entirely agreed to by its host. On some level of being, the individual's ontological attraction to the good persists against destructive habits. Rather than adaptation, this model will maintain eradication of internalized oppression as a possibility and a hope.

Poststructuralists recommend abandoning the belief that humans have a nature in favor of the view that the self is socially constructed through contending discourses. In oppressive societies we are inevitably fragmented and "multi-voiced."[16] Internalized oppression presumably is one of these "voices." Poststructuralists welcome the divided self because this provides a range of discourses and voices from which to choose. Unfortunately, by rejecting all claims about human nature, they are unable to establish any normative basis for choosing one voice over another. The perspective to be offered provides some tentative guidelines for distinguishing the internalized voices of oppression from more human sounding voices.

Let us turn now to an examination of Thomas for insights that shed light on the divided subjectivity of the oppressed. First I highlight selected aspects of Thomas's understanding of habit and virtue. Next I present Thomas's model of a qualitatively different type of habit—vice. I then use these insights to illustrate certain features of the internalized oppression of white working-class men. I then return to Thomas to examine what he means when he says that habits become like a second nature to us. In conclusion, I summarize some implications of Thomas's perspective for liberation.

HABIT

Habits are sustained ways of being moved, thinking, and acting, which through repeated experience, choice,[17] and action have become second nature to us.[18] Moral habits are qualities of character that dispose us well or badly to our end, the flourishing of our nature. A virtue is a good habit, a "characteristic condition relevant to a thing's nature"; vices are bad habits contrary to inherent nature.[19]

For Thomas, of course, the flourishing of our nature does not mean satisfaction of our desires as narrowly understood in a capitalist culture. Too often people are misled into believing that satisfaction of any want will lead to fulfillment. Thomas, in contrast, believes that there are truly human desires, and these must be distinguished from acquired tastes. More accurately, Thomas speaks of truly human attractions; humans are so constituted as to be naturally attracted to the good-for-humans, the ultimate good being enjoyment of God. Habits are thus fundamentally relational—they reflect how well or poorly we relate to the good (ultimately to God) for which we have ontological wellsprings of desire.[20]

According to Aquinas humans possess at the time of birth a specific human set of potentialities. Young ones are born with certain powers (if they are born undamaged[21]) such as the capacities to improve reasoning, make appropriate choices, and be moved by appropriate objects. Children are inherently motivated to unfold and develop these capacities, ultimately because they are moved by their final end to return to God and enjoy communion with God. Young people do not need to be coerced or positively reinforced into engaging intelligently with their environment. Learning about their environment and improving the effectiveness of their interactions is something they do with zest and ease if not mistreated, physically damaged, or otherwise hindered.[22] Responsive engagement with the true goods that attract them "actuates" their potentialities. Moral and intellectual habits can be developed relatively easily by young people who are raised in communities that have adequately reflected on what is conducive to human well-being and have institutionalized virtuous relations.

Any aspect of human behavior and functioning having a range of possible expressions can come under the guidance of habits.[23] In the Thomistic understanding, our nature would remain unperfected, our potentialities unrealized, without habits. In fact, Thomas shares with Aristotle the belief that it is characteristic of human nature to receive habits.[24] By acquiring habits, our intellectual, volitional, and affective powers can be developed fully. Habits give directionality to our inherent capacities since they may be realized and exercised in different ways in various cultures.[25]

As we mature and come into adulthood we can improve our capacity to reflect upon our habits and the quality of our relationship to various goods. Increasingly we can choose the habits from which we would like to act. We can also intentionally resist acting on the basis of undesirable habits. As Thomas reminds us even our will must be perfected by virtue.[26] We may will to act on a habit or act contrary to it, since habits are not determining, but guiding. We still have freedom to choose to act within the habit or outside it.[27] This is true of virtues as well as vices.

To understand the important Thomistic notion of habit more clearly, we might contrast it with modern ideas of habit. The meaning of habit in modern times has become quite narrow compared to its meaning in Aquinas. *Webster's* dictionary informs us that "habit implies a doing unconsciously or without premeditation, often compulsively."[28] *Webster's* also gives "addictions" as a synonym for habit. Such habits might range from the trivial (biting the nails or tapping the fingers) to the serious (drug addiction or sexual compulsion). In a therapeutic culture, addictions have eclipsed habits in the psychological lexicon. Whether trivial or serious, addictive habits imply automatic, rigid activities needing to be stopped. Some positive notion of habits does remain, but this generally refers to customary activities rather than qualities of character. We wish that we had the good habit of rising early and exercising before our workday or that we were in the habit of answering our correspondence promptly. And we speak of losing habits again as customary activities rather than as qualities of being. We no longer call our parents every Sunday or write in our journal each night before retiring.

Aquinas's perspective differs in four major ways from current usage. First, Thomas affirms habits as relational qualities of character, rather than simply activities. Second, the current focus on habit as addiction implies a lack of freedom to act outside, or contrary to, the habit. In contrast, Aquinas maintains that the individual remains completely free to act contrary to either a virtue or a vice (difficult as the latter may be). Third, the current focus on addiction implies powerlessness to act differently. In contrast, Aquinas assumes that even the most depraved retain their natural inclination to the good and the inherent power to act on this inclination,[29] although understandably this may be quite difficult in practice. Fourth, the current reduction of habits to addictions does not capture Aquinas's use of habit to include a large category of positive and desirable habits, the virtues. The positive notion of habit, these virtues, are so important to Thomas's understanding of the moral life, and so different from our current negative and reductionist ideas of habit, that they deserve a separate treatment here.

WHAT KIND OF HABITS ARE MORAL VIRTUES?

There are different types of habits of which moral virtues are a special type. For the purpose of this essay I will highlight only five characteristics of virtuous habits. I have chosen these five characteristics because they are essential to any virtue. Furthermore, they illustrate how Aquinas's model differs from contemporary accounts of habit and from the accounts of internalized oppression briefly described in the introduction.

Moral virtues are a type of habit that (1) affords a clear perception of reality; (2) enables effective engagements with the environment; (3) incorporates voluntarily chosen and sustained commitment; (4) permits flexible thought and action within the operation of the virtue while preserving freedom of choice to act viciously; and (5) embodies appropriate passion. These desirable habits differ in kind from vices, which are deprived of these characteristics.

Clear Perception of Reality.

Virtuous habits are distinctive because they perfect the moral agent's capacity to perceive reality clearly. Prudence is the specific virtue that perfects the capacity for clear perception since it includes both clear apprehension of the goods-for-humans and "right reasoning about what is to be done."[30] Since being virtuous is meant to result in effective engagement with the world and effective engagement requires accurate perception, all four moral virtues require the ability to see reality clearly. As Aquinas says, the moral virtues, by necessity, involve prudence.

What is meant by having a clear perception of reality? From the largest perspective, Thomas answered this question by writing the entire *Summa theologiae*. A clear perception of reality means understanding humans' emanation from God and our inherent desire to return to God. As creatures having emanated from God, our final end is the enjoyment of God. God, as it were, is always calling or attracting us to God's self, with whom it is our nature to have a free relationship.

A clear perception of reality also includes understanding our nature as humans. According to Thomas, what is true about humans is that our common humanity results from being created in the image of God and the consequences of our having fallen away from God. Although our natural attraction to the good is disordered by the fall, it is not thereby destroyed. Humans remain teleologically inclined toward certain things that practical reason affirms as good-for-humans. Thomas sketches these natural inclinations that function as wellsprings of desire for the good-for-humans. They include such things as aware touch, love, reproduction and care of the young, learning, cooperative living, and enjoyment of God. Their contraries we find naturally repugnant.

Practical reason, in recognizing these teleological inclinations, apprehends what is good for us. Thomas argues that our natural inclinations point toward goods that are simultaneously affirmed as good by practical reason. The natural inclination to learn, for example, points to the basic good of knowledge. The primary precepts of the natural law consist of those basic human goods toward which we are teleologically attracted and which practical reason has judged as indeed good-for-us.[31] Although to some extent we can recognize the good with the help of a natural habit Thomas called *synderesis*,[32] discernment of natural law is aided by instruction and experience.

A characteristic of virtuous habits is that they help us discern what is good for us in our daily lives. Charity, for example, helps us see how the common good is conducive to our individual good.[33] Prudence, for example, helps us sort through the multiplicity of confusing choices, helping us reach "the common end of the whole of human life," the good proper to humans. "Prudence is good deliberation about matters pertaining to the whole of human life and the ultimate end of human life."[34]

What else is true for humans that is essential for a clear perception of reality? The realization that everyone is susceptible to the acquisition of bad habits. Because we have inclinations perfectible by virtue, we can fail. We can fail to develop in accord with our nature. Another aspect of our common humanity is our vulnerability to acquiring bad habits. Thus as humans we live with the tension of being both completely capable yet hindered. Our natural inclinations and the goods toward which they point are true of all humans now (we already have the capacity to be moved by these goods). Yet they simultaneously remain as elusive goals (we have not yet completed our participation in these goods). When we look at a world distorted by oppressive relations, Thomas's perspective on reality reminds us that everyone remains capable of virtue yet everyone falls short. No one is immune to the distortions imposed by oppressive relations.

If we acquire the virtuous habits that help us remember these truths about humans, then we should not become confused by the selfish, competitive, or abusive behavior of ourselves or others. Only a false perception of reality would lead us to conclude that these vices are the inherent characteristics of humans. A clear perception of reality includes seeing the extent to which humans act inhumanely while remembering the inherently good nature of these same humans. No one is inherently victim or oppressor.

Another aspect of seeing reality clearly is having an accurate perception of a specific situation. For this we need the allied virtues of prudence—memory of the past, insight into the present, and shrewdness about future consequences.[35] Past experience forms a basis for responding well to the present in trying to secure a desirable future. The need for remembrance ought to be taken in a personal as well as a collective sense. If either individual or collective memory is suppressed or mystified (which I will explain later), the possibility of a virtuous engagement with the present is curtailed and goals for the future will be skewed. For example, one cannot be prudent if one fails to notice oppression and engage the whole situation. Or to put it positively, seeing reality clearly also involves understanding the dynamics of oppression and its effects on humans in the present. Lacking these allied virtues leads to wrong or incorrect concepts ("imagines distortae").[36]

This first characteristic of moral virtue—a clear perception of reality—highlights how deforming and mystifying internalized oppression is. Internalized oppression obscures from us an accurate picture of our universe, ourselves, and our true good. Nevertheless, our attraction to God (and other goods) can give us the power to emerge from oppressive relationships—even when we have deeply ingrained habits of internalized oppression. These acquired habits obscure but do not obliterate our natural directedness toward God. This relationship to our Final Good is ontologically prior to any oppressive relationship, and so has the power to overcome it.

I have shown that the first characteristic of moral virtue is the ability to see reality clearly. Yet right apprehension is not sufficient. Virtues are also oriented toward action. Prudence perfects practical reason and hence involves thinking undertaken with a view toward action. Since all human action is teleological, prudence enables a person to compare and contrast, choose and command for the sake of an end. Virtues should therefore help us interact with our environment effectively. A second characteristic of moral virtues is their improvement of our responsive engagement with the world.

Effective Engagements with the Environment.

Aquinas makes clear that there is no single right way to pursue the good. If we have a fairly accurate perception of the good (and the capacity to be moved by it, as I will show later), prudence helps set the relative ends and choice of means along the way. Although we are naturally inclined toward the good, there are multiple ways to perfect our abilities to perceive, deliberate, judge, and act in our pursuit of the good.[37] Thus an effective interaction always involves choice.

An effective interaction is fresh and tailor-made for the exact situation. Prudence is the habit with which humans are able to compare present situations to old, and through a process of comparison, notice what is new and different about the current situation and act appropriately ("collationem agitur"). Prudence requires knowledge of the universal principles of reason as well as accurate perception ("sub ratione veri") of the singulars of each situation ("ad infinita singularia").[38] Thus prudence helps humans discriminate between even very similar situations, by helping them notice subtle differences. An appropriate engagement with a situation means we cannot be sloppy or lazy by relying on previously worked-out solutions. Prudence can provide summary rules and generalizations from past experiences but these can only inform and do not determine the fitting response.[39] Fresh thinking, not rigid adherence to a set of rules, is the way of prudence. The classical virtue called *gnōmē*, for instance, is interpreted by Aquinas as the prudential judgment about when departure from common rules is warranted.[40]

An effective interaction also entails flexible thinking. A prudential interaction is qualitatively different from the conditioned responses identified by behaviorist psychology. In that view people rigidly respond the same way to situations that appear similar enough. Unlike conditioned humans, virtuous people flexibly choose how to act. Their learning from past experiences is not determining. Information about past choices and their results remain as accessible information, useful in the process of deliberation and discernment.[41] Virtues expand our choices; conditioned responses corrupt and limit them.

Effective engagements require acting on one's flexible thinking. This is not the same as acting on one's thoughts. Thomas calls the ability to generate a fitting engagement with the real situation before us (and not what it reminds us of) "right reason about things to be done." In colloquial English, we praise the person who "thinks" and lament the person who acts "thoughtlessly." These are morally laden judgments, for the person judged to be thinking is deemed to be thinking prudentially. Flexible thinking involves thinking freshly and appropriately about the situation at hand, the end sought, and how best to reach that end. Thinking in this moral sense is not just the presence of thoughts, because one's thoughts could be lacking prudence. That is, one's thoughts could be mere repetitions of conditioned responses, of previously worked-out solutions for similar situations. Or one's thoughts could be misinformation in the form of stereotypes or prejudices ("imagines distortae"). Acting thoughtlessly or without prudence is the failure to notice and discern a fitting interaction with the unique person in this unique situation. Parents act thoughtlessly when they treat their child as they did last week or last year, failing to notice how the child has changed. Colleagues act thoughtlessly when they fail to listen attentively to another colleague because they "know" what the other person is going to say. "Thinking" and "having thoughts" are not the same thing. Flexible thinking is needed to generate appropriate interactions.

Under conditions of oppression, prudent interactions with reality may look different from those under conditions of relative freedom and security. For example, Mingnon H. Anderson reminds us of the coercion and severely limited options endured by African American women. "For all of us who lived the misery of being made to be something other than what we were; for all of us now living who picked cotton and bore children unwanted and still find ourselves in strange fields and lying on cold beds, there are changes still due and coming."[42] Often the oppressed are faced with the narrow choice of submitting or enduring greater evils, possibly death. The decision to submit can be seen as a prudential affirmation of the good of life. To decide on the side of life, to will to continue living can be a powerful form of resistance. And if submission is chosen without internal agreement that such an outrage is ever right, then the engagement with reality has even more integrity.

Voluntarily Chosen and Sustained Commitment.

Alasdair MacIntyre astutely perceives Aquinas's dialectic between the discernment of the good and the acquisition of virtue. We make a commitment to what we think is the good based on an understanding of natural law. This commitment ideally is nurtured in communities in dialogue about the nature of the good, with counsel from trustworthy elders ("counsel of the wise"). In making and living out this commitment, we both acquire virtue and discover if indeed the good we have pursued is the true good of our being.[43] We cannot acquire the moral virtues by living in prolonged doubt about the nature of the good and the nature of reality—commitment and community are necessary. This sustained commitment in a just community molds our passions, thoughts, and deeds. Ideally our attitudes toward self and others are consistent with reality, that is what we can discern about humans' inherent nature and natural law. Virtuous commitments embrace goods appropriate to our nature.

Virtuous actions by definition proceed from commitments that are voluntarily sustained.[44] Aquinas discusses voluntariness under his definition of what constitutes a human act. Coercing someone to work for social justice does not engender a virtuous habit. The person often ends up hating the coercer as well as performing good deeds perfunctorily. Such actions would not be true human actions because they lacked voluntariness—they proceeded from an enforced commitment. Even more serious, such coerced commitments rest on an incorrect perception of reality, namely that people do not inherently seek the good and therefore have to be coerced into doing so. The reverse mistake would be to assume that since humans are inclined to the good, we do not need to make explicit our commitments, maintain expectations, or meet requirements. Vapid permissiveness is also based on faulty views of reality, namely that our nature determines us and our feelings automatically reflect our nature. In contrast, Thomas affirms that virtues perfect our nature and that virtues are also necessary to perfect our passions. Voluntary commitment to the good-for-humans is a necessary characteristic of a virtuous habit.

Voluntariness is crucial to emphasize in a discussion of the habits of the oppressed. Like the sea captain during a storm who faces a choice of dumping his valuable cargo or going down with his ship, many oppressed persons find their options limited by the "storm" of oppression.[45] Under conditions of oppression, some of the attitudes the oppressed adopt are similarly "chosen." The available set of options are themselves coercive, oppressive, and contrary to inherent inclinations and natural law. For instance, many slaves in the United States were forced to assume an attitude of subservience or be killed. In order to enhance their survival, some slaves may have decided to assume an air of inferiority. African American women who needed to shuffle, look diffident, and say "yes massah, yes massah" were exercising the virtue of prudence by sustaining life. This demeanor of subservience was not spontaneously desired, but was demanded by their situation and adopted for survival. In a situation of freedom no one would spontaneously adopt a stance so contrary to her inherent dignity.

Although imposed by oppression, this demeanor of subservience in Thomas's terms is quasi-voluntary.[46] *If* the women were appearing to conform without inwardly agreeing to this false view of their humanity, then the stooped shoulders could be discarded freely in the safety of their own homes. Katie Cannon suggests in *Black Womanist Ethics* that such internal freedom was possible because of the virtue of quiet grace—the strength to "refuse to become inwardly brutalized."[47] Other women might have been beaten into believing—through no fault of their own—that such a false view of their humanity was in fact true. Thereafter, they might believe in their own inferiority and seem unable to abandon the attitude of subservience, even in safe environments. Their allegiance to an oppressive view of themselves would be internalized and become habitual. (I discuss this distortion of commitment under internalized oppression.)

Flexibility within the Virtue and Freedom to Choose outside It.

Aquinas emphasizes that virtues, unlike dispositions, are hard to change, endure, and lack internal conflict.[48] The inveterateness of a virtue should not imply rigidity, for this would not reflect a prudential intelligence. As I indicated earlier, prudence is the key virtue that ensures that we maintain flexibility *within* the operation of any virtue, accuracy in our discernment, and effectiveness in our interactions. For instance, the virtue of courage does not require one predetermined action; at times the courageous thing may be to speak up, at others, to keep silent.

A person chooses to act on the basis of a virtue, since she is not bound to use it, it being subject to the will. Yet this choice, once habituated, becomes so ingrained as to recede from consciousness, and the choice disappears from awareness. Yet freedom of choice remains operative because Aquinas clearly indicates that people remain free to act on reasoning outside the virtue.[49] I say "reasoning" because the decision to act outside of a virtue would most likely be based on confused and pseudo-thinking of the kind found in conditioned responses or vices. For example, the courageous person is also free to act *outside* the habit of courage and to succumb to timidity and fearfulness. This explains why even a virtuous person can tell a lie or inflict harm. Virtues are not determining, but guiding. *Within* the virtue there is flexibility to fashion a creative interaction with the environment while freedom of choice also remains to act *outside* the virtue.

Appropriate Passion.

Following Aristotle, Aquinas says that passion should be appropriate in its object, intensity, duration, and purgation (catharsis).[50] "The man who is angry at the right things and with the right people, and, further, as he ought, when he ought, and as long as he ought, is praised."[51] Lack of passion (numbness), introspective brooding, or a failure to cry or rage may be ways in which the passions have yet to be integrated by the virtues. Overwhelming passion may impede sound judgment. Nevertheless he recommends catharsis as a way to reduce emotional distress, presumably restoring a person to sound judgment: "tears and groans are actions befitting a human who is in sorrow or pain" since "tears and groans naturally assuage sorrow."[52] Indeed G. Simon Harak has argued that passions are the ground of all virtues, since virtuous appetites enable us to be moved by true goods and repelled by true evils.[54]

Thomas' analysis of the appropriateness of passion is more complex than is typically presented because of his appreciation for our organic unity.[55] He does not separate passion from its bodily components. A passion has several integrated expressions: an internal movement or feeling (he felt frightened when his car skidded out of control); physical catharsis (nervous laughing, trembling, and sweating); and verbal expression ("I feel scared"). Virtues help a person decide which of these emotional expressions to reveal and to whom (while trembling he speaks clearly to the police, saving the full expression of his fears for a friend).

Virtuous habits allow us to be moved and to express verbally or physically our passion while thinking simultaneously. Thomas, not suffering from the Enlightenment's bifurcation of reason from emotion (and both from the body), sees no contradiction in the possibility of a person simultaneously trembling, thinking brilliantly, and acting boldly.

Evaluating a passions' appropriateness is a complex political and moral task. Aquinas unfortunately ignores the question of coercive power in this context. *Who* decides what emotional expressions are appropriate? Indeed most oppressed groups are thought by dominant groups to be inappropriately emotional. And some emotional stances (sullen withdrawal, compulsive cheerfulness) may represent strategies of resistance adopted for survival.[56] Rarely is the pain of subjugation seen as legitimate.

In summary, virtuous habits are consistent with our nature as embodied thinkers capable of being moved by the appropriate objects. The moral virtues broaden our choices, sharpen our discernment, and improve our interactions with the environment. Virtuous habits bear no resemblance to the unthinking automatisms described by *Webster's*.[57] For a consideration of the type of habits only remotely similar to the modern usage of habit, we turn to vice.

WHAT KIND OF HABITS ARE VICES?

Aquinas does not provide a separate treatise on vice other than questions 71-73 in the *prima secundae*. Instead, after his discussion of each primary virtue and its allied virtues in the *secunda secundae*, he proceeds to discuss each corresponding vice. This results in a lack of parallelism in his work. While he addresses the characteristics of virtuous habits, he does not give as much attention to vice's *characteristics* as a habit. Instead he focuses on sinful actions that are contrary to each virtue under discussion.

Thomas does make one significant contribution to the task of conceptualizing the type of habit that characterizes vice. This is his definition of vice in the *prima secundae* written in 1269, three years earlier than his treatise on prudence and its vices. Thomas defines vices as habits contrary to human nature and the essence of virtue. "While virtues incline us to that which aligns with nature, vices incline us away from those goods appropriate to our species-nature."[58]

Thomas never analyzes the kind of habit that would be contrary to human nature and the essence of virtue. Indeed, virtue and vice may not be contrary to each other at every point. I have carefully selected those five areas in which vicious habits must be contrary to the essence of virtue. I plan to show that vice is a *qualitatively* different *kind* of habit than virtue. Vices are not just the same kind of prudential, flexible, emotionally appropriate habits simply turned to a wrong end.[59] A vice is a type of habit that *by Thomas's definition* must (1) prevent a clear perception of reality; (2) interfere with effective engagements with the world; (3) be imposed involuntarily and sustained with unthinking allegiance; (4) lack flexibility within the habit, but permit freedom of choice outside it; and (5) prevent or distort appropriate emotional response.

Prevent a Clear Perception of Reality.

Aquinas asserts that anything that is contrary to human reason is a vice. "Vice is contrary to human's nature, in so far as it is contrary to the order of reason."[60] This assertion should not be interpreted with a too narrow focus on reason, because humans possess an organic unity of body, mind, and soul. Vices are habits that affect our voice, vision, and vitality. Yet at the heart of vice is an inability to perceive reality clearly.

Being unable to see reality clearly means misapprehending our place in the universe and becoming confused about our end in God. We become mistaken about what is true about humans and therefore the nature of the good proper to us. Failing to see reality correctly means not recognizing the basic human inclinations and the goods toward which they point. The good becomes obscured from us, and we are unable to discern which of our many longings are genuinely human. We become mistaken about the overall good that gives truly human shape to our lives. We become repulsed by true goods and attracted by false ones.

Forgetting that we were meant for virtue, the habits of vice begin to look and feel natural. We forget that everyone—including ourselves—has the potential for virtue. Some people, perhaps even ourselves, appear inherently inclined toward sloth or greed or injustice. Other people mistakenly appear immune to the effects of oppression; they may appear to us to be without vice. The world appears to consist of good and bad people, rather than to consist of inherently good people who have developed good and bad habits.

Lacking prudence, vices deprive or distort our memory of the past, insight into the present, and shrewdness about the future. The past becomes mystified, distorted, or forgotten. With a distorted past, the possibility of an effective engagement with the present is curtailed. Plans for the future become misguided. The history of oppression becomes denied or mystified, ending the possibility of just restitution in the present.

Interfere with Effective Engagements with the World.

Vices engender ineffective interactions with our environment. Foolhardiness, thoughtlessness, fickleness, negligence, and inconstancy replace the ability to flexibly and creatively engage each new situation.[61] Instead of attending to the future, vices encourage hopelessness, despair, or false bravado. A person lacking prudence might still be able to choose and command a course of action, but be unable to execute the good intention. Immobilization replaces the ability to act.

The hallmark of an effective interaction is that it is fresh and tailor-made for the situation. Instead of attending to particulars of the present circumstance, vices encourage prejudgments based on superficial similarities, misinformation, or ignorance. These distorting habits mean we begin to rely on previously worked-out solutions. We settle for close approximations rather than the challenge of really noticing what is different and unique and then formulating a fresh engagement.

As we have seen, an effective engagement requires flexible thinking. Vices replace flexibility with rigidity. Past information—rather than useful information from which to formulate a new approach—becomes determining. Our options become limited and our interactions repetitive. Rather than fresh thinking, vices invite us to rehearse old solutions to old problems. For example a thief, busily creating a new technical solution to the stubborn lock before him, is not using his creative intelligence to challenge his habit of stealing. From within his habit each new situation looks like a new opportunity to steal, not an opportunity to leave the habit behind.

Lacking the ability to see reality clearly, vicious habits consistently lead to ineffective engagements with reality. Inflexible and ineffective responses are repeated even though they bring increased distress to moral agents and to those around them.

Imposed Involuntarily and Sustained with Unthinking Allegiance.

We recall that virtues involve a voluntarily chosen and sustained commitment to the good. Vices fail this qualification. Are vices voluntarily chosen commitments? At first it would seem that Aquinas thinks so, because the *action flowing from the operation* of a vice would not be a genuine human act if it lacked voluntariness. A closer reading of Aquinas, however, suggests that the *acts that gave rise to the vice* could be involuntary; whereas the *decision to act on* the basis of a vice remains voluntary. (Although the presence of a full-blown vice greatly curtails the individual's freedom, Aquinas always maintains that humans are free to choose differently. "The habit that resides in the soul does not of necessity produce its operation, but is used by a human when willed."[62])

Thomas understands humans to be attracted naturally to truly human goods and repulsed by things that are bad for us. Virtue perfects this natural attraction and repulsion, while vice corrupts it. Saddled with vices, for instance, a person might find learning repugnant and ignorance attractive. The obvious question is, What happens to people so that their natural inclinations can be overridden? Who would voluntarily give up their zest for life, love, community, learning, or God?

Thomas notes that vices can be acquired as a result of three different involuntary experiences: injury, contagion, and ignorance. First, the basis for some vices lies in painful experiences of illness or injury. "A corrupted disposition could either be a habit acquired through practice which is to be turned against nature, or result from a sickly habit on the part of the body. . . ."[63] Certainly we decide to act in a certain way in response to pain, so that our response is voluntary. When we are in great physical or emotional pain due to an injury, we may find it difficult to think. "Passion is sometimes so strong as to take away the use of reason."[64] Our decisions under such circumstances may be shortsighted or regrettable. In this sense we are the authors of our own habits. But we did not necessarily choose to be injured or ill. It is in this sense that the acts that give rise to the vice are "involuntary."

Second, the basis of other vices is generated by a process akin to contagion. "Humans are prone to sin, only because of the sins of others preceding. . . ."[65] When others wound us we may be hurt in such a way that we choose against the good. Third, some people are attracted to the wrong goods through ignorance, which could lay the groundwork for a bad habit. In both these instances, people did not choose contagion or ignorance. Their unhappy response to such painful realities—when their thinking is greatly disrupted due to overwhelming passion—may lay the foundation for what may later become a full-blown vice. Although the situations that gave rise to a vice may have been involuntary initially, the resulting vice is their unique creation.

Although Thomas does not mention it, oppression is a fourth way in which habits are involuntarily acquired. Born into oppressive societies filled with humans burdened with bad habits imposed from every imaginable sort of hurt, we are raised in environments rendered noxious and nonhuman. We then mistreat each other out of the pain of our own mistreatment. Thus the originating experiences of many vices seem to be imposed initially from without. No one in their right mind would voluntarily choose to be hurt in those ways or to acquire the resulting vices. Attractions to false goods are installed or imposed on people—we are not inherently attracted to death, isolation, or ignorance.[66]

These four processes of becoming attracted to nonhuman goods (injury, contagion, ignorance, oppression) share in common that they are hurtful. These four processes are also similar in that they impact the body. Too often in our post-Enlightenment culture we are tempted to split passion from the body. Thomas steadfastly assumes the unity of body with what we today would call "psychological" processes. Thus when people are violated—whether through injury, contagion, ignorance, or oppression—the pain is received physically/emotionally. It is part of the physical movement of a passion to avoid harm. When this is not successful the body spontaneously seeks physical catharsis of the pain (weeping, trembling). A major aspect of how vices are acquired is through enforced physical demands that are inhuman, such as being compelled to smile while in pain, to laugh when angry, to keep "a stiff upper lip" when in sorrow. The habitual assumption of such bodily demeanors helps account for the gradual development of a vice from originally involuntary experiences.

It seems safe to conclude that people must be hurt (accidentally or intentionally) into giving up their natural repulsion to things contrary to their natural good. Therefore, the hurtful experiences that form the basis of many vices must be involuntary.

Vices offer only a simulacrum of virtuous commitment. Thoughtless allegiance rather than prudential choice characterizes the commitment to such habits. They become "natural" to us and sustained with blind devotion. Aquinas notes how our vices may eventually become "lovable" to us.[67] (The degree of culpability, blame, and/or sinfulness of this allegiance, particularly under conditions of exploitation, warrants further exploration.) Such habits are often perceived to be the way things are and inalterable ("you can't change human nature"). It is sad and ironic that something so inherently foreign and hurtful eventually becomes familiar and deceptively natural.

Rigidity within the Vice; Freedom of Choice outside It.

Unlike virtues, vices do not contain flexibility *within* the habit. Once cemented into persistent habits, vices lack prudence about what is to be done *within the operation of the habit*. "Since when a human acts against any virtue, he acts against prudence. Without prudence no moral virtue is possible."[68] A habit of this kind yields only repetitive feelings, chronic physical postures, and a type of habituated thinking. Its thoughts are the product of attempts to think during the original painful experience(s) that generated the vice and may have enhanced the person's survival at the time. But in the present, this habitual thought is no longer reliable. Persons acting within such a habit may feel that they are thinking but are in actuality rigidly repeating the same thoughts and coming to the same conclusions. Thus persons operating on such a rigid habit continually perceive only a narrow range of choices, leading to behavior quite contrary to prudential deliberation. They often escalate their own pain and that of others.

Nevertheless flexible reason exists *outside* the habit. Even rigid habits do not destroy practical reason. Aquinas observes, ". . . a bad habit does not corrupt reason altogether, some of which remains unimpaired. . . ."[69] Earlier in the same article Aquinas notes a difference between an action committed *through vice* and an action committed *by a person who has a vice*. Acting through a vice yields sin, since a decision has to be made to act on the basis of the vice.[70] An action committed through vice will reflect the rigidity of the habit. There is no prudence—no fresh thinking—*inside* the vice, only habitually recycled thoughts and feelings. For the person choosing to operate through a vice of irresponsibility for example, the choice of acting responsibly does not appear to be an option. Within the habit there is no flexibility—the person repeatedly comes up with the same narrow range of responses (e.g., "It's someone else's job") to a great variety of different situations. Once the decision is made to act through the habit, practical reason is put at the service of the habit's ends. The laggard then can be quite creative about how to avoid the next task. Thus, acting through a vice can marshal the person's practical reason and will into serving quite destructive and nonhuman ends.

In contrast, an action committed *by a person who has a vice* may or may not be sinful since the person is free to act through the vice or to act outside it. "When a habit exists in a human, he is able not to use the habit, or produce a contrary act."[71] The moral agent is capable of deciding—rationally, flexibly, and voluntarily—to think, feel, will, and act against the vice, even if she has the vice. This decision has to be made from outside the vice because there is no prudential thinking within it. Acting outside a vice will involve the whole person. She will need to change her tone of voice, her facial expression, and her physical demeanor. She will need to challenge the thoughts she has, the words she utters, and the actions she undertakes. The person frequently has a long history of attempting to decide against it sufficiently and constantly enough to end its chronic operation.

Once a person becomes aware of the existence of the rigid habit and realizes that it is contrary to inherent nature then she can consistently and conscientiously seek to decide outside it and against it. Once she is aware of the possibility of this choice, her subsequent decision to act through the habit versus outside the habit constitutes a human act because it is voluntary.[72]

The concept of freedom to act outside a habit can be difficult for modern readers to grasp. Many of us forget that everyone has the potential for virtue and have begun to think that some people are inherently bad or are damaged so early in life that they are powerless to act differently. Thomas is neither so pessimistic nor so hopeless about the fallenness of God's creatures. Virtue and vice primarily describe relationships between humans and the good. We are not powerless in the face of a vice because we are cooperative, inherently social, and ontologically related to God. Our inherent wellsprings of attraction to the good remain even if we have become deeply inured to evil. Thomas has a deep conviction about our freedom to be moved by love for those goods appropriate to human nature—no matter how entrapped and tangled in vice we may be. We can be empowered to act outside a habit because, despite our vices, we retain our capacities to think and act toward appropriate goods. "That which inclines the will to evil is not always a habit or a passion, but at times is something else. Moreover, there is no comparison between choosing good and choosing evil. Evil is never without some good of nature."[73] No one can ever entirely abandon their natural love for the good, for what is natural cannot be wholly lost.[74]

Inappropriate Passion.

A vice involves inappropriate passion with respect to object, duration, intensity, and/or purgation. A vice includes all the painful emotions contained in the hurtful experience that generated the vice. A vice includes any thoughts that accompanied the originating experience. A vice also distorts our natural attractions and repulsions. A person, if acting within a vice when engaging a new situation, will have painful feelings, inappropriate thoughts, and skewed attractions and repulsions. For example, if a female professor wrongly criticizes a male colleague, he may be reminded of how he felt when he was unjustly criticized by his fifth-grade female teacher. Over time he may have acquired a habit from that earlier experience since he probably was not allowed to heal from his wounds by expressing his emotions appropriately.[75] As a young male he probably knew that showing anger toward his elders was dangerous. He may thus have a habit of being unteachable because to him all criticism seems unjust. In the present moment he can either act appropriately toward his colleague or act within his habit. If he chooses to act on the basis of his habit, he will undoubtedly re-experience old feelings of humiliation and anger. The correct object of these feelings may be his fifth-grade teacher. But since his anger and humiliation feel like appropriate responses to him, he may decide to act on these painful feelings in the present moment, especially since he was wrongly criticized in the present situation. The feelings contained in the habit may be much more intense and last longer than warranted by the situation. Even if he did seek out an appropriate person to whom to express his feelings, unfortunately, he may not be capable of purging his anger. Having internalized the misinformation that men become dangerous when they become angry, his habit now inhibits his emotional recovery.

In summary, vicious habits differ *qualitatively* from virtuous habits. Vices (a) inhibit an accurate assessment of reality, (b) interfere with effective engagements with reality, (c) are imposed involuntarily and sustained through a simulacrum of commitment, (d) exhibit no flexibility within the operation of the habit, and (e) perpetuate inappropriate emotional responses to new situations. Vices proliferate distress for the individual and for the society.

INTERNALIZED OPPRESSION CONSISTS OF VICE-LIKE HABITS.

In this section I will use Thomas's model of vice to highlight certain characteristics of internalized oppression. As an illustration I will focus on ordinary lives, on the internalized oppression among white working-class men.[76]

In *The Hidden Injuries of Class*, Richard Sennett and Jonathan Cobb argue that class society perpetuates the myth that *ability* "sets a person apart from the masses." Ability is allegedly "the badge of individual worth" and the means to "transcend one's social origins."[77] Those not respected as being "above the masses," such as manual laborers, are presumed to lack ability. Manual workers have internalized class oppression when they ascribe their lack of social standing to their own inability and develop habits of inadequacy and worthlessness.

What does Thomas's model of vices tell us about these men's internalized oppression?

Inaccurate Perceptions of Reality.

Internalized oppression, like vicious habits, prevents accurate assessments of reality. Sennett and Cobb note that manual workers, "looking up the ladder of social hierarchy from where they stand, they imagine they see fewer and fewer people who have been allowed the freedom to develop personal resources that others will value."[78] Those few at the top of the class system have some inner ability, so it appears, that common laborers lack. Those at the bottom become consigned to a "limbo of nonability." "The badges of inner ability people wear seem, in sum, unfairly awarded—yet hard to repudiate."[79] Consequently some men blame themselves for their inadequacy rather than question the evaluation scheme that uses differences to mask injustice.

> . . . [S]ociety injures human dignity in order to weaken people's ability to fight against the limits class imposes on their freedom . . . by convincing them that they must *first* become legitimate, must achieve dignity on a class society's terms, in order to have the right to challenge the terms themselves.[80]

The socially imposed habits of inadequacy and worthlessness are mystified as personal character faults. Instead they should be seen as the logical consequence of social arrangements that promise reward for merit but fail to deliver. "Class is his personal responsibility, despite the fact he never had a chance."[81]

Some social psychologists describe a vice-like habit that has its roots in a recording of a painful incident.[82] Their descriptions of how a recording forms the root of a habit are remarkably similar to Aquinas's account of how vices are acquired. A recording is formed when a physically or emotionally painful experience simply overwhelms the inherent human capacity for appropriate engagement. Nevertheless information from the senses was still received since the body and memory recorded the impact of the trauma. Rather than being evaluated, the painful incident is stored as a rigid accumulation, exhibiting the characteristics of a complete, literal recording of all aspects of the incident. The recording includes everything that occurred at the time of the incident—all the visual, auditory, tactile, and kinesthetic content of the experience. The recording includes the words and sounds heard, the emotions felt, and all the thoughts present in the person's mind at the time. An overwhelmingly distressing experience may leave its victim with a rigid imprint of undigested information instead of data enhancing the perception of reality. As Gail Phetersen observes:

> [I]nternalized oppression. . . becomes embedded in personality at the expense of identity and freedom and without regard to

external reality. Oppression seems to breed a package of psychological processes that distort reality. . . .[83]

The core of internalized oppression is a false view of reality. By agreeing with the oppressor, the subjugated may not regard their subordinate status as unjust, but natural. They may not see their suffering as condemnable, but as deserved. They may not see that their source of security rests in forming alliances with their peers. Instead they may compete with members of their own group for the oppressor's favor. If workingmen's feelings, thoughts, and actions mirror the view that they lack what it takes, their behavior contributes to the impression that the stereotype is true. Erica Sherover-Marcuse observes that over time these acquired habits take on a "'natural' appearance and a life of their own."[84] As we shall see later, Thomas suggests that people acquire a second nature that becomes lovable to them. These natural-looking habits unfortunately become an excuse for further stigmatization.

Ineffective Interactions with the Environment.

Internalized oppression sets up working-class men to mistreat others, partly because they have become convinced that mistreatment is deserved. In acting within their habits, they are pulled to try to do so in a more comfortable role in the re-enactment than their original role as victim. Given the rigid choice (perceived from within the vice) of "being degraded or degrading others," workers often "do unto others as was done unto them." They thus may impose distress on other persons whom they try to force into their original role.[85] This phenomenon is the principal channel for the spread of vices by contagion.

For instance, a working-class father may browbeat his children with the message that unless they get an education and make something of themselves they'll end up like him. He may act within his habit of internalized oppression, presenting himself to his children as a warning rather than an enviable model. ("Son, I will be proud of you when you climb up to where you are ashamed of me.") In the process he hurts his children, possibly laying the basis for their internalized oppression.[86] Having internalized the norms and values of the dominant group, manual workers often "mistreat others in an unconscious imitation of their own suffering"[87] and in an ineffective bid to heal their divided self. Thus the oppressed inadvertently help recycle oppression.

According to Aquinas, people are deeply motivated to regain their attraction to true goods, to reclaim a more accurate sense of themselves, and to purge the painful emotions that interfere with their functioning. Sennett and Cobb might concur:

> ... the psychological motivation instilled by a class society is to heal a doubt about the self rather than create more power over things and other persons in the outer world. ... People act to restore themselves rather than to possess and dominate.[88]

Unless of course, they are convinced by the advertising and culture that the way to restore themselves is *through* domination and possession. Unable to restore themselves truly, people often rigidly replay their habits in the hope that someone will notice their suffering and help them. Acting within a vice, unfortunately, causes further harm to the oppressed as well as to others.

Acquired Involuntarily and Sustained Mindlessly.

Like a vice, a habit such as worthlessness is acquired in response to involuntary wounds. Young working-class boys are not likely to agree willingly that their worth derives from how they can isolate themselves from their peers and abandon friends as inferior. As Sennett and Cobb dryly observe, "Validating the self through distinctive personal merit is not a matter of spontaneous desire. . . ."[89] Painful experiences are necessary to force youngsters into agreeing with the belief that their human worth is based on their ability to separate themselves from their peers. Sennett and Cobb describe numerous distressing experiences in elementary schools that could form the core of working-class boys' internalized oppression.

> The kids in Watson School didn't feel betrayed only because others were getting approval, but because they felt the Freds and Vincents [the ones favored by the teachers as most likely to "make it"] were using their powers and that approval not towards aiding them, but toward escaping the situation and progressing by themselves.[90]

The resulting habit of worthlessness is based in such experiences as "desertion by others."[91]

However, one traumatic experience of classism (or racism or sexism) by itself is not enough to generate a chronic habit of worthlessness. A habit is not formed unless a young working-class boy continually replays the thoughts and feelings from the incident. Usually the young person is motivated to rehearse the incident by the hope of obtaining attention. A natural reaction to a wound is to secure help, purge the emotion, and tell the story of what happened. His attempts to tell someone about his experience, however, may be met with ridicule, blame, or silencing. When a rational and appropriate need to secure loving attention remains unmet, a rigid habit of seeking attention may result. As a result of additional disappointments when these inappropriate attempts to secure aid fail to work, the boy may become locked into seeking attention. By now he is on his way to developing a full-blown habit within which he may operate repetitively, despite the habit's failure to produce the desired result.[92]

Daily social intercourse, the structures of ordinary life, and the pervasive cultural milieu also reinforce a fledging habit. Sherover-Marcuse observes that "no oppressed group can remain immune to the institutionally and socially empowered untruths which purport to 'justify' its oppression."[93] By the time young men have reached adulthood, they may have exercised some choice in the development of their habits. Their habits are their own and not exactly like any others. Nevertheless their choices were constrained and distorted by the realities of class society.[94] Sennett and Cobb conclude:

> The real impact of class is that a man can play out *both* sides of the power situation in his own life, become alternately judge and judged, alternately individual and member of the mass. This represents the "internalizing" of class conflict, the process by which struggle between men leads to struggle within each man.[95]

Looking without and looking within he agrees that class society is right—men like him are indeed failures for not making something of themselves.

Like a vice, internalized oppression is sustained by unthinking allegiance. Sherover-Marcuse observes that such

> "thinking," like other forms of mystified consciousness, represents a disturbance of the learning process, a disturbance which itself is the consequence of social oppression and which in turn serves to perpetuate it. In other words, mystified consciousness is not the result of freely functioning intelligence, but of distorted and illogical thought.[96]

This unthinking repetition of the habit perpetuates mistreatment of one's group. Operating within such habits, a man may not be adept at evaluating the true worth or abilities of other manual laborers. For instance, he may attack working-class leaders for "thinking they're better than the rest of us."

Flexibility outside the Habits of Internalized Oppression, Not within Them.

Internalized oppression permits choice *outside* the habit but not within it. In the presence of triggers in ordinary life that remind a working-class man of the pivotal events in which he accepted the reality of his limitations, he faces a tough choice; act on his habit or act like a worthwhile human with ability.

A man's valiant efforts to claim his dignity as a full human unfortunately are likely to be met with further mistreatment; he may be threatened with humiliation or violence for stepping out of line. Without accessible discourses that portray manual laborers as inherently dignified, worthy of respect, and as having valid claims to good working and living conditions, he is likely to choose to act on the habit of worthlessness. Of course, freedom of choice remains outside the habit.

Internalized Oppression Rooted in Painful Emotion.

The internalized habit of worthlessness is bound up with painful emotions from experiences of classism. While the initial response to oppressive mistreatment may make sense (shame or anger), as a rigid and generalized emotional response to similar situations, it quickly proves dysfunctional. When painful emotions from the past are acted on, they interfere with elegant engagements with the present.

An additional component of internalized oppression is the workers' belief that their painful feelings are their personal problem. Mystified as a failure of personal happiness, painful emotions reinforce the workers' sense of inadequacy. Seeking to numb their feelings through alcohol or self-control unfortunately reinforces their internalized oppression.

To recapitulate the argument thus far, internalized oppression consists of vice-like habits. Internalized oppression begins with involuntary experiences that are wounding and confusing. Unable to name and condemn these experiences as wrong and unjust, the oppressed are unable to heal from these experiences. Furthermore, unable to obtain the real help they need, they may begin to develop a habit of replaying their misinformation and painful feelings in unsuccessful bids for help. Reinforced by a classist society, they act on their developing habits to their own detriment and that of others. Internalized oppression becomes a second nature that then feels true and looks natural. It will be difficult for them to identify and dismantle their internalized oppression when both internal and external voices make their habit of inferiority seem natural.

The enforced acquisition of vices explains the oppressed's collusion with injustice. I have yet to explain the capacity of the oppressed for sustained resistance to oppression. For this explanation, I turn next to the Thomistic distinction between nature and second nature. This distinction can help the oppressed identify and dismantle their internalized oppression. In addition, this distinction helps explain why rebellion against injustice is possible by people burdened with internalized oppression. I now turn to the distinction between nature and second nature and its implications for liberation.

NATURE AND SECOND NATURE.

According to Aquinas, humans have a nature with qualities and potentialities formed in the image of God. In the Garden of Eden we were rightly ordered souls in proper relation to self, neighbor, and God. Disobedience to God and the transmission of original sin biologically through generations disordered this original righteousness.[97] The nature resulting from the Fall is the universal condition of all humans upon conception. Although disordered by original sin, this nature has an innate tendency toward good ("there is a certain natural appetite for good in conformity with reason"[98]) and a habit of *synderesis* by which we can know the primary principle of the natural law ("good is to be sought and done and evil avoided"). Human nature is dynamic.[99] The first movement of the will is toward love, since the will is moved by our ultimate end in God.[100]

Despite the diminishment wrought by the loss of original righteousness, human nature, like all of God's creation, is good. Copleston describes Aquinas's conception of ontological goodness.

> For every being is actual so far as it is being, and actuality involves perfection. And a perfection is 'desirable' either by the thing which possesses it or by something else. Being and good . . . have the same denotation, though 'good' here signifies being considered in relation to will, desire, or natural inclination or tendency. If, therefore, every being is 'good' . . . it is obvious that no being can be completely evil.[101]

Thus Aquinas stands in opposition to a doctrine of total depravity. Aquinas cannot hold that anyone is bad by nature, not even the devil. "But the law written on the human heart is the natural law and cannot be erased."[102] A so-called "bad nature" must be attributed to bad customs or habits[103] or a disordered will or appetite. "If a human is attracted to evil, this is due to a corruption or disorder in the foundations of the human."[104]

It is a characteristic of our nature to develop virtue. But much can interfere along the way. We are vulnerable to misfortune and bad luck. As we have seen, this vulnerability can result in the acquisition of vice. This vulnerability also characterizes our nature, so that our nature is capable of both virtue and vice. Since our nature is not neutral, virtue is deemed natural while vices must be condemned as a deformation.

There are two problems with Thomas's presentation of nature. First, he treats the Garden of Eden as an historical event in the life of the species and original sin as a biological transmission. Second, he does not question the small class of people involved in formulating his universal claims about nature. A full exploration of these problems is beyond the scope of this paper; I will briefly indicate alternative lines of argument.

First, one could argue that the Garden of Eden occurs in the history of each individual, not of the species. Every human begins life innocently[105] and fully intact. Original sin is a historical condition into which humans are born, which even before birth impinges on and limits the full flourishing of the infant's humanity.[106]

Second, one could argue that the method of arriving at claims about human nature should have as a goal the inclusion of the voices and stories of all peoples. Such claims could emerge from the memories of suffering and resistance from which the oppressed begin to delineate what they find necessary for human flourishing. Such claims would then be tested in a concrete praxis of ending oppression. This praxis must include activities aimed at eliminating internalized oppression as well as habits of domination. Such praxis might mitigate against (but not necessarily prevent) the reification of a single group's perspectives into universal claims.[107] By implication, any resulting perspectives on human nature should remain open to revision in the light of continued praxis.

Despite these difficulties, Aquinas's claims about nature presented above can contribute to liberation efforts. Politically and practically his perspective is far more effective in countering internalized oppression than either the view that we are blank slates (constituted by experience or discourses) or that we are innately wicked. Positing humans as blank slates creates the theoretical possibility that some people could be thoroughly and completely victimized to create a class of people for whom there is no hope. Positing humans as innately wicked "fails to take adequate notice of the corrupting effects of oppression, promotes despair and hopelessness,"[108] and blames people for the vices acquired in response to mistreatment.[109] Such a view ascribes to nature acquired vices and makes these unchangeable. Universal claims must remain suspect because they may mask difference and reify the particular. Nevertheless it is in *practice* that we should test the liberatory potential of Thomas's view that people are inherently dynamic, flexible, motivated by love, *and* have acquired habits that may occlude (*not* obliterate) their birthright.

What is meant by second nature? Second nature consists of those habits giving unique specification to our inherent nature.[110] It refers to those habits—whether good or bad—that appear natural.[111] Aquinas uses several phrases for second nature such as "quasi" nature and a "kind" of nature. Second nature will include habits both contrary to *and* conforming to human nature. Thus a person's second nature will be a mixture of virtues and vices.

What is the relation of nature to second nature? Vices, aspects of second nature, cannot destroy nature.[112] The ontological attraction to the good remains because reason can never be conjoined to evil. Virtues, also aspects of second nature, do not limit nature. For instance, although it is natural for humans to develop language, English is a habit, a specification of an open-ended power. Habits direct the functioning of any given individual; he now thinks in the categories and symbols of his native tongue. Yet this acquired habit of English does not alter his nature as a being capable of learning many languages and perceiving the world differently. If certain *potentia* were not developed these *potentia* still exist. Even if a working-class man were not allowed to acquire the intellectual virtue of mathematical reasoning, and developed a habit of internalized oppression ("I can't learn math"), his *capacity* to learn math remains nonetheless intact.

Internalized oppression is an aspect of second nature. Just as people do not become their good or bad habits essentially, so people do not become their internalized oppression essentially, although it may greatly restrict their functioning. People with bad habits are potentially free to develop virtues that enable them to act and think more in tune with their nature.[113]

One of the crucial contributions of Thomas's model is the distinction that can be made within second nature. His model allows the oppressed to distinguish between those aspects of second nature developed in accord with nature from those aspects of second nature bent out of shape by mistreatment. In the normative sense of "human," virtues reflect what is most human about us. In contrast, internalized oppression is nonhuman and alien to us. Thus it becomes possible to contrast the human with her internalized oppression. The "human" here refers to those humanly developed aspects of her second nature. Humans are flexible, internalized oppression is rigid; humans are dynamic, internalized oppression is static; humans create new solutions to old problems, internalized oppression perpetuates ineffective approaches; humans remember, internalized oppression causes us to forget; humans hope, internalized oppression breeds despair; humans discern, internalized oppression is reactive; humans think, internalized oppression confuses.[114]

Moreover, the distinction between human and nonhuman aspects of second nature changes the terms of a current debate. Current debate pits nature against culture by trying to distinguish those characteristics that are genetic from those that are cultural. In contrast, Thomas's distinction invites exploration of which aspects of our second nature are flexible and dynamic and which are rigid and static. All aspects of second nature are cultural for it is our nature to live in society and be engaged with our environment. There is no expression of humanity that is not culturally influenced—even our biological powers such as reproduction are expressed in particular cultural milieus. The crucial question is not to determine what is biologically natural (which strips away our most distinctive human creation, culture). Rather, Thomas reminds us that the significant question is: "What expression of humanity seems most free from vice-like habits and is prudentially flexible, loving, cooperative, and intelligent?"

This concludes my presentation of those aspects of Thomas's thought that provide a model for conceptualizing the phenomenon of internalized oppression. We have examined his understanding of habit, virtue and vice, and nature and second nature. Next we examine the implications of Thomas's model for liberation.

His model helps address three problems: (1) how the oppressed's empowerment to resist injustice can be explained; (2) how the oppressed can distingish their internalized oppression from more human ways of being; and (3) how the oppressed can expose discourses that ascribe internalized oppression to their inherent nature.

CONCLUSION: CONTRIBUTIONS OF THOMAS'S MODEL TO LIBERATION.

(1) How does Thomas's model help explain how the oppressed are capable of resistance? The oppressed's capacity for resistance is explicated by distinguishing between flexible and rigid aspects of second nature. Rarely are people totally consumed by vices. Aspects of their virtuous second nature can be acted upon to challenge injustice. Freedom to act outside of a vice always remains as a choice. The option of acting in accord with nature furnishes a resource for powerful liberatory action outside internalized oppression. Moreover, the human is always available as a natural ally against his or her nonhuman habits,[115] given the ontological attraction to the good. All oppressed peoples have unrecorded histories of resistance to oppression and, in particular, unapplauded resistance to their internalized oppression.[116]

(2) How do Thomas's assumptions about human nature aid in the identification of internalized oppression? Thomas claims that humans are intelligent and inherently social. Moreover we are motivated by love, inclined to the good, and capable of being moved by appropriate objects. These claims offer the oppressed some guidelines by which to identify their internalized oppression. Confused by voices within and confounded by voices without, the oppressed have some

guidelines about which voices to listen to and act on. Liberationists, unfortunately, have often discarded all claims about human nature as inevitably oppressive. This rejection often results in the adoption of the blank-slate view of human nature.[117] Thomas offers an alternative to a blank-slate discourse by showing that substantive claims about human nature can aid, rather than hinder, liberation efforts. Such claims should be tested in liberatory practice to discover if they do help the oppressed identify their internalized oppression. Once they have identified it, the oppressed presumably are in a better position to develop strategies to tackle the ways it sabotages their efforts.

(3) What does Thomas's model reveal about oppressive ideologies? His model reveals that they operate by ascribing to nature what should be ascribed to second nature. Women for example have rightly protested against essentialist claims about "female nature" that have perpetuated misogyny. Specifically Thomas's claim that humans share a fundamental common humanity counters this oppressive legacy. Thomas thinks we share a common humanity because of the monotheism underlying his doctrine of creation and his interpretation of eternal law as a universal reality. His belief that we all descended from the same parents strengthens his idea that everywhere human nature shares the same fundamentals.[118] Any tentative claim made about human nature must therefore be assumed to be true of everyone. Arguments that males and females—slave, Jew, or homosexual—are different in their basic fundamentals must smuggle in ancillary, and contradictory, claims.

Unfortunately, Aquinas does smuggle in contradictory claims. He immediately qualifies the universality of the *imago dei*—which implies the radical commonality of all natures—by noting that in a secondary sense, women do not possess the *imago dei* because women were created from Adam's rib and because women were created for man.[119] Women are therefore deficient.[120] Not only are ruling men held out as the model against which women (and potentially other groups) may be found wanting, the "deficiencies" of women are assigned to their inherent nature rather than to their acquired second nature. Thus is misogyny perpetuated. Thomas immediately qualifies himself two articles later by reaffirming that "the image of God is common to both sexes, since it is in the mind in which there is no distinction of sex."[121]

At this juncture, the modern thinker can attempt to develop Aquinas's thought as he might have, had he been aware of the misogynist aspects of his own second nature. If Aquinas's understanding of human nature and habit can produce in the hands of liberationists a fresh understanding of internalized oppression, then the fact that his own applications fall short of this should not stand in our way.[122] A consistent thinker would have to dispense with Aquinas's notion of deficient natures as a significant departure from the tone of his entire system.[123] The existence of a common human nature implies that the burden of proof should be placed on those who wish to ascribe significant differences to fundamental nature. They will need to demonstrate that differences are *not* due to acquired habits or customs. Thus, a third major contribution of Aquinas's model to liberation to our third question is the *prima facie* assumption that differences should be ascribed to second nature.[124]

This *prima facie* assumption counters the tendency to think of vices as natural and unchangeable aspects of a given personality or temperament ("some people are just competitive"). This assumption should encourage us to improve the accuracy of our speech. It signals the difference between saying "she is competitive" (or jealous or cold) versus "she has a habit of competitiveness" (or jealousy or coldness). The first may be a true statement—she is competitive and it may describe her accurately as a being with that characteristic. (Of course, the characterization may be wrong, depending on who is doing the characterizing and who is encouraged to be competitive in a particular culture.) The danger lies in using "is" to indicate her inherent nature, that she does not have any possibility of acting cooperatively, outside the habit. Encouraged by an oppressive milieu, we too often ascribe habits to nature.[125]

Furthermore, discussions of oppression often risk portraying the subjugated as *entirely* consisting of their internalized oppression. This portrayal also collapses second nature into nature. Thomas's model prevents mistaken regard of the oppressed as essentially poor victims who lack self-worth. African American feminists have in particular protested being treated as inherent victims.[126] They insist (rightly) that Anglo-Americans should notice the manifold ways they have preserved their humanity and the humanity of others in their communities. Their communities nurture practices that sustain the acquisition of virtues and skills appropriate to surviving the economic, political, and ideological barriers encountered. Thomas's model reminds us how oppressed people have been able to retain their humanity and develop virtuous habits, despite the destructive habits they have encountered in others and which they may have consequently internalized.

Demonizing oppressors also collapses second nature into nature. Thomas's model should prevent us from demonizing oppressors. Perpetrators have intact natures and their oppressive ways should be seen as part of their second nature. This model challenges the view that some people are corrupt by nature. It also challenges the desire to distance ourselves from our enemies by thinking that they are inherently evil in a way that we (innocent victims) are not. Thomas's model requires that we insist that perpetrators are humans too, though with deeply vicious second natures that make human functioning truly difficult. This insistence does not undercut in any way righteous outrage against outrageous evil. Humans embodying such habits deserve complete respect while their vices deserve none.[127]

In conclusion, Aquinas's insights remind us that undoing internalized oppression is a moral practice in its own right. The project of eliminating internalized oppression ought to be seen as a demanding moral practice of acquiring virtue and abandoning destructive habits. This practice of undoing our allegiance to these habits can be undertaken simultaneously with other liberation efforts. The complete eradication of internalized oppression stands as a challenge and a possibility. But to neglect this project would be to ignore the corrupting influence of internalized oppression on all liberation efforts. Getting Egypt out of the people is as important as getting the people out of Egypt.

NOTES

I wish to thank Maureen Kameza, Ulrike Wiethaus, Christine Overall, G. Simon Harak, S. J., Steven Boyd, and members of the Society of Christian Ethics for helpful comments on earlier drafts of this essay.

1. Much of what is developed here could apply to oppressors' habits, but there are important differences that will be explored in a subsequent work. Since many people occupy dual roles (both oppressed and oppressor), this essay also artificially separates what may be aligned closely in experience.

2. For a similar definition see Gail Pheterson, "Alliances Between Women: Overcoming Internalized Oppression and Internalized Domination," *Signs* 12, no. 1 (Autumn 1986): 148. Internalized oppression is widely recognized within sociological, psychological, and liberation literature. Some relevant literature would include Paulo Freire, *Pedagogy of the Oppressed* (New York, N.Y.: Continuum, 1970); Erving Goffman, *Stigma: Notes on the Management of Spoiled Identity* (New York, N.Y.: Prentice-Hall, 1963); Albert Memmi, *The Colonizer and the Colonized* (Boston, Mass.: Beacon Press, 1965); Marilyn Frye, *The Politics of Reality* (Trumansburg, N.Y.: Crossing Press, 1983); Erica Sherover-Marcuse, *Emancipation and Consciousness* (Oxford: Basil Blackwell, 1986). For the internalized oppression of women see Jean Baker Miller, *Toward a New Psychology of Women* (Boston, Mass.: Beacon Press, 1976) and bell hooks, *Feminist Theory: From Margin to Center* (Boston, Mass.: South End Press, 1984); of the blue-collar working class see Richard Sennett and Jonathon Cobb, *Hidden Injuries of Class* (New York, N.Y.: Vintage Press, 1972); of Jews, see Albert Memmi, *Portrait of a Jew* (New York, N.Y.: Viking Press, 1971); of African Americans, see Cherrie Moraga and Gloria Anzaldua, eds., *This Bridge Called My Back: Writings by Radical Women of Color* (Watertown, Mass.: Persephone Press, 1981) and Patricia Hill Collins, *Black Feminist Thought* (Boston, Mass.: Unwin Hyman, 1990).

3. Ada Maria Isasi-Diaz, "Toward an Understanding of *Feminismo Hispano* in the U.S.A.," in Barbara Andolsen, ed., *Women's Consciousness, Women's Conscience* (San Francisco, Calif.: Harper and Row, 1985), p. 56.

4. The reader might bear in mind feminist criticisms of a hierarchy of being (see Rosemary Ruether, *Sexism and God-Talk* [Boston, Mass.: Beacon Press, 1983], pp. 72–85); post-Kantian awareness of the situatedness of thought (see H. R. Niebuhr, *The Responsible Self* [New York, N.Y.: Harper and Row, 1963]); post-Hegelian awareness of history as a major analytic category besides nature (see Charles Taylor, *Hegel and Modern Society* [New York, N.Y.: Cambridge University Press, 1979]); and feminist criticisms of ahistorical essentialism (see Chris Weedon, *Feminist Practice and Poststructuralist Theory* [Oxford: Basil Blackwell, 1987]; Flax, *Thinking Fragments* [Berkeley, Calif.: University of California Press, 1990]; Diana Fuss, *Essentially Speaking* [New York, N.Y.: Routledge, 1989]; and Elizabeth Spelman, *Inessential Woman* [Boston, Mass.: Beacon Press, 1988]).

5. See G. Simon Harak, S. J., *Virtuous Passions* (Mahwah, N.J.: Paulist Press, 1993). Harak uses modern science, in dialogue with classical authors like Aquinas, to show how deeply the self is formed by the other in interactions and how important it is for our freedom that our paradigmatic other be God.

6. See Phillipa Foot's assessment of Aquinas in *Virtues and Vices and Other Essays in Moral Philosophy* (Berkeley, Calif.: University of California Press, 1978), which was one of the early philosophical treatments of virtue with a sympathetic interpretation of Aquinas. Jean Porter's *The Recovery of Virtue* (Louisville, Ky.: Westminster/John Knox Press, 1990) is a philosophical investigation of Aquinas's contributions to several modern theoretical debates in ethics.

7. Natural law as used in this essay refers to metaethical judgments about goods appropriate to nature and conducive to human flourishing. I treat natural law as a metaethical grounding for ethical norms, not a set of moral injunctions. The excessively prescriptive interpretation of natural law as a way of classifying human acts (characteristic of the manualists) I regard as a vast departure from Thomas's spirit and method.

The debate on how Thomas saw natural law—metaethical and/or normative—remains unresolved, leaving open the question of how he moves from his set of judgments about what is good for human well-being to concrete rules and virtues. The status of any resulting moral norms, such as John Finnis's requirement that one must never act against a fundamental good, is therefore also highly debated. While both the method by which one moves from metaethical judgments about goods to specific norms and the status of those norms remain pressing issues, both lie outside the focus of this essay. For revisionist interpretations of natural law see Anthony Battaglia, *Toward a Reformulation of Natural Law* (New York, N.Y.: The Seabury Press, 1981); Germain Grisez, "The First Principle of Practical Reason," *Natural Law Forum* 10 (1965): 168-202; John Finnis, *Natural Law and Natural Rights* (Oxford: Clarendon Press, 1980); and a critique of such attempts in Russell Hittinger, *A Critique of the New Natural Law Theory* (Notre Dame, Ind.: University of Notre Dame Press, 1987). James F. Keenan's *Goodness and Rightness in Thomas Aquinas's Summa theologiae* (Washington, D.C.: Georgetown University Press, 1992) does not address the issue of natural law per se, but his investigation of Thomas's meaning and use of "goodness and rightness" points to the need to stop seeing natural law and virtue as unrelated.

8. For a critique of two major feminist approaches, see Judith W. Kay, "Politics without Human Nature? Reconstructing a Common Humanity," *Hypatia* vol. 9, no. 1 (Winter 1994): 24–36, in which I argue for the need for explicit hypotheses about human nature as a component of feminist politics.

9. For a good discussion of liberal feminists, see Alison Jaggar, *Feminist Politics and Human Nature* (Totowa, N.J.: Rowman and Allanheld, 1983), chap. 2.

10. Barrington Moore, *Injustice: The Social Bases of Obedience and Revolt* (White Plains, N.Y.: M.E. Sharpe, 1978), p. 61.

11. Mary Daly, in particular, adopts this perspective. See her *Gyn/Ecology* (Boston, Mass.: Beacon Press, 1978), pp. 39, 52–64.

12. Jean Grimshaw makes this observation about radical feminists in *Philosophy and Feminist Thinking* (Minneapolis, Minn.: University of Minnesota Press, 1986), chap. 4.

13. For a good discussion of the dogmatic strain in Marx and Marxists, see Erica Sherover-Marcuse, *Emancipation and Consciousness* (Oxford: Basil and Blackwell, 1986), chap. 1.

14. See for example, Carol Gould, *Marx's Social Ontology* (Cambridge, Mass.: The MIT Press, 1978). For a contrasting interpretation of Marx, see Norman Geras, *Marx and Human Nature: Refutation of a Legend* (New York, N.Y.: Schocken Books, 1983).

15. Nancy Chodorow, *The Reproduction of Mothering: Psychoanalysis and the Sociology of Gender* (Berkeley, Calif.: University of California Press, 1978), pp. 206–9.

16. See Weedon, *Feminist Practice and Poststructuralist Theory;* Flax, *Thinking Fragments* chap. 1; and Linda Nicholson, ed. *Feminism/Postmodernism* (New York, N.Y.: Routledge, 1990).

17. The voluntariness of this choice may be in question, as I discuss later under internalized oppression. The oppressed did not choose to acquire internalized oppression, even though repeated choice encouraged by an oppressive environment has transformed a disposition (an orientation intermittently exercised and easily discarded) into a true habit (enduring and difficult to change).

18. Thomas uses phrases that are frequently translated as second nature: "quae est quasi quaedam natura," "est habitus in modum naturae" (*ST* I-II.56.5); "secundum quod consuetudo et habitus vertitur in naturam" (*ST* I-II.78.2); and "habitus similitudinem habet naturae deficit tamen ab ipsa" (*ST* I-II.53.1ad1). *ST* refers to *Summa theologiae*. I use the Latin text of the Blackfriar's edition, New York, N.Y.: McGraw-Hill Book Co., 1963–1969, although the translations are my own. Henceforth all references will be to the *Summa theologiae* unless otherwise noted.

19. "Directe quidem virtus importat dispositionem quandam alicujus convenienter se habentis secundum modum suae naturae: unde Philosophus dicit quod 'virtus est dispositio perfecti ad optimum; dico autem perfecti, quod est dispositum secundum naturam'" (I-II.71.1).

20. I-I.54.3.

21. Throughout the remainder of the paper I assume that people are not brain damaged in ways that interfere with thinking, volition, and/or feeling.

22. I.77-83. Undue hindrance may stunt or distort operation of these powers.

23. Each power that can be diversely ordered to acting requires a habit by which it is well disposed to its act. "Dicendum quod omnis potentia quae diversimode potest ordinari ad agendum indiget habitu quo bene disponatur ad suum actum" (I-II.50.5). Habits are dispositions of something that is in potentiality in regard to nature. "Habitus sunt dispositiones quaedam alicujus in potentia existentis ad aliquid, sive ad naturam, sive ad operationem vel finem naturae" (I-II.54.1).

24. I-II.49.4. See also: Virtue is natural to a human in respect to his specific nature [species-nature] insofar as certain naturally known principles in regard to both thought and action are in humans' reason naturally; these are like the seeds of intellectual and moral virtues, insofar as there is in the will a certain natural appetite for good in accordance with reason. "Utroque autem modo virtus est homini naturalis secundum quamdam inchoationem. Secundum quidem naturam speciei inquantum in ratione hominis insunt naturaliter quaedam principia naturalitater cognita tam scibilium quam agendorum; quae sunt quaedam seminalia intellectualium virtutum et moralium,

inquantum in voluntate inest quidam naturalis appetitus boni, quod est secundum rationem" (I-II.63.1).

25. Even though a power is simple as to essence, it is multiple in capacity, inasmuch as it extends to many specifically different acts. "Ad secundum dicendum quod potentia, etsi sit quidem simplex secundum essentiam, est tamen multiplex virtute, secundum quod ad multos actus specie differentes se extendit. Et ideo nihil prohibet in una potentia esse multos habitus specie differentes" (I-II.54.1ad2).

26. I-II.50.5.

27. III.78.2; cf. I-II.71.4.

28. Philip B. Gove, ed., *Webster's Third International Dictionary* (Springfield, Mass.: G & C Merriam Publishers, 1981).

29. I-II.81.2; cf. I-II.85.2.

30. "Prudentia vero est recta ratio agibilium" (I-II.57.4).

31. Thomas discusses the basic inclinations and goods in the treatise on law, I-II.94.1 & 2. The natural law consists of a self-evident axiom (good is what all things seek after); a primary principle (good is to be sought and done and evil to be avoided); primary precepts (which specify goods-for-humans such as knowledge); and secondary precepts (normative obligations and prescriptions). Natural law is the group of values or goods that the practical intellect delivers as a result of judging the objects of our natural tendencies as good.

32. I-II.79.12.

33. II-II.47.10.

34. "Ad tertium dicendum quod prudentia est bene consiliativa de his quae pertinent ad totam vitam hominis et ad ultimum finem vitae humanae" (I-II.57.4a3).

35. II-II.48.1. I have only listed three of the allied virtues here; the other five are reason, understanding, openness to being taught, circumspection, and caution: ("cognoscitiva, scilicet memoria, ratio, intellectus, docilitas, solertia, praeceptiva, applicando cognitionem ad opus, scilicet providentia, circumspectio et cautio").

36. II-II.51.3

37. II-II.47.6 and 8.

38. II-II.47.1

39. II-II.47.2.

40. II-II.48.

41. I-II.58.5, 57.6, and 58.4.

42. Mingnon H. Anderson, *Mostly Womenfolk and A Man or Two: A Collection* (Chicago, Ill.: Third World Press, 1976), p. 8.

43. Alasdair MacIntyre, *Whose Justice? Which Rationality?* (Notre Dame, Ind.: University of Notre Dame Press, 1988), p. 180.

44. I-II.6.1.

45. I-II.6.6.

46. "[V]oluntarium secundum quid" (I-II.6.6).

47. Katie Cannon, *Black Womanist Ethics* (Atlanta, Ga.: Scholar's Press, 1988), p. 127. Compare what Bruno Bettelheim says of Jewish survivors of

concentration camps: "They also came to realize what they had not perceived before; that they still retained the last, if not the greatest, of the human freedoms: to choose their own attitude in any given circumstance. . . . [T]his, and only this, formed the crucial difference between retaining one's humanity . . . and accepting death as a human being . . . : whether one retained the freedom to choose autonomously one's attitude to extreme conditions even when they seemed totally beyond one's ability to influence them" *Informed Heart* (New York, N.Y.: Avon Books, 1960), p. 158.

48. I-II.49.2a3; also 49.3.

49. "Et ideo sicut potest contingere quod aliquis habens habitum vitiosum prorumpat in actum virtutis, eo quod ratio non totaliter corrumptiur per malum habitum sed aliquid ejus integrum manet, ex quo provenit quod peccator aliqua operatur de genere bonorum" (I-II.78.2). And also, "Quod ratio non semper in suo actu totaliter a passione impeditur: unde remanet ei liberum arbitrium, ut possit averti vel converti ad Deum. Si autem totaliter tolleretur usus rationis, jam non esset peccatum nec mortale nec veniale" (I-II.77.8ad3).

50. Neither Aquinas nor Aristotle specified what they meant by catharsis. I follow Thomas Scheff's and Don Bushnell's theory that a complete emotion cycle of catharsis includes three interdependent elements: (a) a biological sequence involving stimulation (e.g., loss), arousal (grief), climax (weeping), and relaxation (repose); (b) a cognitive component (the person views the loss as both participant and observer); and (c) a social context (whether permission to complete the cycle is granted or withdrawn). Thomas Scheff and Don Bushnell, "A Theory of Catharsis," *Journal of Research in Personality* vol. 18 (1984): pp. 238–64, at pp. 244, 256–57.

51. Aristotle, *Nicomachean Ethics,* David Ross, trans. (Oxford: Oxford University Press, 1980), IV: 5, 1125b28; I-II.24.1.

52. "Lacrymae et gemitus naturaliter mitigant tristitiam" (I-II.38.2).

53. "[Prudentia] . . . quod non fit sine appetitu recto" (II-II.47.4); "Sed prudentia non consistit in sola cognitione, sed etiam in appetitu" (II-II.47.6).

54. Harak, *Virtuous Passions,* chap. 4.

55. For an excellent corrective to Cartesian misreadings of Aquinas see Harak, *Virtuous Passions,* especially chap. 2.

56. I thank Ulrike Wiethaus for this observation.

57. Some virtues may give the appearance of being automatic and unthinking. For example, an honest woman might say that she is honest automatically, but more accurately she proceeds without undue deliberation about whether or not honesty is a good policy. The virtue of honesty involves almost intuitive evaluation of the appropriate ways to be honest in each particular situation, a process of evaluation made laborious for the person without such a habit.

58. Aristotle, quoted by Aquinas in I-II.71.1. Aquinas defines vice: "Sed secundum id quod directe est de ratione virtutis, opponitur virtuti vitium: vitium enim uniuscujusque rei esse videtur quod non sit disposita secundum quod convenit suae naturae" (I-II.71.1).

59. I-II.49.4a3.

60. "Homo autem in specie constitutur per animam rationalem. Et ideo id quod est contra ordinem rationis proprie est contra naturam hominis inquantum est homo; quod autem est secundum rationem est secundum naturam hominis inquantum est homo" (I-II.71.2).

61. "[T]emeritas, imprudentiae, inconsideratio, inconstantia, negligentia" (II-II.53.2).

62. "Sed habitus in anima non ex necessitate producit suam operationem, sed homo 'utitur eo cum voluerit'" (I-II.71.4).

63. "Talis autem dispositio corrupta vel est aliquis habitus acquisitus ex consuetudine, quae vertitur in naturam, vel est aliqua aegritudinalis habitudo ex parte corporis . . ." (III.78.3).

64. "Quia passio quandoque quidem est tanta quod totaliter aufert usum rationis" (I-II.77.7).

65. Aquinas alludes to the process of contagion in I-II.80.4, "inquantum induxit primum hominem ad peccandum, ex cujus peccato infantum vitiata est humana natura ut omnes simus ad peccandum proclives." Patrick McCormick's discussion of contagion differs from Thomas. McCormick uses the analogy of a pathological virus that infects all that it touches. This portrays persons as overly passive, hapless in the face of sin, and ignores our capacity for resistance (Patrick McCormick, *Sin as Addiction* [New York: Paulist Press, 1989], pp. 110–20).

66. As Thomas says, "Uno quidem modo, per hoc quod homo habet aliquam dispositionem corruptam inclinatem ad malum, ita quod secundum illam dispositionem fit homini quasi conveniens et simile aliquod malum, et in hoc, ratione convenientiae, tendit voluntas quasi in bonum" (I-II.78.3).

67. Habits are lovable to us as they are connatural and like a second nature. "Quia unicuique habenti habitum est per se diligibile id quod est ei conveniens secundum proprium habitum, quia fit ei quodammodo connaturale, secundum quo consuetudo et habitus vertitur in naturam" (I-II.78.2).

68. "Quia cum homo agit contra quamcumque virtutem agit contra prudentiam" (I-II.73.1).

69. See note 49.

70. Whatever is a principle of a voluntary act is a subject of sin: "quod non peccatur nisi voluntate sicut primo movenete" (I-II.74.2).

71. "Unde simul habitu in homine existente, potest non uti habitu, aut agere contrarium actum" (I-II.71.4).

72. Those acts are properly called human that are voluntary because the will is in the rational appetite, which is proper to a human (I-II.6, preface).

73. "Quod illud propter quod voluntas inclinatur ad malum non semper habitus est vel passio, sed quaedam alia"; and "Quia malum numquam est sine bono naturae, sed bonum potest esse sine malo culpae perfecte" (I-II.78.3ad3,ad4).

74. "Quod naturalis amor, etsi non totaliter tollatur a malis, tamen in eis pervertitur per modum jam dictum" (II-II.25.7ad2).

75. Scheff and Bushnell argue that an interrupted emotion cycle of catharsis does not facilitate healing from trauma and often leads to compul-

sions and other symptoms. An interrupted emotion cycle means that: (a) the biological response is not completed; (b) the person is under- or overdistanced from the pain; and/or (c) the social permission to complete the cycle is denied ("Theory of Catharsis," p. 257). See note 50.

76. The example here focuses on white, blue-collar working-class men. There may be similarities to other members of the working class, e.g., men and women of color or white women.

77. Sennett and Cobb, *Hidden Injuries*, p. 62. For related works see Stanley Aronowitz, *False Promises: The Shaping of American Working Class Consciousness* (New York, N.Y.: McGraw Hill, 1974); Harry Braverman, *Labor and Monopoly Capital: The Degradation of Work in the Twentieth Century* (New York, N.Y.: Monthly Review Press, 1974); Patricia C. Sexton and Brendon Sexton, *Blue Collars and Hard Hats* (New York, N.Y.: Random House, 1971); and Michael Lerner, "Stress at the Workplace," *Catalyst* 8 (1980): 75–82.

78. Sennett and Cobb, *Hidden Injuries*, p. 73.

79. Sennett and Cobb, *Hidden Injuries*, p. 118.

80. Sennett and Cobb, *Hidden Injuries*, p. 153

81. Sennett and Cobb, *Hidden Injuries*, p. 97.

82. The following discussion of human response to trauma closely parallels that found in Bruno Bettelheim, *The Informed Heart*, pp. 119–130, 282, 288. Compare John Dewey's discussion of bad habits in *Human Nature and Conduct* (New York, N.Y.: The Modern Library 1930), part One, section II.

83. Pheterson, "Alliances," pp. 158–59.

84. Sherover-Marcuse, *Emancipation*, pp. 4–5.

85. For a good discussion of the phenomenon of "jumping to the other end of the stick" (in which some inmates of German concentration camps identified with the Nazi guards, imitating their mistreatment of inmates), see Bettelheim, *Informed Heart*, pp. 168–74, 286.

86. Sennett and Cobb, *Hidden Injuries*, p. 128.

87. Sherover-Marcuse, *Emancipation*, p. 4.

88. Sennett and Cobb, *Hidden Injuries*, p. 171.

89. Sennett and Cobb, *Hidden Injuries*, p. 152.

90. Sennett and Cobb, *Hidden Injuries*, p. 270.

91. Sennett and Cobb, *Hidden Injuries*, p. 270.

92. For an examination of how efforts to seek help with distress affect much social interaction see Charles Derber, *The Pursuit of Attention: Power and Individualism in Everyday Life* (Cambridge, Mass.: Schenkman Publishers, 1979).

93. Sherover-Marcuse, *Emancipation*, pp. 4–5.

94. It is incorrect to blame the oppressed for their internalized oppression. These habits were acquired in response to involuntary mistreatment. Nevertheless the oppressed can be held responsible, though not necessarily blameworthy, for choosing to act on these habits. They should not usually be held blameworthy, however, because they often lack a better picture of themselves that would assist them to identify internalized oppression as "not themselves."

95. Sennett and Cobb, *Hidden Injuries*, pp. 97–98.
96. Sherover-Marcuse, *Emancipation*, p. 154, n. 9.
97. I-II.85.1.
98. "... inquantum in voluntate inest quidam naturalis appetitus boni, quod est secundum rationem" (I-II.63.1).
99. "Nature is the principle of motion or movement," Aristotle quoted in I-II.58.1. See also Anton Pegis, *At the Origins of the Thomistic Notion of Man* (New York, N.Y.: Macmillan, 1963), pp. 44–47.
100. I-II.56.3a1.
101. F. C. Copleston, *Aquinas* (New York, N.Y.: Penguin Books, 1986), pp. 151–52.
102. "Augustinus dicit in Confess., 'Lex tua scripta est in cordibus hominum, quam nec ulla quidem delet iniquitas.' Sed lex scripta in cordibum hominum est lex naturalis. Ergo lex naturalist deleri non potest" (I-II.94.6.)
103. "Habitus autem malus dicitur qui disponit ad actum non convenientem naturae" (I-II.54.3).
104. "Unde quod ad malum ejus appetitus declinet contingit ex aliqua corruptione se inordinatione in aliquo principiorum hominis" (I-II.78.1).
105. I follow Alice Miller's argument about innocence as a reality of the child's situation, not as a romantic idealization of children. Miller states: "A baby is defenseless and as yet bears no responsibility for others; as yet, he owes nobody anything. But this fact does not contradict the frequent observation that children can behave very cruelly, just as cruelly as they have been treated by others" (*Banished Knowledge*, Leila Vennewitz, trans. [New York, N.Y.: Anchor Books, 1991], p. 46).
106. See Timothy E. O'Connell's description of original sin as a situation that the baby discovers, experiences, encounters, and protests. *Principles for a Catholic Morality*, rev. ed. (San Francisco, Calif.: Harper and Row, 1990), pp. 83–84.
107. Such a practice is well-described in liberation literature; a particularly good example is Sharon Welch, *A Feminist Ethic of Risk* (Minneapolis, Minn.: Fortress Press, 1990), chap. 7.
108. I am indebted to Christine Overall for these points in a personal letter.
109. Alice Miller exposes the oppressive aspects of the myth of the wicked child in chapter three of *Banished Knowledge*.
110. I-II.53.1, 2; 58.5; and 78.2.
111. For examples of Thomas's references to second nature and related phrases see n. 18.
112. "Quod, sicut dicitur in VII *Ethic.*, habitus similitudinem habet naturae, deficit tamen ab ipsa. Ed ideo, cum natura rei nullo modo removeatur ab ipsa, habitus difficile removetur" (I-II.53.1ad1).
113. Note that the possibility of eliminating vices does not imply in Thomas's framework that some properly developed second nature is waiting in the wings to be brought out at the first possible invitation. Dismantling old habits and acquiring new ones is tedious, lengthy, and uncertain. The

potential for virtue exists—but ending allegiance to internalized oppression and learning appropriate ways of acting are ongoing projects requiring sustained commitment.

114. It would be a misinterpretation to suggest that the distinction between aspects of our second nature implies an inherent dichotomy or dualism in the human psyche. We were not born with fragmented selves, but became fragmented due to disorder in the world. Only a few rare saints perhaps possessed an undivided self. They perhaps had a second nature devoid of internalized oppression. The rest of us have internalized oppression. Our overall functioning will be a mixture of flexible and rigid behaviors, appropriate and inappropriate passions. Yet internalized oppression is only an aspect of our second nature; it is not all of us. I make this distinction between nature and second nature using non-Thomistic sources in "Politics without Human Nature? Reconstructing a Common Humanity," *Hypatia* (Winter 1994): 40–41.

115. This is a theoretical possibility. In practice, we may possess neither the resources nor the skills to enable persons who are deeply enmeshed in vice to recover.

116. See Cannon, *Black Womanist Ethics*, pp. 104–5; and Sherover-Marcuse, *Emancipation*, p. 140.

117. In her first book Sharon Welch begins with Michel Foucault's version of a blank-slate discourse, and then, brought to the brink of despair, she entertains the innately evil discourse (*Communities of Resistance and Solidarity* [New York, N.Y.: Orbis, 1985], pp. 78–88). In her latest book she fortunately abandons the nihilism and relativism of Foucault and discusses the creation of a human identity (*A Feminist Ethic of Risk*, p. 150).

118. Christian theologians have traditionally cited original sin as the root of our commonalities rather than inherent nature. See I-II.81.1.

119. I.93.4.

120. See Carol Whitbeck's analysis of Aristotle and the theme of woman as partial man. "Theories of Sex Difference," in *Women and Values*, Marilyn Pearsall, ed. (Belmont, Calif.: Wadsworth Publishing Co., 1986), p. 34

121. "Sed quia imago Dei utrique sexui est communis, cum sit secundum mentem in qua non est dinstinctio sexuum" (I.93.6ad2).

122. This is a paraphrase of Weedon, *Feminist Practice*, p. 13.

123. A traditional reading of Thomas concludes that women and men are not fundamentally different, but possess complementary gifts that (conveniently) fit the existing division of labor. Many feminists have argued instead that men and women are each full complements and do not need each other in order to be whole. See Ruether, *Sexism and God-Talk*, pp. 96, 113.

124. Aquinas differentiates between species-nature (specific nature) and individual makeup. He does not claim that individuals are identical, only that everyone has the same species-nature. See I-II.63.1.

125. Thomas's claims about human nature correct some liberationists who charge that the term nature refers to rigid, undynamic essences. Thomas assumes that humans are dynamic and characterized by an inherent ability

to generate a fresh supply of intelligent engagements with reality. From his perspective, humans are not rigid and static—vices are. Regarding nature as undynamic is another example of ascribing the characteristics of second nature to nature.

   126. Cannon, *Black Womanist Ethics*, chap. 1; and Patricia Hill Collins, *Black Feminist Thought* (Boston, Mass.: Unwin Hyman, 1990), pp. 32, 44.

   127. II-II.25.6.

Taking Women's Experience Seriously: Thomas Aquinas and Audre Lorde on Anger

DIANA FRITZ CATES

TAKING WOMEN'S EXPERIENCE SERIOUSLY.

Women's experience raises moral questions, provides moral perspectives, reveals moral excellences, and admits of moral failures that have not been analyzed adequately by mainstream ethicists. Privileged white male ethicists, in reflecting upon their own experience and the experience of those with whom they are most familiar, have been successful at illuminating certain features of moral experience, some of which appear to be shared by all human beings. Other features, however, have been relegated to the shadows. Some of the latter features, when they are finally brought into the light of day, may reveal themselves to be peculiar to women; others may turn out to be shared across gender lines. Feminist ethicists urge their fellow ethicists to attend, in any case, to the diversity and complexity of women's experience in an effort to elucidate as fully as possible the moral experience of humans.

A fundamental principle of feminist ethics, then, is that "ethics must take women's experience seriously." But what does this mean? For Virginia Held, it means that ethics must "bring women's experience into the domain of moral consciousness" and count it as being "equal" in significance to the experience of men "in the construction or validation of moral theory."[1] It is only by making moral theory "deal with" experiences that are, at present, more typical of women than of men that we can hope for a future ethic that is "suitable for all humans in all contexts."[2]

For Margaret Farley, taking women's experience seriously means becoming aware of "the disparity between received traditional interpretations of [women's] identity and function within the human community and [women's] experience of themselves and their lives."[3] It means testing proposed moral principles, norms, and conceptions of well-being against women's experience of their own reality.[4]

For Ada Maria Isasi-Diaz, taking women's experience seriously includes seeking to be "converted" empathetically to a heartfelt understanding of the injustice suffered by *Feminista Hispana* and others who are oppressed because of their racial, ethnic, national, sexual, and class particularities. It means engaging in ethical reflection about the requirements of justice *as* a person who is vulnerable to the realization that "what is true and good for others [as oppressed] might well be true and good for [me, as oppressor]."[5]

For Katie Cannon, taking women's experience seriously includes recognizing that "[r]acism, gender discrimination and economic exploitation, as inherited, age-long complexes," have had a profound impact on the moral experience of black women.[6] It requires discerning what is ethically desirable for black women in light of "the circumstances, the paradoxes and the dilemmas that constrict Blacks to the lowest range of self-determination."[7]

Common to all of these perspectives is the view that good ethical reflection seeks to discover, articulate, assess, and apply moral principles, norms, visions, and values that emerge from and, in turn, shape the moral experience of diverse human beings, including those who have never before had a discernible voice in academic ethical discourse. Good ethical reflection attends carefully to the changing reality of moral experience. Taking *women's* experience seriously as ethicists means observing women's experience in as much of its variety as we can manage, empathizing with it, considering carefully how best to describe it, clarifying it without oversimplifying it, and subjecting it to analysis and evaluation in light of a well-deliberated, but open-ended vision of the good. It means doing all of this with the aim of enriching our understanding of what it is to do well at being human and thus becoming more deliberate in our attempts to improve the ordinary lives of women and men.[8]

Ethicists who wish to take women's experience seriously have many resources from which to draw. We can draw directly from the expressed experiences of past and present women. We can take advantage of various feminist analyses of these experiences. We can also make use of traditional ethical sources. Some feminist ethicists choose not to use the latter any more than they have to because these sources tend, in their view, to be oblivious to the reality of women's lives. Mary Hunt, for example, believes that, "[traditional] sources only distract since they are rooted in patriarchal worldviews that systematically pass over the particular experiences of women. Using them as starting points only reinforces what needs to be replaced. . . ."[9] Others choose to make considered use of materials written by men. Mary Daly, for example, uses Thomas Aquinas's analysis of the passions as a partial basis for constructing her radical feminist philosophical theory of the virtues. "I have chosen medieval naming of the passions as a springboard for Elemental Naming of them," she explains, "for there is a refreshing vigor, clarity, bluntness, and complex simplicity in that analysis that is lacking in contemporary psychobabble."[10] Thomas's analysis cannot simply be "taken as is and applied to women's situation," Daly argues, but it can be "used as a tool by Shrewd women" to "attain/regain Earthy/Elemental wisdom about the passions."[11]

June O'Connor offers a broad perspective on the issue of sources. She writes:

> Good ethics as I envision it and work at it, looks to multiple voices for wisdom and insight. . . . It looks to the experience described as revelation as well as to the experience of reason; it taps the wisdom that comes from intuition, from history, from both group experience and personal experience; it listens to creative imagination and to feeling, for it recognizes that truth and goodness can be perceived affectively as well as intellectually; it welcomes myths, rituals, proverbs, experiences, beliefs, and traditions as sources pertinent to furthering the religio-ethical task. No one of these sources alone is, or can be, sufficient. But each can offer its voice, shedding light on the question at hand. Religious ethics and philosophical ethics, benefitting from the breadth of view offered by specific historical traditions, should place all of these sources on their agenda for inquiry and assess their contribution in relation to one another.[12]

From this perspective, it appears unwise to dismiss traditional theological or ethical materials on the grounds that those who wrote them were not women and were not particularly interested in women's lives. There are features of human experience that all or most human beings seem to share, and some male scholars have captured some of these features well.[13] We must recognize, however, that there are important differences in the experiences of many women and men, as these have been shaped within the context of different male-ordered societies. It thus seems reasonable to anticipate that scholars like Thomas Aquinas have managed to get part, but not all, of the human picture right.

In what follows, I present a feminist ethical analysis that demonstrates part of what it is, in my view, for ethics to take women's experience seriously. I aim, specifically, to examine one woman's experience of a painful moral struggle. The woman is the late Audre Lorde—a black, lesbian poet and essayist whose writings have left an indelible mark on the hearts and minds of many ethicists. The moral struggle to which Lorde gives expression concerns the meaning and value of anger in the lives of black women in America. The principal source that I use to interpret, describe, clarify, and analyze Lorde's experience is Thomas Aquinas's account of anger in the *Summa theologiae*. I use this account because it is the best that I have encountered to date.[14] It is detailed, probing, revealing, and it brings much-needed clarity to a complex human phenomenon.[15]

Some readers will object that using Thomas, in effect, to systematize Lorde's experience could not possibly do justice to the uniqueness, the intricacy, and the depth of her experience. Indeed, no theoretical framework could. It must be acknowledged, however, that unless we subject our own and each other's experience to careful, critical, systematic, and thus nonself-deceptive analysis, using the best analytical tools at our disposal, the experience in question will remain largely opaque and impenetrable to ethical reflection. It will, accordingly, remain ineffectual in helping many who theorize about the right and the good to realize that they do so from an overly constrained experiential base. It is, of course, important that we not analyze our own and each other's experience in a way that makes of this experience a mere specimen for self-interested poking and probing. We can do our best to avoid this sort of objectification by remaining bound in our analysis by a heartfelt concern for women's and men's well-being.

I use Thomas's analysis of anger, then, to shed light on certain aspects of Audre Lorde's moral experience. I wish to elucidate Lorde's experience in order to frame as clearly as possible some of the philosophical issues to which it gives rise—issues with which Lorde invites all of us, as human beings, to wrestle. Using Thomas's analysis of anger in this way promises to reveal its remarkable contemporary significance. But it also promises to raise some unsettling questions. As we shall see, a central question concerns the ways in which Thomas's description of anger does and does not fit the experience of persons on the "underside" of modern western society.

THOMAS AQUINAS ON ANGER.

Let us begin with an analysis of Thomas on anger. I begin with Thomas, rather than Lorde, because my thinking about anger is, as a matter of fact, deeply Thomistic. Years of wrestling with Thomas's treatment of anger have disposed me to encounter analyses like Lorde's with Thomas's questions already in mind. Intellectual honesty seems to require this admission. Approaching women's experience with Thomas in mind does not, however, preclude the possibility of thinking new thoughts about anger outside of a Thomistic framework. It simply provides a helpful starting point. Whether this starting point is, in the end, a credible one is an assessment that can be made only after Thomas's analysis has been considered.

Thomas argues in his *Summa theologiae* that anger is a passion. Strictly speaking, a passion is a movement of the sense appetite.[16] The appetite is a power by which the self is moved to seek what is suitable and avoid what is unsuitable.[17] The sense appetite, in particular, is a power by which the self is moved to seek what the senses apprehend as delectable and avoid what the senses apprehend as odious.[18] Sense apprehensions that elicit movements of the sense appetite include apprehensions of the exterior senses, such as the sense of hearing, but they also include apprehensions of the interior senses, such as the sense of particular reason (*ratio particularis*). Particular reason is a power that apprehends the relative advantages or disadvantages attached to the attainment or avoidance of particular objects of sense.[19]

As Thomas's description of the sense of particular reason suggests, the interior sense apprehensions of human beings have "a certain affinity and proximity" to the powers of intellect that, "so to speak, [overflow] into them."[20] Ordinarily, human beings who apprehend an object as disadvantageous by means of the senses find that their powers of intellect are, at the same time, making it possible for them to make this disadvantageousness intelligible in terms of a conception of the good. Thus, human sense apprehensions tend always to be accompanied by apprehensions of the intellect.[21] Nevertheless, Thomas wants to maintain a distinction between interior sense apprehensions and intellective apprehensions.

First, interior sense apprehensions can take only sensible particulars as their intentional objects. Unlike intellective apprehensions, they cannot abstract universals from particulars. Particular reason, for example, can form an intention regarding the usefulness of a particular object; it can even compare the relative usefulness of different objects; but Thomas says that it can do so only by "some sort of collation" that falls short of an appeal to the category of the useful as an aspect of the good.[22]

Second, interior sense apprehensions are embodied in that they are "performed through a corporeal organ."[23] Just as exterior sense apprehensions take place through changes wrought in organs like the ears,[24] interior sense apprehensions take place through changes wrought in organs like the brain. The operation of particular reason, says Thomas, is performed by means of "a certain particular organ, namely, the middle part of the head."[25] By contrast, apprehensions of the intellect have their *origin* in sense apprehensions,[26] but they "so far [exceed] the corporeal nature that [they are] not even performed by any corporeal organ."[27]

Movements of the sense appetite that are elicited by sense apprehensions of particular objects are similarly particular and embodied. First, they are particular in that they are movements toward or away from objects that are apprehended by interior and exterior senses as suitable or unsuitable in their particularity. Just as sense apprehensions tend in humans to be accompanied by intellective apprehensions, so movements of the sense appetite tend in humans to be accompanied by movements of the intellective appetite, such that the whole self is moved by the object as it is apprehended.[28] Nevertheless, Thomas distinguishes movements of the sense appetite from those of the intellective appetite on the grounds that the intellective appetite is inclined toward objects that the intellect apprehends as "good according to the common notion of good," whereas the sense appetite is inclined toward objects that the senses apprehend as desirable in their singularity: "the sensitive appetite does not consider the common notion of good, because neither do the senses apprehend the universal."[29]

Second, movements of the sense appetite are embodied in that they "are properly to be found where there is corporeal transmutation."[30] Movements of the sense appetite have as their "material element" a "natural change of the organ; for instance, *anger* is said to be *a kindling of the blood about the heart.*"[31] Movements of the intellective appetite, by contrast, are not embodied in the same sense. They cause certain resonances in the body,[32] but they do not themselves take place in and through changes in the body. Thomas distinguishes movements of the sense appetite from movements of the intellective appetite on the grounds that "there is no need for corporeal transmutation in the act of the intellectual appetite: because this appetite is not exercised by means of a corporeal organ."[33]

To say that anger is a passion is thus to say that anger is an embodied movement of the sense appetite toward or away from an object that is apprehended by the external and internal senses as suitable or unsuitable in its particularity. It is to say this with the recognition, however, that sense apprehensions tend not to occur apart from intellective apprehensions, and movements of the sense appetite tend not to occur apart from movements of the intellective appetite. This caveat turns out to be particularly important in the case of anger, for anger is a passion and, as such, it is a movement of the sense appetite; yet it requires a certain contribution from the intellect in order to emerge in its distinctively human form.

Anger is a movement of the sense appetite. To be more specific about the sort of sense appetitive movement it is, we must follow Thomas through another distinction. Thomas divides the sense appetite into two parts: the concupiscible sense appetite and the irascible sense appetite. He says that,

> In order to make this clear, we must observe that in natural corruptible things there is needed an inclination not only to the acquisition of what is suitable and to the avoiding of what is harmful, but also to resistance against corruptive and contrary agencies which are a hindrance to the acquisition of what is suitable, and are productive of harm.[34]

The inclination to acquire or avoid that which is apprehended simply and straightforwardly as suitable or unsuitable to the senses is a movement of the concupiscible appetite. The inclination to resist blocks or attacks that hinder this seeking or avoiding is a movement of the irascible appetite. The irascible appetite empowers the self to resist, overcome, and rise above any obstacles that inhibit the movement of the concupiscible appetite.

Movements of the concupiscible appetite include love and hate, desire and aversion, joy and sorrow. Love, desire, and joy refer to the threefold movement wrought in the sense appetite by an object that is apprehended by the senses as suitable. Hate, aversion, and sorrow refer to the contrary threefold movement wrought by an object that is apprehended by the senses as unsuitable:

> In the first place, therefore, good causes, in the appetitive power, a certain inclination, aptitude or connaturalness in respect of good: and this belongs to the passion of *love:* the corresponding contrary of which is *hatred* in respect of evil.—Secondly, if the good be not yet possessed, it causes in the appetite a movement towards the attainment of the good [loved]: and this belongs to the passion of *desire* or *concupiscence:* and contrary to it, in respect of evil, is the passion of *aversion* or *dislike.*—Thirdly, when the good is obtained, it causes the appetite to rest, as it were, in the good obtained: and this belongs to the passion of *delight* or *joy:* the contrary of which, in respect of evil, is *sorrow* or *sadness*.[35]

Concupiscible passions are thus movements of initial attunement, elicited desire, and subsequent possession of a particular good or evil.

Movements of the irascible appetite include hope, despair, fear, daring, and anger. When the self desires to attain some future good to which the concupiscible appetite has acquired an initial attunement, but is kept from this attainment by some obstacle, then the movements of hope or despair are elicited. Either the self hopes, in which case the appetite is inclined to reach for what the self regards as an arduous, but nonetheless possible good.[36] Or the self despairs, in which case the appetite is inclined to withdraw from what the self regards as desirable, but impossible.[37] When the self desires to avoid some future evil to which the concupiscible appetite has acquired an initial hatred, but is kept from this avoidance by some obstacle, then the movements of daring or fear result. Either the self shows daring, such that the appetite is inclined to struggle against the threatening evil.[38] Or the self shows fear, such that the appetite is inclined to shrink from the threatening evil.[39] "It follows, therefore, that daring results from hope; since it is in the hope of overcoming the threatening object of fear, that one attacks it boldly. But despair results from fear: since the reason why a man despairs is because he fears the difficulty attaching to the good he should hope for."[40]

When the self desires to avoid some evil to which the concupiscible appetite has acquired an initial hatred, but the self cannot avoid the evil because the evil is already *present*, then anger may result. There is no movement of the irascible appetite that is contrary to anger (in terms of the duality of approach and withdrawal). Either the appetite is moved to resist and attack the present evil, in which case the self undergoes the irascible passion of anger. Or the appetite is moved to succumb to the present evil without a struggle, in which case the self suffers the simple concupiscible passion of sorrow. To withdraw from a present evil just *is* to succumb to it in sorrow.[41] Anger is actually caused by contrary passions, so that it contains, in effect, contrariety within itself. As we shall see, it is caused by sorrow accompanied by hope.[42]

For Thomas, anger is thus a movement of resistance or attack that takes place within the irascible part of the sense appetite. We are now in a position to examine in detail the causes, the objects, and the effects that Thomas attributes to this movement. The causes of anger can be considered in two ways: "first, on the part of the object [at which the anger is aimed]; secondly, on the part of the subject [who feels the anger]."[43] On the part of the object, anger is caused by an injury that has been committed against us.[44] Anger is caused, in particular, by the commission of a slight. A slight is an act that reveals that the one who commits it has "slight esteem" for us, that he "thinks little" of us, "care[s] little" about our well-being, or "seems not to care much" for our friendship.[45] A slight is an act that derogates our "excellence."[46]

Our excellence consists in any matters at which we excel and are recognized by others in the community to excel. The actual possession of an excellence and the communal recognition of that excellence are bound together in Thomas's analysis.[47] Wisdom, health, skills, wealth, power, superior social status, strength, and manliness are all considered by Thomas to be excellences.[48] It is clear that Thomas, following Aristotle, would also wish to include the virtues and the goods of friendship on this list. Implicit in Thomas's brief discussion of human excellence is, I believe, the assumption that it is our excellence that makes us distinctively who we are, and it is our excellence that makes us objectively lovable.[49] Hence when someone slights our excellence, he undermines the very basis of our self-understanding and self-esteem: he injures the goods that we esteem in ourselves (e.g., he cheats us out of our wealth or he accuses us of being cheap, inhibiting our claim to generosity in either case) and he does so in a way that is visible to other members of the community (who will no longer come to *us* when they need financial assistance). Insofar as we understand and esteem ourselves as others understand and esteem us, a slight makes us feel deficient, then, not only by causing in us some deficiency, but also by making us look deficient to people in whose regard we have a personal stake.

The cause of anger on the part of the object, then, is a slight committed against our excellence. Thomas clarifies that a slight is only likely to elicit anger when it is unmerited and thus unjustified. Thomas refers to Aristotle: "Wherefore the Philosopher says (Rhct. ii.3) that *men are not angry,—if they think they have wronged some one and are suffering justly on that account; because there is no anger at what is just.*"[50] In addition, "deficiency or littleness in the person with whom we are angry, tends to increase our anger, in so far as it adds to the unmeritedness of being despised."[51] The examples that Thomas gives to illustrate this point are telling: "For just as the higher a man's position is, the more undeservedly he is despised [by those inferior to him]; so the lower it is, the less reason he has for despising [those who are superior]. Thus a nobleman is angry if he be insulted by a peasant; a wise man, if by a fool; a master, if by a servant."[52]

These examples are telling because they reveal the extent to which Thomas's experience of anger was socially constructed out of an enduring, taken-for-granted, and publicly shared sense of appropriate social order that he and other members of his thirteenth-century European community inherited from Aristotle and other classical thinkers.[53] They are telling because they cause us to reflect upon the extent to which our own experiences of anger are socially constructed in terms of the sexism, racism, and classism of twentieth-century America. Many women, for example, report that it is difficult for them to get angry with sexist men. One reason is because these women are not, at bottom, convinced that sexist slights are unmerited. They have been conditioned by our still-sexist society to regard themselves as so deficient relative to the "excellence" of men that being treated *as* deficient causes little offense. Notably, Thomas says that, "if the person, who inflicted the injury, excel[s] very much, anger [toward him] does not ensue, but only sorrow."[54]

Thomas goes on to say that an unmerited slight is most likely to elicit anger when it is done on purpose. "For if we think that some one has done us an injury through ignorance or through passion, either we are not angry with them at all, or very much less: since to do anything through ignorance or through passion takes away from the notion of injury, and to a certain extent calls for mercy and forgiveness."[55] However, when someone knowingly and intentionally treats us as if we were of little account he gives expression to a considered judgment that we *are* of little account. His contemptuous judgment constitutes an injurious blow to some aspect of our goodness and thus a blow to the honor that we are due because of that aspect of our goodness. A deliberate injury of this sort angers us more than anything.[56]

We noted earlier that the causes of anger can be considered on the part of the object (i.e., the slighter) and on the part of the subject (i.e., the slighted).[57] As we have seen, the cause of anger on the part of the object is an unmerited slight committed against the subject, usually on purpose. On the part of the subject, there are several causes that are together sufficient to elicit anger.[58] One cause is the desire to seek what is good for us and repel what is evil. Like every other passion, anger is rooted in "natural" self-love.[59] A person does not get angry unless he perceives that his excellence has been slighted, and he does not perceive that his excellence has been slighted unless he perceives some good in himself that is worth promoting and being promoted by the community of which he is a part.[60]

A second cause of anger on the part of the subject is the initial sorrow that results when someone slights our excellence. "Now it is evident that nothing moves a man to anger except a hurt that grieves him: while whatever savors of defect is above all a cause of grief."[61] The movement of the sense appetite in response to a slight does not terminate in sorrow, however, when we perceive that we possess an excellence that is worthy of being protected, promoted, and honored by others. A third cause of anger on the part of the subject is our excellence itself.[62]

> Now it is evident that the more excellent a man is, the more unjust is a slight offered him in the matter in which he excels. Consequently those who excel in any matter, are most of all angry, if they be slighted in that matter; for instance, a wealthy man in his riches, or an orator in his eloquence, and so forth.[63]

On the other hand, if our excellence is well-established in the eyes of the people who matter most to us, then we may regard a slight to that excellence as trivial. "If a man be despised in a matter in which he *evidently* excels greatly, he does not consider himself the loser thereby and therefore is not grieved: and in this respect he is less angered."[64]

A fourth cause of anger on the part of the subject is the denouncing of an unmerited slight that has indeed injured our excellence: "wherefore the Philosopher says *(Ethic.* vii.) that *anger, [drawing] the inference that it ought to quarrel with such a person, is therefore immediately exasperated.*"[65] When we get angry, it is because we have drawn the inference that a slight committed against us must be denounced. We draw this kind of inference quickly and impulsively, and our sense of *what* follows from *what* can easily be distorted by "the commotion of the heat urging to instant action."[66] As we have seen, Thomas defines anger as a movement of the sense appetite that arises in response to sense apprehension. This implies that the inference at issue is not, in itself, a judgment of "universal reason." It may *become* such if "universal reason . . . so to speak, overflows into [it]" (I.78.4ad5), but it may, instead, remain resistant to reason: "of all the passions, anger is the most manifest obstacle to the judgment of reason."[67]

A fifth cause of anger on the part of the subject is the hope of getting back at the offender for committing the unmerited slight.[68] It is not enough that the slight be denounced; it must also be avenged. It is not enough that the offender be resisted; he must also be punished. He must be made to suffer for what he has done. Why? What good could possibly be accomplished by making the offender suffer? We can pursue this question by examining Thomas's discussion of the object of anger. The object of anger must not be confused with the cause of anger on the part of the object. The object of anger is what the angry person tends toward and (at the same time) away from in her anger, whereas the cause of anger on the part of the object is the act that elicits this tendency in the angry person. Thomas says that the object of anger is twofold. Anger tends *away from* a particular evil, namely, "the noxious person, on whom it seeks to be avenged," and it tends *toward* a particular good, namely, "the vengeance, which it desires to have."[69]

First, anger (i.e., the angry person) tends away from the person who has committed the slight. It tends away from this person as evil. Thomas says that anger is caused, in part, by sorrow. Thus, the object of anger would seem to overlap somewhat with the object of sorrow inasmuch as both anger and sorrow tend away from a present evil. Bear in mind, however, that anger (unlike sorrow) is a movement of the irascible part of the sense appetite, which means that there is an arduousness associated with it. Thomas says that there is an arduousness associated with both the tending away from the noxious person and the tending toward vengeance.[70] Thomas does not account for this arduousness except to say that it has something to do with the "magnitude" (magnitudine) of the evil object.

What does Thomas mean by the claim that anger's movement is arduous in that it tends with particular difficulty *away from* an evil of magnitude? He likely means that the offended person finds it difficult to dodge the offender's efforts to diminish his good, to make him appear diminished to others, and thus to make him *feel* diminished. The angry person finds it difficult to dodge the offender's efforts because the offender is someone of considerable standing in the eyes of the offended person. The offender is also someone of standing in the broader community: when he talks, people listen. This makes it difficult for the offended person to dismiss what the offender says. Where the offender is someone who commands little attention or esteem, the offended person is not likely to bother with him.[71]

Second, anger (i.e., the angry person) tends *toward* the vengeance that it seeks to execute. "Vengeance consists in the infliction of a penal evil on one who has sinned."[72] The angry person seeks to inflict evil on the offender by punishing him, "and the nature of punishment consists in being contrary to the will, painful, and inflicted for some fault. Consequently an angry man desires this, that the person whom he is hurting, may feel it and be in pain, and know that this has befallen him on account of the harm he has done the other."[73] It is important to note that the angry person seeks to carry out such punishment "in so far as it has an aspect of good, that is, in so far as he reckons it as just."[74] Under what conditions can such punishment be reckoned as just? When the person who executes it intends in his vengeance "the maintaining of justice and the correction of defaults."[75]

How can causing an offender pain contribute to "the maintaining of justice and the correction of defaults"? The offender has committed an unmerited slight against the offended person. In doing so, the offender has deprived the offended person of a good that is rightfully hers. He has failed to show her the respect and honor that she is due.

In response to this injustice, the offended person desires that justice be restored. How can causing the offender pain restore justice? Thomas says that, "by means of punishment the equality of justice is restored, in so far as he who by sinning has exceeded in following his own will suffers something that is contrary to his will."[76] What Thomas is getting at, I believe, is that justice is restored when the offender is made to suffer pain against his will, not simply because this "evens out" the pain suffered by the offender and the offended person, but because the offender is thereby made to feel constrained in the exercise of his will as the offended person was made to feel constrained in the exercise of her will, thereby reestablishing a certain balance of (duly constrained, interpersonal) power.[77]

The angry person desires more than this, however. She also desires "the correction of defaults," i.e., a correction of the inappropriately low regard that the offender has for her. It is not enough that the offender constrain his will to *express* his contempt for the offended person, say, through fear of further punishment. The offender must also stop *feeling* the contempt he has for the offended person. He must acquire the regard toward the offended person that the latter is due. Thomas does not say this explicitly, but he implies it when he says that acts of confession, repentance, and the begging of pardon on the part of the offender tend to appease an offended person's anger because these acts are an explicit recognition of the higher position or excellence of the offended person: "according to Prov. xv.1: *A mild answer breaketh wrath*: because, to wit, they [offenders] seem not to despise, but rather to think much of those before whom they humble themselves."[78]

Thomas is saying that the (second aspect of the) object of anger is punishment—a punishment that will make the offender suffer for his past failure to constrain the exercise of his will and a punishment that will, at the same time, rectify the offender's faulty regard for the offended person. The angry person wants, in effect, to force the offender to take her excellence seriously. But how can anyone force another to take due note of her excellence when the other does not see the excellence and does not care to see it? How can anyone force another to regard as excellent qualities for which he has little regard? Forcing the other to suffer humiliation or some other loss of goods seems unlikely to make him revere the punisher, unless of course the punisher wishes to be revered simply for her power to effect pain. Forcing the other to suffer humiliation or some other loss of goods could shake the offender up a bit, take some of the hot air out of his overinflated self-regard. It could thereby force him to raise his regard for the offended person indirectly by forcing him to lower his relative regard for himself. On the other hand, such punishment could just as readily cause the other to laugh in the offended person's face, thus deepening the slight. When an offended person lashes out in anger she reveals that the offender has gotten to her. She reveals the extent to which her self-regard is predicated on the regard of the offender, which makes her vulnerable to further slight.

Recall once again that anger is, for Thomas, a movement of the irascible part of the sense appetite, which means that there is a certain arduousness associated with both the tending away from the noxious person and the tending toward vengeance: "for the movement of anger does not arise, unless there be some magnitude about both these objects; since *we make no ado about things that are naught or very minute*, as the Philosopher observes (*Rhet.* ii.2)."[79] We are now in a position to discern part of what makes the angry person's tending *toward* vengeance so arduous. The vengeance that the angry person seeks is intended to bring about what the angry person regards as a just state of affairs between her and her offender, but the offender has likely made a considered judgment that the offended person and his relationship with her are of relatively small account. In such a case, it is unlikely that the angry person's punishment of the offender will effect the requisite reordering of regard. The arduousness in the desire for vengeance is intensified to the extent that it is preceded by the arduousness associated with anger's sorrow, namely, the recognition that the offender has the power to diminish the offended person's excellence and he has the power to make this diminishment visible to significant others.

I am pressing Thomas's analysis here, but in a way that I think is broadly consistent with his insights. Pressed in this way, Thomas's analysis makes visible an aspect of anger that ordinarily remains hidden from view, namely, the angry person's intense desire to force someone to take her seriously, yet her painful suspicion that serious regard on the part of others is not the sort of thing that can be forced. Pressed in this way, Thomas's analysis also exposes the "doublethink" inherent in the angry person's consciousness, namely, her ordinary assurance that certain of the qualities that she possesses are excellences, coupled with the nagging realization that these excellences are not recognized by someone who has (at least some of) the power to define excellence and to name the people who possess it. Her excellence cannot, in the end, count as excellence unless it is counted as such by certain people who wield a certain amount of power.[80]

As we have seen, Thomas holds that anger is a desire to punish someone for unjustly slighting our excellence. Consider, finally, two of the effects that anger has on the person who undergoes such a desire. One is a powerful disturbance in the body:

> ... because the movement of anger is not one of recoil, which corresponds to the action of cold, but one of prosecution, which corresponds to the action of heat, the result is that the movement of anger produces fervor of the blood and vital spirits around the heart, which is the instrument of the soul's passions. And hence it is that, on account of the heart being so disturbed by anger, those chiefly who are angry betray signs thereof in their outer members. For, as Gregory says (*Moral.* v. 30) *the heart that is inflamed with the stings of its own anger beats quick, the body trembles, the tongue stammers, the countenance takes fire, the eyes grow fierce, they that were well known are not recognized. With the mouth indeed he shapes a sound, but the understanding knows not what it says.*[81]

Although Thomas identifies this bodily commotion as an *effect* of anger, elsewhere he acknowledges that it is partly constitutive of anger itself, where anger is construed as a movement of the soul "in respect of a bodily transmutation."[82] Thomas says, for example, that "the commotion of the heat urging to instant action . . . is the material element of anger."[83] It is important to keep the bodily aspect of anger in view. Anger seeks vengeance, not as a clear-headed, logical response to a carefully measured injustice, but as a physically charged, impulsive reaction to an immediately sensed offense. The language of justice should not mask the fact that anger is, for Thomas, fundamentally a movement of the sense appetite that follows somewhat, but can also resist, the guidance of universal reason.

A second effect of anger is pleasure: "the movement of anger arises from a wrong done that causes sorrow, for which sorrow vengeance is sought as a remedy. Consequently as soon as vengeance is present, pleasure ensues, and so much the greater according as the sorrow was greater.—Therefore if vengeance be really present, perfect pleasure ensues, entirely excluding sorrow, so that the movement of anger ceases."[84] In light of our previous analysis of anger's object, it appears that, in order for vengeance to effect perfect pleasure in the offended person, it has to effect the regard on the part of the offender that the offended person thinks she is due. There may be *some* pleasure simply in feeling the power to make the offender feel constrained in the exercise of *his* power. There may be *some* pleasure simply in making the offender feel small, such that the offended person emerges in the punishing moment feeling bigger than the offender. But it would seem to be less than fully satisfying for an offended person to emerge feeling big in a respect for which she was not even slighted. Vengeance may, for example, make the offender *terrified* of the offended person, which means that he now regards more highly the offended person's power to injure him, but it may be that the respect in which the offended person really wants to be regarded highly is her artistic talents or her homemaking skills.[85]

In sum, Thomas holds that anger is an embodied movement of the irascible part of the sense appetite whose nature can be specified with reference to its causes, objects, and effects. The causes of anger are an unmerited slight to one's excellence, a self-loving desire to be justly regarded for one's excellence, a sorrow over the injury inflicted on that excellence, a denouncing of the injury, and a hope of avenging it by causing its perpetrator pain. The objects of anger are the perpetrator of the slight regarded under the aspect of evil, and vengeance toward him regarded under the aspect of good. Anger seeks vengeance as a means to the reestablishment of right relationship. Finally, the effects of anger are a powerful bodily commotion and a pleasure that attends the righting of a wrong.

Thomas's description of anger is remarkably astute, in my judgment, but it does not tell the whole story about anger—even as we have begun to extend its boundaries. Already we have reason to suspect that attending to western women's experiences of anger (and to the experiences of other marginalized people) will expose dimensions of anger that remain hidden in Thomas's analysis. We should not, I think, expect women's experiences of anger to undermine Thomas's account completely. Most men *and* women learn some version of anger as our passions are educated into western society, and Thomas's account seems to capture one such version very well.[86] We should, however, expect some women's experiences to raise questions of Thomas's account—questions that must be addressed before its descriptive adequacy can be assessed. We should expect this especially from women who have struggled long and hard "to git man off [their] eyeball."[87]

A feminist ethical analysis of anger requires that we assess a classic treatment like Thomas's as persons with an empathetic awareness of the problems and ambiguities evident in the angers of women. As an initial foray into this thick brush, let us turn to Audre Lorde's experience of anger.[88] Consider, in particular, some of the ways that Lorde's experience can be illuminated by Thomas's analysis and yet, at the same time, reflect back upon that analysis a critical light of its own.

THOMAS AND LORDE IN CONVERSATION.

Two of the essays that appear in Audre Lorde's *Sister Outsider* deal directly with anger. One essay, "The Uses of Anger: Women Responding to Racism,"[89] focuses on Lorde's anger toward white women. A second essay, "Eye to Eye: Black Women, Hatred, and Anger,"[90] focuses on Lorde's anger toward other black women. In what follows, I take these two essays as an expression of central aspects of Lorde's experience of anger. Lorde's expression of this experience is evocative, eye-opening, and painfully honest, which makes it a rich resource for ethical analysis. I can unearth only a few of its treasures within the framework of this essay.

Recall that Thomas frames his analysis of anger in terms of the causes, objects, and effects of anger. With regard to the causes of anger, he distinguishes between the cause on the part of the object and the causes on the part of the subject. He says that the cause of anger on the part of the object is an unmerited slight committed against our excellence. Thomas's use of the category "excellence" likely reflects its common usage among the privileged European men of his time. For him, our excellence includes our possession of goods like virtue and friendship, along with the respect that we command for possessing these goods. Our excellence also includes the possession of goods like wealth, power, status, oratory skills, manliness, and the honor associated with these goods. A common cause of anger, in Thomas's world, was a slight by which one person violated what another person regarded as his rightful standing in a well-ordered relationship or in the broader social hierarchy.[91]

The tendency of the powerful to identify their economic, political, and social privileges as excellences that compose an objective scale of value against which all people are to be measured—and the tendency to identify these excellences as natural or divinely ordained—is itself a principal cause of Lorde's anger.[92] For her, unmerited slight often takes the form of the racist and sexist presumption that white men—and white women, through their association with white men—are inherently superior to black women, such that they have "the right to dominance, manifest and implied."[93] Unmerited slight often takes the form of the racist and sexist presumption that white men—and women—have the right to dominate black women's minds and bodies by depriving them, ignoring them, stereotyping and ridiculing them, loathing them, and silencing them through thoughtlessness, intimidation, and violence.

Lorde could agree with Thomas that the cause of anger on the part of the object is an unmerited slight committed against one's excellence. Her experience as a black woman, however, raises potent questions regarding what counts as an unmerited slight against one's excellence and who is to count it as such. In what does one's excellence consist? Does it consist in the possession of certain qualities? If so, which ones? Does it consist in the possession of qualities that *we* prize or in qualities that are prized by others? Which others? On what grounds?

Lorde's experience informs her that her excellence, the ground of her value, lies partly in her humanness, where her humanness is conceived as the power to yearn for and to make truthful and transformative intellectual-emotional connections with persons who are *different* from her.

> We have been raised to view any difference other than sex as a reason for destruction, and for Black women and white women to face each other's angers without denial or immobility or silence or guilt is in itself a heretical and generative idea. It implies peers meeting upon a common basis to examine difference, and to alter those distortions which history has created around our difference. For it is those distortions [rather than our differences themselves] which separate us.[94]

For Lorde, our basic human excellence lies in "our power to examine and to redefine the terms upon which we will live and work; our power to envision and to reconstruct, anger by painful anger, stone upon heavy stone, a future of pollinating difference and the earth to support our choices."[95]

Lorde's experience also informs her that her excellence lies in the particular ways that she chooses to exercise this creative power. It lies in the way that she refuses "to settle for anything less than a rigorous pursuit of the possible in myself, at the same time making a distinction between what is possible and what the outside world drives me to do in order to prove I am human."[96] It lies in her love of black women, which moves her to confront with courage "the tangle of unexplored needs and furies that face any two Black women who seek to engage each other directly, emotionally, no matter what the context of their relationship may be."[97] It lies in the way that she has resisted racism and sexism to survive "in places where there was no light, no food, no sisters, no quarter."[98] It lies in the way that she has chosen to mother:

> I sat listening to my girl talk about the bent world [of the university that] she was determined to reenter in spite of all she was saying, because she views a knowledge of that world as part of an arsenal which she can use to change it all. I listened, hiding my pained need to snatch her back into the web of my smaller protections. I sat watching while she worked it out bit by hurtful bit—what she really wanted—feeling her rage wax and wane, feeling her anger building against me because I could not help her do it nor do it for her, nor would she allow that.[99]

In these and many other ways, Lorde gives expression to the particular excellences that she possesses, excellences that she prizes, even if the guardians of a racist and sexist America do not.

Thomas's description of the cause of anger on the part of the object is adequate to Lorde's experience in that her anger is, indeed, caused by an unmerited slight committed against her excellence. But what she counts as her excellence has little to do with her possession of recognized virtues (although it has a lot to do with her possession of qualities that the dominant culture does not recognize as virtues). It has little to do with the fact that she shares certain goods of friendship with white men and women and therefore feels betrayed when these goods aren't respected (although it has something to do with the fact that many white men and women deem friendship with someone so "different" from them to be impossible). And it has nothing to do with her possession of wealth, recognized social standing, or manliness. What Lorde counts as her excellence is her power to work with others on the margin of the dominant cultural system of values to "define and fashion a world where all our sisters can grow, where our children can love, and where the power of touching and meeting another woman's difference and wonder will eventually transcend the need for destruction."[100] It is when *this* excellence is slighted that Lorde's anger is evoked.[101]

The causes of anger on the part of the subject are specified by Thomas as a love of one's own good, a sorrow over the present injury to one's good, a denouncing of that injury on the basis of one's excellence, and a hoping for revenge. Once again, Lorde's experience of anger, interpreted in light of Thomas's analysis, raises some provocative issues with respect to that analysis. First, it is clear that Lorde loves herself and that, were it not for this love, she would not rage against those who seek to destroy her. Hers is not, however, the "natural" self-love of a privileged person that is rooted in a broad social acceptance. Hers is a subversive self-love that she has had to sustain in the face of blatant hatred:

> The Story Hour librarian reading *Little Black Sambo*. Her white fingers hold up the little book about a shoebutton-faced little boy with big red lips and many pigtails and a hatful of butter. I remember the pictures hurting me and my thinking again there must be something wrong with me because everybody else is laughing and besides the library downtown has given this little book a special prize, the library lady tells us.
>
> Lexie Goldman and I on Lexington Avenue, our adolescent faces flushed from springtime and our dash out of high school. We stop at a luncheonette, ask for water. The woman behind the counter smiles at Lexie. Gives us water. Lexie's in a glass. Mine in a paper cup. Afterward we joke about mine being portable. Too loudly.[102]
>
> Sometimes it feels as [though] if I were to experience all the collective hatred that I have had directed at me as a Black woman, admit its implications into my consciousness, I might die of the bleak and horrible weight.[103]

Born and raised in "a society of entrenched loathing and contempt for whatever is Black and female," Lorde internalized much of this hatred before she even knew what was happening.[104] To some extent, her self-love (i.e., her conviction of her own excellence) led her to resist images of herself that had been propagated by those who hated her, but to the extent that these images became her own, her self-love led her paradoxically to resist herself as the person so imaged.

> Did *bad* mean *Black*? The endless scrubbing with lemon juice in the cracks and crevices of my ripening, darkening, body. And oh, the sins of my dark elbows and knees, my gums and nipples, the folds of my neck and the cave of my armpits![105]

Lorde's self-love also led her paradoxically to resist other black women in whose faces she saw hateful images of herself:

> This cruelty between us, this harshness, is a piece of the legacy of hate with which we were inoculated from the time we were born by those who intended it to be an injection of death. But we adapted, learned to take it in and use it, unscrutinized. Yet at what cost! In order to withstand the weather, we had to become stone, and now we bruise ourselves upon the other who is closest.
>
> *I loved you. I dreamed about you. I talked to you for hours in my sleep sitting under a silk-cotton tree our arms around each other or braiding each other's hair or oiling each other's backs, and every time I run into you on the street or at the post office or behind the Medicaid desk I want to wring your neck.*[106]

Unwittingly, Lorde's self-love led her to resist herself and other black women in terms of a socially contrived measure by which both of them were inevitably condemned:

> If you are like me, then you will have to be a lot better than I am in order to even be good enough. And you can't be because no matter how good you are you're still a Black woman, just like me. (Who does she think she is?) So any act or idea that I could accept or at least examine from anyone else is not even tolerable if it comes from you, my mirror image. If you are not THEIR image of perfection, and you can't ever be because you are a Black woman, then you are a reflection upon me. We

are never good enough for each other. All your faults become magnified reflections of my own threatening inadequacies. I must attack you first before our enemies confuse us with each other. But they will anyway.[107]

As I see it, Lorde's self-love led her to seek the destruction of a self that had been constructed through the internalization of racist and sexist images, but it led her to seek the destruction of this self at least partly in the interest of another self—a self that she experienced to be her own, but whose dimensions she could not yet fully recognize. It led her to reject the first self in the interest of a second self whose excellence she simply could not deny. These are not easy distinctions to make philosophically or psychologically, and it is evident that Lorde struggled to make them even as she wrote.

Thomas is right to say that self-love is a cause of anger, but Lorde's experience raises questions about the self whose interests anger seeks to defend. Is this a self that identifies itself, to a significant degree, with privileges like wealth and social status? It seems natural for such a self to defend *its* interests by seeking to ensure the survival "of a system for which racism and sexism are primary, established, and necessary props of profit."[108] Is anger, for some of us, a passion that serves the maintenance of the status quo? Is our education into anger done in the service of our unquestioned privilege? Or is the self whose interests anger seeks to defend a self that continually calls such identifications into question? It seems natural for this second sort of self to defend *its* interests by seeking to establish authority over its own definition and by seeking to acquire a share of the resources needed to actualize its self-defined self. Is anger, for some of us, a passion that serves the subversion of the status quo? Is our education into anger done in the service of an alternative vision of justice? Lorde's experience, conflicted as it is, reveals that those who appear to have little reason for getting angry with the powerful (because they appear to have little excellence to defend) get angry with the powerful partly because of a love for the self whose identity remains beyond the grasp of the image-makers.[109]

One cause of anger on the part of the subject, then, is the self's love for itself. A second cause of anger on the part of the subject is sorrow over a slight. For Thomas, anger is caused partly by the pain of being diminished and regarded *as* diminished in the eyes of those whose regard matters to us. For Lorde, too, anger is caused by the pain of being knocked down and regarded as low, especially by those who appear to hold a higher position than us on some publicly endorsed scale of value. Lorde's experience reveals, however, that the cause of anger (at least for some of us) is more the sorrow suffered when we are not treated as equals than the sorrow suffered when our relative standing in a personal or social relationship is diminished. Lorde defines anger as "a grief of distortions between peers."[110] I take her to mean that anger is caused, in part, by the anguish that a person experiences when her peers fail to recognize her as a peer—as a person who possesses equal human dignity and the power to make a unique contribution to the good of society. The anger of many black women, in particular, is caused by the pain suffered when racists and sexists refuse to recognize, prize, and promote black women's power to keep hoping and loving under the most excruciating circumstances—their power "to keep this world revolving toward some livable future."[111]

Lorde's experience reveals that the anger of many black women is also caused by the sense of loss experienced when the internalization of racism and sexism causes black women to mistrust and misjudge each other:

> The language by which we have been taught to dismiss ourselves and our feelings as suspect is the same language we use to dismiss and suspect each other. Too pretty—too ugly. Too Black—too white. Wrong. I already know that. Who says so. You're too questionable for me to hear you. You speak THEIR language. You don't speak THEIR language. Who do you think you are? You think you're better than anybody else? Get out of my face![112]

> It is not that Black women shed each other's psychic blood so easily, but that we have ourselves bled so often, the pain of bloodshed becomes almost commonplace. If I have learned to eat my own flesh in the forest—starving, keening, learning the lesson of the she-wolf who chews off her own paw to leave the trap behind—if I must drink my own blood, thirsting, why should I stop at yours until your dear dead arms hang like withered garlands upon my breast and I weep for your going, oh my sister, I grieve for our gone.[113]

Lorde would thus agree with Thomas that anger is caused, in part, by sorrow, but she would likely urge us to reconsider the nature of this sorrow. For Thomas, this sorrow is commonly the painful experience of being reduced in size relative to those whose regard is important to us. For Lorde, this sorrow is the painful experience of being refused entrance into the ranks of peer altogether because one is thought by those who establish these ranks to be small by nature. For Lorde, this sorrow is also the painful experience of being unable to embrace other of the system's "rejects" as peers because one has internalized, to some degree, the system's message that rejects are not "worth wanting each other."[114] A single slight on the part of a ranked member of society elicits a painful feeling of being alienated and isolated from rejecters and rejects alike.

A third cause of anger on the part of the subject is the denouncing of the injury to one's excellence. Thomas says that anger is caused, in part, by an immediate judgment that one has been injured unjustly and that unjust injuries are bad. With Thomas in mind, we could say that for Lorde, too, anger is caused by an immediate judgment that the slight committed against one was unmerited and that unmerited slights are bad. Lorde's experience reveals, however, that anger is also caused by an immediate judgment that the prevailing social order, which presumes that most slights committed against black women are merited, is itself bad and must be denounced: ". . . if I take the white world's estimation of me as Black-woman-synonymous-with-garbage to heart, then deep down inside myself I will always believe that I am truly good for nothing."[115] Lorde denounces racist and sexist slights partly by denouncing the racism and the sexism in whose terms they appear to be justified: "America's measurement of me has lain like a barrier across the realization of my own powers. It was a barrier which I had to examine and dismantle, piece by painful piece, in order to use my energies fully and creatively."[116] It may be that, for most of us, anger is caused not only by a denouncing of a slight, but also by a denouncing of some larger, amorphous social reality in relation to which we feel objectified, quantified, and judged.[117]

One cause of anger is thus, for Lorde, the denouncing of a particular slight and the unjust social order in terms of which that slight appears to be justified. Lorde makes clear that the denouncing of a slight facilitates an empowering affirmation of the self's value. She goes on, however, to make the observation that the immediate denouncing of a slight sometimes impedes self-affirmation by causing the self to deny just how important the affirmation of others is to the self. Lorde focuses on the way in which her denouncing of a slight from a black woman often serves to disguise how much she needs the respect and love of that woman.

> The anger with which I meet another Black woman's slightest deviation from my immediate need or desire or concept of a proper response is a deep and hurtful anger, chosen only in the sense of a choice of desperation—reckless through despair. That anger which masks my pain that we are so separate who should be most together—my pain—that she could perhaps not need me as much as I need her, or see me through the blunted eye of the haters, that eye I know so well from my own distorted images of her. Erase or be erased![118]

> . . . sometimes it feels like better a righteous fury than the dull ache of loss, loss, loss.[119]

Pressing Lorde's point, it seems that the immediate denouncing of an oppressor's[120] slight can sometimes provide the oppressed with a self-deceptive diversion—a diversion from the painful reality that the oppressed yearn to be received and affirmed by the oppressor in such a way that the oppressor finds himself no longer capable of oppressing. Better to denounce straightaway one's injury at the hands of the "vile oppressor" than to admit how much we long for his transformation into tenderness, compassion, and delight in the fact that we are.

A fourth cause of anger on the part of the subject is the hope for vengeance. Once again, we can address this aspect of anger by turning to a discussion of anger's object. Recall that for Thomas, the object of anger is twofold. On the one hand, the angry person tends in her anger *away from* the person who has injured her excellence, "as something contrary and hurtful, which bears the character of evil."[121] For Lorde, too, we who are angry recoil in our anger from evil ones who have chosen to treat us as if we were negligible. But more than this, we who are angry recoil from evil ones who have come, through no fault of their own, to represent for us the judgment that "people like you and me don't count for much." That is to say, we recoil from our sisters—and from ourselves—because all we can see when we look at each other—and at ourselves in the mirror—is the oppressor's judgment that we are not worth wanting.

Lorde's experience enables us to find deep significance in Thomas's claim that there is a certain arduousness associated with anger's tending away from the present evil of the offender. The reason why it is so difficult for some of us to tend away from this evil is because we are so vulnerable to persons who try to "make" us by insisting that they will only recognize us if we embody the ready-made images that they provide for us.

> Growing up, metabolizing hatred like a daily bread. Because I am Black, because I am woman, because I am not Black enough, because I am not some particular fantasy of a woman, because I AM.[122]

Once we embody these images, it is very difficult for us to tend away from the image-makers as evil. It is very difficult for us to insist that the image-maker's judgment of his own creation is mistaken. Lorde's experience reveals, in a way that Thomas's discussion does not, how difficult it is to resist as evil a person whose judgment of us confirms what we have always been told and what we have therefore learned to tell ourselves, namely, that we will *never* measure up.

The angry person tends *away from* the evil of the person who slights her. But she tends, at the same time, *toward* the good of vengeance against that person. Thomas says that the angry person wants to cause her offender pain in the hope of reestablishing a just relationship with him. It appears that Lorde, too, would say that the angry person wants to cause her offender pain, even though the angry person causes *herself* pain in the process:

> Why do I dream I cradle you at night? Divide your limbs between the food bowls of my least favorite animals? Keep vigil for you night after terrible night, wondering? Oh sister, where is that dark rich land we wanted to wander through together?[123]

Lorde, too, would say that the angry person wants to cause her offender pain in the hope of righting their relationship. In Lorde's language, the angry person wants to bring about change: "Anger is a grief of distortions between peers," she says, "and its object is change."[124] What sort of change does she have in mind? "I do not mean a simple switch of positions or a temporary lessening of tensions, nor the ability to smile or feel good. I am speaking of a basic and radical alteration in those assumptions underlining our lives," including the assumption that racism and sexism are "immutable given[s] in the fabric of [our] existence."[125]

Because the object of her desire is the effecting of a particular sort of relationship, namely, one in which the participants receive and respond to each other as peers in difference, Lorde wants in her anger to cause a particular sort of pain. She does *not* want to cause her offender the pain of guilt:

> Guilt is not a response to anger; it is a response to one's own actions or lack of action. If it leads to change then it can be useful, since it is then no longer guilt but the beginning of knowledge. Yet all too often, guilt is just another name for impotence, for defensiveness destructive of communication; it becomes a device to protect ignorance and the continuation of things the way they are, the ultimate protection for changelessness.[126]

Neither does Lorde want to cause her offender the pain of fear, as fear "seduce[s] us into settling for . . . less than the hard work of excavating honesty."[127] What sort of pain *does* she want to cause her offender? Implicit in Lorde's work, as I read it, is the notion that the angry person wants to make her offender feel the pain of being "brought down to size." But much more than this, the angry person wants to make her offender suffer the realization that his well-being is bound up with the well-being of every other human being, such that when he treats another human being as if she were of little account, he becomes of little account himself. That is to say, the angry person wants to make her offender come to the painful realization that he, too, is a vulnerable and needy relational creature: "I am not free while any woman is unfree, even when her shackles are very different from my own. And I am not free as long as one person of Color remains chained. Nor is any one of you."[128]

The fact that Lorde struggles in her work to avoid causing paralyzing guilt and fear in the objects of her anger reveals an aspect of the arduousness that Thomas thought to be associated with the tending toward just vengeance. Lorde not only faces the resistance of people who openly hate her and seek to maintain the institutionalization of that hatred. She also faces the resistance of people who claim that they want to effect a change in their relationship with her, but are in truth unwilling to surrender any of the power or privileges that they have amassed relative to her. She faces the self-love of white women, for example, who identify themselves partly with the status of their white men and therefore feel deeply threatened by Lorde's call for change. Lorde's experience is that her anger often turns off the people that she most desires to reach; it makes them run away from her rather than turn toward her; it effects alienation, rather than compassion.

For Thomas, the angry person desires vengeance with the intention of reestablishing the just relationship that was upset by the slight. For Lorde, the angry person desires vengeance with the intention of establishing, perhaps for the first time, a relationship that is truly respectful of human equality in difference. Establishing such relations requires rethinking the meaning of justice. What does it *mean* to give to each according to his or her due? What, exactly, is each of us due? Respect for our humanity? Respect for our differences? Which of our differences are *worthy* of respect? In accordance with which vision of the good? Lorde's experience reveals how important it is that such questions be pursued as free as possible from the constraints of racism and sexism.

Finally, consider the effects of anger on the one who experiences it. Like Thomas, Lorde recognizes that anger can effect powerful changes in the body. She speaks of her anger as "a molten pond at the core of me, . . . an electric thread woven into every emotional tapestry upon which I set the essentials of my life—a boiling hot spring likely to erupt at any point, leaping out of my consciousness like a fire on the landscape."[129] I think that, for Lorde, it is this bodily commotion, in part, that can make anger so dangerous and destructive, but it is this same commotion that can make anger so transformative. "Every woman has a well-stocked arsenal of anger potentially useful against those oppressions, personal and institutional, which brought that anger into being. Focused with precision it can become a powerful source of energy serving progress and change."[130]

Thomas argues that pleasure is another effect of anger, at least in cases where anger is effective in securing its desired end. For Lorde, the angry person gets some pleasure from doing what she can to expose and expunge the racism and the sexism of her offenders. She gets some pleasure from doing what she can to create fruitful relationships. Given the incredible resilience of prejudice, however, such pleasure is bound to be short-lived and bittersweet. Lorde implies that the person who struggles for justice in anger gets most of her pleasure from the simple realization that she continues to survive and to struggle. This does not sound much like the perfect pleasure that Thomas deemed possible in the angry man.

CONCLUSION.

Bringing Thomas and Lorde into conversation with each other reveals the contemporary relevance and significance of Thomas's analysis of anger. At the same time, however, it reveals how important it is to construct accounts of human anger in light of a *variety* of human experiences, including the experiences of those who have been consistently marginalized relative to the reigning systems of social value. Thomas's analysis shows that anger is caused by an unjust slight to one's excellence. Our reading of Lorde's experience reveals that we must beware lest the system-builders define what counts as an excellence and a slight to one's excellence in a way that systematically undermines the moral authority of the system-busters. Thomas's analysis shows that anger is caused by a desire to defend the interests of the self. Our reading of Lorde's experience reveals that this can be a desire to defend the interests of a relatively privileged self (so that anger becomes, to a significant extent, an assertion of superiority), or it can be a desire to defend the interests of a disenfranchised self (so that anger becomes more an assertion of basic human equality). Thomas's analysis shows that anger is caused by sorrow at being denied the due regard of others. Our reading of Lorde's experience reveals that, for many of us, this is less a sorrow at losing our previously recognized standing in some interpersonal or broader social order than it is a sorrow at not being regarded as peer.

Thomas's analysis shows that anger is caused by the immediate denouncing of a slight. Our reading of Lorde's experience reveals that anger is often caused by the simultaneous denouncing of the prevailing social order in terms of which the slight appears to be justified. Thomas's analysis shows that anger takes as its object the person who committed the particular slight. Our reading of Lorde's experience reveals the way in which racism and sexism function to make slighted persons, too, the unwitting objects of their own anger, such that they implode on themselves or explode in "horizontal rage." Thomas's analysis shows that anger seeks vengeance with the intention of righting a wrong relationship. Our reading of Lorde's experience reveals that we need to rethink what it is to be in right relationship with persons who are different from us (especially with respect to gender and race). Thomas's analysis shows the power that an embodied anger can have to effect pleasure-inducing ends. Our reading of Lorde's experience reveals the power that an embodied anger can have to enable the oppressed to survive and even to survive with dignity as they struggle against the odds to establish right relationships with each other and with their oppressors.

Bringing Thomas and Lorde into conversation with each other exposes some of the peculiarities of Thomas's analysis, but it also shines light on some of the problematic tensions within angers like Lorde's. It enables us to see, for example, that some of the angers of the oppressed appear to be inadvertently expressive and supportive of a social yardstick according to which certain persons and groups will always come up short. The implicit adoption and reinforcement of this measure that occurs in the feeling and expressing of certain kinds of anger appears to be counterliberative. At the same time, however, it may be that the angers of the oppressed can, to some degree, be formed and used by the oppressed to subvert this very measure and its power over our lives. Examining Thomas and Lorde together as we have done makes clear that there can be no sociopolitical liberation apart from the liberation of our minds, which we must pursue within the framework of our day to day lives.

It is one thing, of course, to determine the way in which anger does, in fact, function in our societies and our lives. It is another to determine the way in which anger *ought* to function in our societies and our lives. This essay has undoubtedly given rise to serious normative questions that cannot be pursued within its limits. I invite readers to pursue some of these questions themselves. Wrestling with descriptive and normative questions regarding anger and other of the human passions is not only an interesting academic exercise. It is part and parcel of the work of virtue.

In conclusion, certain traditional sources can be of use in helping human beings to better understand, assess, and shape the structure of their experience. But these sources have to be used very carefully. They have to be used with a raised awareness of the ways in which definitions of humanness, including definitions of human emotions like anger, can render certain humans invisible to the dominant culture, problematic or even unintelligible to themselves, and overwhelmed with vague doubts regarding whether or not they really *count* as human. Traditional sources can be useful in helping us understand what it means to be human, but we must hold onto their conceptual frameworks loosely enough that we are able to see and understand those humans whose experiences do not fit these frameworks—persons who show us that there may be something seriously flawed in the frameworks themselves. In any case, we ought not to presume that analyses of human experience that are offered by even the most brilliant of men (like Thomas) are, in themselves, sufficient to give us an adequate account of the human. Critical attention must be paid to the experiences of women (and other oppressed persons). If the (partially) analyzed experience of one marginalized black woman is so provocative of ethical insight, imagine the insight that could be gleaned from analyses of so many other women's experiences.[131]

NOTES

1. Virginia Held, "Feminism and Moral Theory," *Women and Moral Theory*, Eva Feder Kittay and Diana T. Meyers, eds. (Totowa, N.J.: Rowman & Littlefield, 1987), pp. 112–4.
2. Virginia Held, "Feminism and Moral Theory," p. 114. For Held, a universal moral theory would be a feminist moral theory in that it would "[reflect] the experience and standpoint of women" as well as men (114).
3. Margaret Farley, "Feminist Theology and Bioethics," in Barbara Hilkert Andolsen, Christine E. Gudorf, and Mary D. Pellauer, eds., *Women's Consciousness, Women's Conscience: A Reader in Feminist Ethics* (San Francisco, Calif.: Harper & Row, 1985), p. 295.
4. Margaret Farley, "Feminist Theology and Bioethics," p. 295.
5. Ada Maria Isasi-Diaz, "Toward an Understanding of *Feminismo Hispano* in the U.S.A.," in Andolsen, Gudorf, and Pellauer, eds., *Women's Consciousness, Women's Conscience*, pp. 52–53.
6. Katie G. Cannon, *Black Womanist Ethics* (Atlanta, Ga.: Scholars Press, 1988), p. 2.
7. Cannon, *Black Womanist Ethics*, p. 3.
8. "Ordinary lives" is a "term of art" used by Charles Taylor "to designate the [everyday] life of production and the family," which is regarded in modern times as "the very centre of the good life." Modern feminists hold that the life of friendship, too, is morally central. Charles Taylor, *Sources of the Self: The Making of the Modern Identity* (Cambridge, Mass.: Harvard University Press, 1989), pp. 13–14.
9. Mary E. Hunt, *Fierce Tenderness: A Feminist Theology of Friendship* (New York, N.Y.: Crossroad, 1992), p. 2.
10. Mary Daly, *Pure Lust: Elemental Feminist Philosophy* (Boston, Mass.: Beacon Press, 1984), p. 198.

11. Daly, *Pure Lust*, p. 199.

12. June O'Connor, "On Doing Religious Ethics." In Andolsen, Gudorf, and Pellauer, eds., *Women's Consciousness, Women's Conscience*, p. 281.

13. I appreciate that, for many of us, "common human experience" looks like a concept used by those in power to render invisible important differences between human beings and thereby to diffuse the potentially explosive power of these differences. Nevertheless, it remains the case that unless we posit the reality of *some* common human experience, we cannot account for the reality of human understanding between selves, nor can we account for the meaningfulness of ethics. For diverse perspectives on the elements of experience that we can and cannot assume human beings to share, see Gene Outka and John P. Reeder, Jr., eds., *Prospects for a Common Morality* (Princeton, N.J.: Princeton University Press, 1993).

14. Thomas's analysis is extended creatively and powerfully by J. Giles Milhaven in *Good Anger* (Kansas City, Mo.: Sheed and Ward, 1989).

15. It should be noted from the start that Thomas got many of his insights on anger from Aristotle. It is beyond the scope of this paper, however, to delineate this connection. See Aristotle, *Rhetoric*, W. Rhys Roberts, trans., *The Basic Works of Aristotle*, Richard McKeon, ed. (New York, N.Y.: Random House, 1941), book II, chaps. 2 and 3.

16. ". . . ratio passionis . . . invenitur in actu appetitus sensitivi. . . ." (I-II.22.3). All references are to the *Summa theologiae*. References to the Latin are to S. Thomae Aquinatis, *Summa theologiae* (Romae: Marietti, 1950). Where the reference is *not* included in the body of the paper, the footnote contains the reference along with additional comments. I follow the translation of St. Thomas Aquinas, *Summa Theologica*, Fathers of the English Dominican Province, trans. (Westminster, Md.: Christian Classics, 1981).

17. I.80.1.

18. I.80.2.

19. I.78.4.

20. ". . . illam eminentiam habitum cogitativa et memorativa in homine, non per id quod est proprium sensitivae partis; sed per aliquam affinitatem et propinquitatem ad rationem universalem, secundum quandam refluentiam" (I.78.4ad5).

21. I am seeking here to interpret Thomas in a way that grasps the unity of the Thomistic self without collapsing Thomas's distinction between intellective and sense apprehensions and appetites. See, e.g., I.78.4, 81.3, 84.6; I-II.46.4. For an excellent discussion of the Thomistic self as a soul-body composite, see G. Simon Harak, S. J., *Virtuous Passions: The Formation of Christian Character* (Mahwah, N.J.: Paulist Press, 1993), chaps. 3–4.

22. I.78.4. In effect, Thomas wants to identify a way of forming intentions about sense objects that is higher than the way nonhuman animals form them, yet lower than the way humans form them with their intellects. It might be helpful to think of the sense apprehensions that elicit passions as lying along the broad middle-range of a continuum. On one end of the continuum would be apprehensions of particulars like "this sensation." On the other end would be apprehensions of universals like "the good."

23. ". . . fit per organum corporale. . . ." (I.78.1).
24. Thomas says that the eyes are an exception in that sight takes place "without natural immutation either in its organ or in its object," which makes it "the most spiritual, the most perfect, and the most universal of all the senses." "Visus autem, quia est absque immutatione naturali et organi et obiecti, est maxime spiritualis, et perfectior inter omnes sensus, et communior" (I.78.3).
25. ". . . determinatum organum, scilicet mediam partem capitis" (I.78.4).
26. I.78.4.
27. "Est ergo quaedam operatio animae, quae intantum excedit naturam corpoream, quod neque etiam exercetur per organum corporale" (I.78.1).
28. I.81.3.
29. "Appetitus autem sensitivus non respicit communem rationem boni: quia nec sensus apprehendit universale" (I.82.5).
30. ". . . passio proprie invenitur ubi est transmutatio corporalis" (I-II.22.3).
31. ". . . unde in definitione motuum appetitivae partis, materialiter ponitur aliqua naturalis transmutatio organi; sicut dicitur quod *ira est accensio sanguinis circa cor*" (I-II.22.2ad3).
32. I-II.24.
33. "In actu autem appetitus intellectivi non requiritur aliqua transmutatio corporalis: quia huiusmodi appetitus non est virtus alicuius organi" (I-II.22.3).
34. "Ad cuius evidentiam, considerari oportet quod in rebus naturalibus corruptibilibus, non solum oportet esse inclinationem ad consequendum convenientia et refugiendum nociva; sed etiam ad resistendum corrumpentibus et contrariis, quae convenientibus impedimentum praebent et ingerunt nocumenta" (I.81.2).
35. "Bonum ergo primo quidem in potentia appetitiva causat quandam inclinationem, seu aptitudinem, seu connaturalitatem ad bonum: quod pertinet ad passionem *amoris*. Cui per contrarium respondet *odium*, ex parte mali.—Secundo, si bonum sit nondum habitum, dat ei motum ad assequendum bonum amatum: et hoc pertinet ad passionem *desiderii* vel *concupiscentiae*. Et ex opposito, ex parte mali; est *fuga* vel *abominatio*.—Tertio, cum adeptum fuerit bonum, dat appetitus quietationem quandam in ipso bono adepto: et hoc pertinet ad *delectationem* vel *gaudium*. Cui opponitur ex parte mali, *dolor* vel *tristitia*" (I-II.23.4).
36. I-II.40.1.
37. I-II.40.4.
38. I-II.45.1.
39. I-II.42.1.
40. I-II.45.2.
41. I-II.23.3.
42. I-II.46.1a2.
43. "Causa autem passionis, ut supra dictum est, dupliciter accipi potest: uno modo, ex parte obiecti; alio modo, ex parte subiecti." (I-II.46.5).

44. Anger can also be caused by an injury committed against other people, but only because they "belong in some way to us: either by some kinship or by friendship, or at least because of the nature we have in common." ". . . irascimur contra illos qui aliis nocent, et vindictam appetimus, inquantum illi quibus nocetur, aliquo modo ad nos pertinent: vel per aliquam affinitatem, vel per amicitiam, vel saltem per communionem naturae" (I-II.47.1ad2).

45. "Oblivio enim parvipensionis est evidens signum: ea enim quae magna aestimamus, magis memoriae infigimus. Similiter ex quadam parvipensione est quod aliquis non vereatur contristare aliquem, denuntiando sibi aliqua tristia. Qui etiam in infortuniis alicuius hilaritatis signa ostendit, videtur parum curare do bono vel malo eius. Similiter etiam qui impedit aliquem a sui propositi assecutione, non propter aliquam utilitatem sibi inde provenientem, non videtur multum curare de amicitia eius. Et ideo omnia talia, inquantum sunt signa contemptus, sunt provocativa irae" (I-II.47.2ad3).

46. "Et ideo quodcumque nocumentum nobis inferatur, inquantum excellentiae derogat, videntur ad parvipensionem pertinere" (I-II.47.2).

47. Thomas says, for example, that ". . . we seek for some kind of excellence from all our goods [which implies that the excellence and the goods are two different things]. Consequently whatever injury is inflicted on us, in so far as it is derogatory to our excellence, seems to savor of a slight." "Ex omnibus autem bonis nostris aliquam excellentiam quaerimus. Et idea quodcumque nocumentum nobis inferatur, inquantum excellentiae derogat, videntur ad parvipensionem pertinere" (I-II.47.2).

48. I-II.47.3, 47.4. I add manliness (virilitas) to the list because Thomas links it with excellence (excellentia) at I-II.48.3ad2, where he links both manliness and excellence with vengeance. At I.92.1 *passim*, ad1, and ad2, Thomas associates the excellence of men with their "naturally" superior intellectual capacities relative to women. It is noteworthy that the Latin word for virtue (virtus) has its root in the word for man (vir).

49. It seems clear that, for Thomas, all human beings are due *some* personal and moral regard simply by virtue of the fact that they are human beings. As we have seen, he says, "If we are angry with those who harm others, and seek to be avenged on them, it is because those who are injured belong in some way to us: either by some kinship or by friendship, or at least *because of the nature we have in common*" (I-II.47.1ad1; my emphasis). It seems equally clear, however, that for Thomas, some human beings are due *more* personal and moral regard than others (beyond the bare minimum that they are due as humans). He says, for example, that "the more excellent a man is, the more unjust is a slight offered him in the matter in which he excels" ["Constat autem quod quanto aliquis est excellentior, iniustius parvipenditur in hoc in quo excellit"] (I-II.47.3), which implies that the kind and amount of personal and moral regard that a person is due depends, to some extent, on his possession of qualities that are not possessed (at least not to the same degree) by all humans. See also Thomas's detailed discussion of the order of charity, where he argues (for example) that, "the better a thing is, and the more like to God, the more is it to be loved: and in this way a man ought to

love his father more than his children, because, to wit, he loves his father as his principle, in which respect he is a more exalted good and more like God." "Et secundum hoc id quod habet maiorem rationem boni est magis diligendum, et quod est Deo similius. Et sic pater est magis diligendus quam filius: quia scilicet patrem diligimus sub ratione principii, quod habet rationem eminentioris boni et Deo similioris" (II-II.26.9).

50. "Unde dicit Philosophus, in II *Rhetoric.*, quod *si homines putaverint eos qui laeserunt, esse iuste passos, non irascuntur: non enim fit ira ad iustum*" (I-II.47.2).

51. "Defectus igitur vel parvitas eius contra quem irascimur, facit ad augmentum irae, inquantum auget indignam despectionem" (I-II.47.4).

52. "Sicut enim quanto aliquis est maior, tanto indignius despicitur; ita quanto aliquis est minor, tanto indignius despicit. Et ideo nobiles irascuntur si despiciantur a rusticis, vel sapientes ab insipientibus, vel domini a servis" (I-II.47.4).

53. Nearly all of the authoritative statements adduced by Thomas to indicate the significance of "slight" and "excellence" to the elicitation of anger are Aristotle's. I am not claiming that Thomas constructed his account of anger deliberately with an eye toward reinforcing the prevailing social order; I am only claiming that his account reflects such an order and that it serves, in fact, to reinforce it. I shall pursue this point further in section III.

54. "Unde si fuerit multum excellens persona quae nocumentum intulit, non sequitur ira, sed solum tristitia . . ." (I-II.46.1). Thomas's precise point here is that anger only arises where there is hope of revenge. When the person who slights us excels very much relative to us, there is little hope of us ever getting that revenge (even if we feel we deserve it). Still, I think this passage points to the fact that people who are thought to be small by those who wield power over them have little basis for thinking that they are anything *but* small. Hence, they are likely to feel sorrow at their smallness, rather than resisting the very charge of smallness. In another question, Thomas says that "men who are weak, or subject to some other defect, are more *easily* angered, since they are more easily grieved" ["Et ista est causa quare homines qui sunt infirmi, vel in aliis defectibus, *facilius* irascuntur: quia facilius contristantur"] (I-II.47.3; my emphasis). This statement seems to be at odds with Thomas's overall view of anger in that a person who is broadly deficient in the possession of excellence would seem to have little grounds for insisting on his excellence. Then again, it is perhaps a mistake to expect that a broadly deficient person would have an accurate understanding of his deficiency.

55. "Si enim putemus aliquos vel per ignorantiam, vel ex passione nobis intulisse iniuriam, vel non irascimur contra eos, vel multo minus: agere enim aliquid ex ignorantia vel ex passione, diminuit rationem iniuriae, et est quodammodo provocativum misericordiae et veniae" (I-II.47.2).

56. I-II.47.2 *passim* and ad3.

57. As the discussion up to this point already suggests, we cannot cling to this philosophical distinction too tightly, for the object is always the object as perceived by the subject (and by others whose perceptions matter to the subject).

58. Thomas uses the term "cause" (causa) in several different senses. In each case, the sense has to be gathered from the context. I shall leave it to the reader to gather the senses in which the term is being used. To specify these in the text would require delving into complex philosophical issues, the discussion of which would take us far off course.

59. ". . . for just as everything naturally seeks its own good, so does it naturally repel its own evil." ". . . sicut enim unumquodque naturaliter appetit proprium bonum, ita etiam naturaliter repellit proprium malum" (I-II.47.1).

60. Thomas does not make a distinction between the excellence that a person possesses (objectively and in the eyes of those who matter most to her) and the excellence that she *believes* she possesses (objectively, but contrary to a particular person's recognition or some broader communal recognition). This is probably due to the fact that the "self" of his time, unlike our own, was so strongly communal. Some such distinction will have to be made, however, if we are to appropriate Thomas's analysis for our time. Many women, for example, recognize certain qualities that they possess as being excellences (and, hence, foundations for proper self-love) even though many of the powerful males in our society refuse to recognize them as such. Thomas offers no clear way of talking about the self-loving anger of people whose assessments of their own excellence differ from the prevailing cultural assessments.

61. "Manifestum est autem quod nihil movet ad iram, nisi nocumentum quod contristat. Ea autem quae ad defectum pertinent, maxime sunt contristantia . . ."(I-II.47.3).

62. Thomas says that, ". . . excellence is the cause of a man being easily angered." ". . . excellentia est causa ut aliquis de facili irascatur" (I-II.47.3).

63. "Constat autem quod quanto aliquis est excellentior, iniustius parvipenditur in hoc in quo excellit. Et ideo illi qui sunt in aliqua excellentia, maxime irascuntur, si parvipendantur: puta si dives parvipenditur in pecunia, et rhetor in loquendo, et sic de aliis" (I-II.47.3).

64. ". . . ille qui despicitur in eo in quo manifeste multum excellit, non reputat se aliquam iacturam pati, et ideo non contristatur: et ex hac parte minus irascitur" (I-II.47.3ad2; my emphasis).

65. I substitute ". . . drawing . . ." for ". . . as if it had drawn. . . ." ". . . unde, in VII *Ethic.*, dicit Philosophus quod *syllogizans quoniam oportet talem oppugnare, irascitur confestim*" (I-II.46.4).

66. ". . . commotionem caloris velociter impellentis . . ." (I-II.48.3ad1).

67. ". . . ira, inter ceteras passiones, manifestius impedit iudicium rationis . . ." (I-II.48.3).

68. I-II.46.1.

69. "Sed ira respicit unum obiectum secundum rationem boni, scilicet vindictam, quam appetit: et aliud secundum rationem mali, scilicet hominem nocivum, de quo vult vindicari" (I-II.46.2).

70. I-II.46.3.

71. Thomas says that, "if a man be despised in a matter in which he evidently excels greatly, he does not consider himself the loser thereby." ". . . ille

qui despicitur in eo in quo manifeste multum excellit, non reputat se aliquam iacturam pati . . ." (47.3ad2). Yet he also says that, "deficiency or littleness in the person with whom we are angry, tends to increase our anger, in so far as it adds to the unmeritedness of being despised." "Defectus igitur vel parvitas eius contra quem irascimur, facit ad augmentum irae, inquantum auget indignam despectionem" (I-II.47.4). To give Thomas the benefit of the doubt on this apparent inconsistency, he may hold that "superior" people have good *reason* to be angry with their "inferiors" in that any slight coming from an inferior person is unmerited. At the same time, however, superior people sense that the slight of an inferior person ordinarily poses no real threat to their superiority. Hence, it can readily be dismissed (see the rest of 48.3ad2).

72. ". . . vindicatio fit per aliquod poenale malum inflictum peccanti" (II-II.108.1).

73. "Est autem de ratione poenae quod sit contraria voluntati, et quod sit afflictiva, et quod pro aliqua culpa inferatur. Et ideo iratus hoc appetit, ut ille cui nocumentum infert, percipiat, et doleat, et quod cognoscat propter iniuriam illatam sibi hoc provenire" (I-II.46.6ad2).

74. ". . . inquantum habet quandam rationem boni, scilicet prout aestimat illud esse iustum . . ." (I-II.46.6). Thomas goes on to say that this is one respect in which anger differs from hatred, "for the hater wishes evil to his enemy, as evil, whereas the angry man wishes evil to him with whom he is angry, not as evil but in so far as it has an aspect of good, that is, in so far as he reckons it as just, since it is a means of vengeance." ". . . sed odiens appetit malum inimici, inquantum est malum; iratus autem appetit malum eius contra quem irascitur, non inquantum est malum, sed inquantum habet quandam rationem boni, scilicet prout aestimat illud esse iustum, inquantum est vindicativum."

75. ". . . conservatio iustitiae et correctio culpae . . ." (II-II.158.2).

76. ". . . per poenam reparatur aequalitas iustitiae, inquantum ille qui peccando nimis secutus est suam voluntatem, aliquid contra suam voluntatem patitur" (II-II.108.4).

77. See J. Giles Milhaven's insightful analysis of this aspect of anger in *Good Anger*, especially chap. 11.

78. ". . . secundum illud *Prov.* 15, [1]: *Responsio mollis frangit iram:* inquantum scilicet tales videntur non despicere, sed magis magnipendere eos quibus se humiliant" (I-II.47.4).

79. ". . . non enim insurgit motus irae, nisi aliqua magnitudine circa utrumque existente; *quaecumque* enim *nihil sunt, aut modica valde, nullo digna aestimamus,* ut dicit Philosophus, in II *Rhetoric*" (I-II.46.3).

80. I do not use a phrase like "people of power" to refer only to people with publicly recognized social power. I use it to refer to any people in the community who have the power to make or break us socially, politically, economically, or personally. Some people have this power by virtue of their social standing, but others have it more by virtue of their being in certain sorts of relationships with us. Most of Thomas's examples refer to people who get angry when someone fails to acknowledge their relative social standing. But some of them refer to people who get angry, say, when a friend fails

to treat them in a way that honors their friendship. He says, for example, that "he that hinders another from carrying out his will, without deriving thereby any profit to himself, seems not to care much for his friendship." "Similiter etiam qui impedit aliquem a sui propositi assecutione, non propter aliquam utilitatem sibi inde provenientem, non videtur multum curare de amicitia eius" (I-II.47.2ad3).

81. ". . . quia motus irae non est per modum retractionis, cui proportionatur frigus; sed magis per modum insecutionis, cui proportionatur calor; consequenter fit motus irae causativus cuiusdam fervoris sanguinis et spirituum circa cor, quod est intrumentum passionum animae. Et exinde est quod, propter magnam perturbationem cordis quae est in ira, maxime apparent in iratis indicia quaedam in exterioribus membris. Ut enim Gregorius dicit, in V Moral., *irae suae stimulis accensum cor palpitat, corpus tremit, lingua se praepedit, facies ignescit, exasperantur oculi, et nequaquam recognoscuntur noti: ore quidem clamorem format, sed sensus quid loquatur, ignorat*" (I-II.48.2).

82. "Passio autem cum abiectione non est nisi secundum transmutationem corporalem" (I-II.22.1).

83. ". . . commotionem caloris velociter impellentis, quae est materialis in ira" (I-II.48.3ad1).

84. ". . . motus irae insurgit ex aliqua illata iniuria contristante; cui quidem tristitiae remedium adhibetur per vindictam. Et ideo ad praesentiam vindictae delectatio sequitur: et tanto maior, quanto maior fuit tristitia.—Si igitur vindicta fuerit praesens realiter, fit perfecta delectatio, quae totaliter excludit tristitiam, et per hoc quietat motum irae" (I-II.48.1).

85. My own experience is that vengeance rarely issues forth in perfect pleasure because it rarely succeeds in effecting the end that the angry person seeks, which is that the offender *freely* regard her with the respect that she deserves.

86. The prominence of this version becomes strikingly clear in Jeffrie G. Murphy and Jean Hampton, *Forgiveness and Mercy* (New York, N.Y.: Cambridge University Press, 1988).

87. Celie attributes this notion to Shug in Alice Walker, *The Color Purple* (New York, N.Y.: Washington Square Press, 1982), p. 179.

88. Audre Lorde was a woman, but she was a woman who understood what it meant to be a woman in light of what it meant (to her) to be a black person, a lesbian, a writer, a mother, and so on. One cannot separate Lorde's femaleness from the other aspects of her identity, and I have no intention of doing so in what follows. I *do* focus explicitly, as Lorde does, on relevant aspects of Lorde's femaleness and her blackness, but I do not mean to imply thereby that either of these aspects of Lorde's identity can, in the end, be well-articulated or understood apart from the others. All I can really hope to do in this essay is to begin a (heated) conversation about the relationship between anger, self-identity, and self-affirmation.

89. Audre Lorde, "The Uses of Anger: Women Responding to Racism," *Sister Outsider* (Freedom, Calif.: The Crossing Press, 1984).

90. Audre Lorde, "Eye to Eye: Black Women, Hatred, and Anger," *Sister Outsider* (Freedom, Calif.: The Crossing Press, 1984).

91. Notice how easily Thomas assimilates social, political, and economic goods to the good of virtue: "To honor a person is to recognize him as having virtue, wherefore virtue alone is the due cause of a person being honored. Now it is to be observed that a person may be honored not only for his own virtue, but also for another's: thus princes and prelates, although they be wicked, are honored as standing in God's place, and as representing the community over which they are placed . . . and in the same way parents and masters should be honored, on account of their having a share of the dignity of God Who is the Father and Lord of all." ". . . honor est quoddam testimonium de virtute eius qui honoratur, et ideo sola virtus est debita causa honoris. Sciendum tamen quod aliquis potest honorari non solum propter virtutem propriam, sed etiam propter virtutem alterius. Sicut principes et praelati honorantur etiam si sint mali, inquantum gerunt personam Dei et communitatis cui praeficiuntur. . . . Et eadem ratione parentes et domini sunt honorandi, propter participationem divinae dignitatis, qui est omnium Pater et Dominus" (II-II.63.3).

92. Notice, e.g., what Thomas says with respect to the excellence of manliness: "As regards the individual nature, woman is defective and misbegotten, for the active force in the male seed tends to the production of a perfect likeness in the masculine sex; while the production of woman comes from defect in the active force or from some material indisposition, or even from some external influence; such as that of a south wind, which is moist, as the Philosopher observes (*De Gener. Animal.* iv.2)." ". . . per respectum ad naturam particularem, femina est aliquid deficiens et occasionatum. Quia virtus activa quae est in semine maris, intendit producere sibi simile perfectum, secundum masculinum sexum: sed quod femina generetur, hoc est propter virtutis activae debilitatem, vel propter aliquam materiae indispositionem, vel etiam propter aliquam transmutationem ab extrinseco, puta a ventis australibus, qui sunt humidi, ut dicitur in libro *de Generat. Animal.*" (I.92.1ad1). He also says that, "there is another kind of subjection, which is called economic or civil, whereby the superior makes use of his subjects for their own benefit and good; and this kind of subjection existed even before sin. For good order would have been wanting in the human family if some were not governed by others wiser than themselves. So by such a kind of subjection woman is naturally subject to man, because in man the discretion of reason predominates." "Est autem alia subiectio oeconomica vel civilis, secundum quam praesidens utitur subiectis ad eorum utilitatem et bonum. Et ista subiectio fuisset etiam ante peccatum: defuisset enim bonum ordinis in humana multitudine, si quidam per alios sapientiores gubernati non fuissent. Et sic ex tali subiectione naturaliter femina subiecta est viro: quia naturaliter in homine magis abundat discretio rationis" (I.92.1ad2).

93. Lorde, "Uses of Anger," p. 124.
94. Lorde, "Uses of Anger," p. 129.
95. Lorde, "Uses of Anger," p. 133.
96. Lorde, "Eye to Eye," p. 173.
97. Lorde, "Eye to Eye," p. 163.
98. Lorde, "Uses of Anger," p. 133.

99. Lorde, "Eye to Eye," p. 158.
100. Lorde, "Eye to Eye," p. 133.
101. One could argue that for Thomas, humanness is an excellence that all human beings possess equally and for which all are thus due equal regard (where "humanness" is defined in terms of the "natural inclination to act according to reason") (I-II.94.3). But it appears that in his judgment, different human beings possess even this humanness to different degrees (I.92.1; cf. I.109.2ad3). Different degrees of rational capacity, in addition to different degrees in the realization of these capacities, entitle persons to different degrees of respect (even if at some minimal level there is a kind of equality). For further discussion of the notion of "equal regard" in Thomas, see Jean Porter, *The Recovery of Virtue: The Relevance of Aquinas for Christian Ethics* (Louisville, Ky.: Westminster/John Knox Press, 1990), chap. 5.
102. Lorde, "Eye to Eye," p. 148.
103. Lorde, "Eye to Eye," p. 171.
104. Lorde, "Eye to Eye," p. 151.
105. Lorde, "Eye to Eye," p. 149.
106. Lorde, "Eye to Eye," pp. 159–60.
107. Lorde, "Eye to Eye," pp. 159–60.
108. Lorde, "Uses of Anger," p. 128.
109. Lorde's experience discloses some of the liberative power of a modern (as opposed to a medieval communal) understanding of the self, according to which individuals have the (limited) freedom and the responsibility to transcend, expose, and explode oppressive cultural constructions of their individuality.
110. Lorde, "Uses of Anger," p. 129.
111. Lorde, "Eye to Eye," p. 175.
112. Lorde, "Eye to Eye," p. 169.
113. Lorde, "Eye to Eye," p. 156.
114. Lorde, "Eye to Eye," p. 153.
115. Lorde, "Eye to Eye," p. 168.
116. Lorde, "Eye to Eye," p. 147.
117. Racism and sexism are not easily made the objects of a well-focused anger. Lorde acknowledges that, "As Black women, we have wasted our angers too often, buried them, called them someone else's, cast them wildy into oceans of racism and sexism from which no vibration resounded, hurled them into each other's teeth and then ducked to avoid the impact. But by and large, we avoid open expression of them, or cordon them off in a rigid and unapproachable politeness. The rage that feels illicit or unjustified is kept secret, unnamed, and preserved forever" ("Eye to Eye," pp. 166–7). Mary Daly characterizes this kind of paralyzing anger as a "plastic passion": ". . . plastic passions are free-floating feelings resulting in more and more disconnectedness/fragmentation. Since they are characterized by the lack of specific and nameable causes, they must be 'dealt with' endlessly in an acontextual way. . . . Since they have no perceivable causes, they function to serve the mechanisms of 'blaming the victim'" *Pure Lust*, pp. 200–201.
118. Lorde, "Eye to Eye," p. 154.

119. Lorde, "Eye to Eye," p. 164.

120. Here, the oppressor is, in a sense, another black woman in whose eyes Lorde sees the downcast look of the privileged white male oppressor. I make my point, however, with regard to the oppressor *behind* the oppressor (i.e., the one who engineers the illusion in the first place).

121. I-II.46.2.

122. Lorde, "Eye to Eye," p. 152.

123. Lorde, "Eye to Eye," p. 154.

124. Lorde, "Uses of Anger," p. 129.

125. Lorde, "Uses of Anger," p. 128.

126. Lorde, "Uses of Anger," p. 133.

127. Lorde, "Uses of Anger," p. 128.

128. Lorde, "Uses of Anger," pp. 132–3.

129. Lorde, "Eye to Eye," p. 145.

130. "Uses of Anger," p. 127. Recall Thomas's analysis of the passions as movements of the sense appetite that can be guided by universal reason. We could say that, focused with precision and ordered toward the good of right relationship, the commotion of the oppressed person's anger can be communicated in such a way that it sets up a commotion with the oppressor, thereby effecting a change in mutual passional regard.

131. For probing, insightful, and encouraging comments on an earlier draft of this paper, I wish to give special thanks to Don Davis, James Gubbins, G. Simon Harak, S. J., Christopher Johnson, J. Giles Milhaven, and James F. McCue.

Child Abuse and Embodiment from a Thomistic Perspective

G. SIMON HARAK, S. J.

In his reflections on modern culture, Charles Taylor observes that, "this culture puts a great emphasis on relationships in the intimate sphere, especially love relationships. These are seen to be the prime loci of self-exploration and self-discovery and among the most important forms of self-fulfillment."[1] Such "ordinary life" relationships, he observes, are "crucial because they are the crucible of inwardly generated identity."[2] A person's relationship with his or her parents is surely one of the prime loci of self-exploration and self-discovery. What happens to a person's identity when physical abuse is placed into that crucible?

This chapter will examine the phenomenon of child abuse from the perspective of Thomas Aquinas's theology of embodiment. I will begin with a working definition of child abuse and a discussion of its effects upon the victim.[3] My additional goal in the first part of this chapter is to enter a little bit into the world of the abused child, as has Alice Miller, for example, in her seminal works on this topic. Thus, I will use not only research studies, but also various works of literature to further illumine the plight of the abused child. I employ this strategy because I believe both that our ethical studies should be characterized by wisdom and compassion, and that a deeper understanding of the plight of the abused child will lead us to greater appreciation of Thomas Aquinas's presentation. We will find that Thomas will help us to discuss the effects of abuse morally and theologically, and to respond to such suffering with sensitivity and even with healing.

Thomas never directly considers children in his theology, let alone the effects of child abuse. I believe, however, that his attention to the role of the *passions* in the formation of character provides a unique forum for discussing the plight of those suffering the effects of abuse, and that Thomas can fruitfully and constructively engage the current discussion of child abuse at this point. In looking for a way in which Thomas might address this current problem, then, we will focus primarily on his *Treatise on the Passions*.[4]

This attempt to bring Thomistic insights to the discussion of child abuse will reveal a deeper understanding of Thomas as well. In the *Treatise on the Passions*, Thomas consistently emphasizes the self in passion, the self as "suffering" the action of another. That emphasis gives us a hermeneutic by which we focus more on the action of the other than on the action of the self in Thomas's theology. And that in turn more clearly displays the foundational activity of the divine other in Thomas's system. I am personally inclined, because of my Eastern Catholic background, to attend more to the status of divine action than to human action in my reading of Thomas's theology. Yet this attention and this hermeneutic is surely warranted by the structure of the *Summa theologiae* itself, which begins with, and returns to, God. Furthermore, Thomas's regard for the primacy of divine love may explain why his discussion of passions is the longest (and, I believe, the least understood) treatise in the *Summa*, since Thomas wants to emphasize what God does for us and to found our moral efforts first upon God's gifts.

Thomas's attention to the other (to which we are in passion) in the *Treatise* prepares us for a right understanding of the virtuous life and is consistent with his systematic commitment to the divine other throughout the *Summa*. The *Treatise on the Passions*, with its constant description of the other as agent in interaction with the self, precedes the discussion of *habit* (itself a relational notion in Thomas), which in turn precedes his discussion of the virtues and the vices. In this chapter's particular area of interest, we need to appreciate the full moral impact of the abusive other upon the child and how such an abusive action can lead the self to destructive habits. Thomas's insistence on the primacy of the human being's passion for God, however, will answer the abused person's need for a healing power that can undermine even the deformative powers of abusive parental love. Our need to answer this cry for healing can lead us to rediscover Thomas's deep theological commitment to the divine other who is our first parent, our best healer, and the one who grounds all our empowerment (virtue). In sum, I hope that this chapter will shed a new yet authentic light on both the current discussion of child abuse and the understanding of Thomas.

CHILD ABUSE AND ITS EFFECTS.[5]

In *The Encyclopedia of Child Abuse*, Clark and Clark tell us that, "The earliest and most enduring problem in the study of child abuse has been the development of a useful, clear acceptable (and accepted) definition of 'abuse.'"[6] But although modern researchers acknowledge that, "There will never be a final definition of maltreatment that will be satisfying to professionals and families, and that will remain relevant to future generations," they note nonetheless that, "Relative agreement has been achieved concerning many grossly deleterious acts that are considered child maltreatment by the majority of past and present societies."[7]

The American Association for Protecting Children reported in 1987 that there had been 2,200,000 abuse and neglect reports received by state agencies in the previous year.[8] Not all of those complaints were founded. (The Association estimates about one-third to one-half were.) But not all cases of true child abuse were reported. Nevertheless, that figure can give us some idea of the extent of the problem.

Here we will concentrate specifically on physical abuse of the child.[9] The National Center on Child Abuse and Neglect defines physical abuse as "an act of commission by a parent or caretaker which is not accidental and . . . which results in physical injury, including fractures, burns, bruises, welts, cuts and/or internal injuries."[10] That is the definition of abuse we will use in this chapter, although we recognize its limitations.[11] In focusing on physical abuse, I am not ignoring psychological abuse. I am, however, already accepting a Thomistic insight: that embodiment indicates a more thoroughgoing enactment of will. That is, while verbal abuse (shouting, insults, name-calling) indubitably harm a child, physical attacks (often, but not necessarily, accompanied by verbal abuse) upon a child cause physiological as well as psychological damage, and so are a more comprehensive violation.

Studies reveal that virtually all abused children share characteristics that begin in the abusive home and continue through adulthood.[12] Let us now explore six major characteristics of physical abuse in greater depth.

The Appropriation of the Abuser's Attitudes toward the Abused.

Morton Schatzman's *Soul Murder* presents us with one of the most fascinating studies of the effect of physical punishment upon the interior life of the victim of abuse. He reports on the life of

> Daniel Paul Schreber (1842-1911), an eminent German judge, [who] went mad at forty-two, recovered, and eight and a half years later went mad again. It is uncertain if he ever was fully sane, in the ordinary social sense, again. Psychiatrists and psychoanalysts consider him a classic case of paranoia and schizophrenia. His father, Daniel Gottlieb Moritz Schreber (1808-1861), who supervised his upbringing, was a leading German physician and pedagogue. . . . He proposed to 'battle' the 'weakness' of his era with an elaborate system of child-rearing aimed at making children obedient and subject to adults. . . . He sired two sons; Daniel Gustav, the elder, went mad too and killed himself.[13]

Schatzman's purpose in *Soul Murder* is to compare the writings of the father, Daniel Gottlieb, on child rearing[14] to the journal (*Memoirs*) of the son, Daniel Paul, describing the patterns of his mental illness.[15] In so doing, he finds some startling correspondences that allow us to understand many of the effects of child abuse.

In his writings on correct child rearing, the father, Daniel Gottlieb, frequently counseled corporal punishment for children, stating, for example, that "the most important thing is that the [child's] disobedience should be *crushed* to the point of regaining complete submission, using corporal punishment if necessary."[16] But the father also devised various physical constraints for the children—devices that would compel good posture by strapping a child's head to his shoulders, for example, or by binding her to the bed in which she slept. Thus, the bodies of the Schreber children were under constant assault. We can find evidence for the psychological effects of these bodily violations in the memoirs of the son, written toward the end of his life. We read, for example,

> From the first beginnings of my contact with God up to the present day my body has continuously been the object of divine

miracles. . . . I may say that hardly a simple limb or organ in my body escaped being temporarily damaged by miracles, nor a single muscle being pulled by miracles, either moving it or paralysing it according to the respective purpose. Even now the miracles which I experience hourly are still of a nature to frighten every other human being to death. . . .[17]

Switching back and forth between the *Memoirs* of the son and the pedagogical teachings of the father, Schatzman draws parallels between the son's ongoing experience of the "bodily miracles" and the father's description of the various physical devices for controlling the bodily demeanor of the child. The correspondence, some fifty years later, is uncanny. For example, Daniel Paul writes about "miracles of heat and cold,"[18] which Schatzman compares to the hot and cold baths that his father counseled should be administered to a child. The son writes about the "compression-of-the-chest-miracle,"[19] which Schatzman parallels with the father's invention of the *Geradhalter* ("Straight-holder"): an iron bar attached to a table and resting against the child's chest, making it uncomfortable for the child to lean forward; it also had straps fitted around the child's head to keep his head straight. Fifty years later in his *Memoirs*, the son still speaks of any movement of looking toward a sound as being "accompanied by a painful blow directed at my head; the sensation of pain is like a sudden pulling inside my head which calls forth a very unpleasant feeling . . . and may be combined with the tearing off of part of the bony substance of my skull—at least that is how it feels."[20]

Schatzman's comment on all this makes a point that has become well-established by the 1990s. "The son thinks the 'miracles' are enacted upon objective anatomical organs of his body. He does not see that he is *re*enacting his father's behavior toward his body. Schreber suffers from reminiscences. His body embodies his past."[21]

Schatzman's observation is most interesting for our study. That is, the embodied self seems to remember the abuse it has received and to continue that abuse no matter how long it has been since the actual physical abuse has stopped. The abuse has been appropriated, or taken on, by the victim himself. Through the studies of Schatzman and others, we find that it is inadequate to say that the abuse has been appropriated by the victim merely through the psychological process known as internalizing the attitudes of the abuser (though indeed that occurs). It seems more accurate to say that the attitudes of the abuser are appropriated by becoming *embodied* in the victim of abuse.

In a penetrating study of the religious roots of child abuse and its long-term effects, Philip Greven concurs with the above assessment: "Our minds and bodies absorb the blows and pain in childhood and react to them in a multitude of ways for the remainder of our lives, forming a substratum of early experience that continues to be manifested in an astonishing variety of forms in our adult psyches."[22] In this ongoing bodily reenactment of abuse, the abused person shows that he has somehow taken on, or appropriated, the original abuser's dispositions, and especially the abuser's anger toward the abused child (or against his "self-will").

I write "somehow" because most modern thinkers find it difficult to account adequately for this very important phenomenon: why and how external *physical* activity (such as abuse) can create such interior states as disposition, intention, and choice. I have argued elsewhere that this inability is due to the lingering effects of Cartesianism on our understandings of the relationship between body and soul.[23] Thus we will have to wait until our study of Thomas Aquinas with his rich understanding of the interplay between body and spirit to grasp the full impact of physical abuse upon the soul. Current scientific research, however, may point the way to appreciating how body and spirit interact. That research shows that in any experience of interaction with another, the body is physically changed in some way, for example in its posture, heart rate, skin conductance level, or hormonal level. Prolonged, habitual interactions can physically reconfigure the body. Melvin Konner, for example, has shown that an enriched environment for laboratory rats caused physically observable differences in the brain and its neurological patterns.[24] From such studies we can see that the anger, consistently enacted upon the body of the abused, can cause the embodied self to become configured to abuse, affecting the patterns of disposition, intention, and choice in an abused person.

In considering the appropriation of the will of the abuser, Schatzman writes, "Many psychoanalysts have dwelled upon the motives of the person who projects; few have pondered the experience of the person *upon whom* someone else projects parts of himself, which he tries to master 'in' the other person for what he imagines is the other's sake."[25] Tracy Nagurski graphically conveys this appropriated intention in a poem addressed to her incestuous father:

you taught me so well
to hate myself,
my body,
that i don't need you anymore
to hurt me,
fuck me physically
or emotionally.
i do very well on my own now.[26]

In extreme cases, embodied and internalized anger may lead one to such anger at the self (or more properly, toward the self as embodied) that one is led to suicide, as was Schreber's first son. However we find the most theologically interesting connection between abuse of the outer self and destruction of the inner self reflected in the title of Schatzman's work: *Soul Murder*. Daniel Paul Schreber himself describes that murder of the soul when he writes, "At the time when my nervous illness seemed almost incurable, I gained the conviction that soul murder had been attempted on me by somebody. . . ."[27] And for Schreber, "soul murder" refers to the idea "widespread in the folklore and poetry of all peoples that it is somehow possible to take possession of another person's soul."[28] This is the reason that we are summoning Thomas to give a theological account of the effects and healing of abuse: it is because this abuse of the body becomes a striking at the soul. Essentially, the *soul* of the abused person needs to be freed from possession, redeemed from its death.

Silencing.

Closely related to the notion of soul murder is how physical abuse profoundly silences the victim. We have already read how Schreber thought it was "the most important thing" to achieve "complete submission" in the child. Greven gives us many examples of how religious parents are counseled to use physical abuse to achieve this complete submission. He cites John Robinson, who tells us that "surely there is in all children, though not alike, a stubbornness, and stoutness of mind arising from natural pride, which must, in the first place, be broken and beaten down . . ." for "Children should not know, if it could be kept from them, that they have a will of their own, but in their parents' keeping. . . ."[29] Susanna Wesley, mother of John and Charles, writes, "When a child is corrected it *must be conquered*. . . .

And when the will of a child is *totally subdued*, and it is brought to revere and stand in awe of the parents, then a great many childish follies and inadvertencies may be passed by. . . . I insist on the *conquering of the will of children* betimes, because this is the only strong and rational foundation of a religious education. . . ."[30] And Greven assiduously demonstrates how the same kind of attitude persists in the writings of "many fundamentalists and other Protestants who advocate corporal punishment," such as J. Richard Fugate, the Reverend Jack Hyles, and especially James Dobson, author of the enormously popular *Dare to Discipline*.

We find a theologically significant analogy here, between the disparity of power between the parent and the child, and the disparity of power between God and the human being. It is almost as though those who abuse with religious warrant sense that correspondence and enforce their will upon the child with absolute authority. The result, again, is that the child embodies and internalizes the abusive will of the parent, to the complete detriment of the child's own will. Before such an imposing exercise of "divine" authority, the child's own will is *silenced*. Let us be clear, however. That silence is not the silence of Job when the vindicating glory of the Lord is finally revealed. Nor is it the silence of deep communion that characterizes the contemplative. It is, in fact, the demonic *doppelgänger* of those silences, a silence whose similarity to those enriching silences makes it all the more insidious. Psychologist Sáldor Ferenczi tells us that

> The overwhelming power and authority of the adults renders [the children] silent. Often they are deprived of their senses. . . . [F]ear, when it reaches its zenith, forces them automatically to surrender to the will of the aggressor, to anticipate each of his wishes and to submit to them; forgetting themselves entirely, to identify totally with the aggressor.[31]

Perhaps the most profound understanding of the power of physical pain to silence the victim comes not from studies on child abuse, but from Elaine Scarry's penetrating study of the effects of torture, *The Body in Pain*. Scarry tells us that "physical pain is language-destroying."[32] She explains that "Physical pain does not simply resist language but actively destroys it, bringing about an immediate reversion to a state anterior to language, to the sounds and cries a human being makes before language is learned."[33] "The purpose of [torture]," she wants us to understand, "is not to elicit needed information but visibly to deconstruct the prisoner's voice. The prolonged interrogation . . . also graphically objectifies the step-by-step backward movement along the path by which language comes into being and which is here being reversed or uncreated or deconstructed."[34] In the course of her work, Scarry shows how the silenced victim's voice is replaced with the "incontestably real" will of the regime that inflicts pain. She also encourages us by showing that Amnesty International works precisely "to restore to each person tortured his or her voice . . . to present regimes that torture with a deluge of letters and telegrams, a deluge of voices speaking on behalf of, voices speaking in the voice of, the person silenced. . . ."[35]

It would seem, then, that another feature of the redemption for the survivor of abuse would be the empowerment of the child vis-a-vis the abusive parent, a restoration of right relationship we might call justice. Put theologically, we might say that we need to empower the victim of abuse to speak—to speak from within a strong sense of *justification* of the self, and to speak especially as an individual distinct from her or his parent. We need to present the liberating Word of God to exorcise from the victim the imposed silence of abuse.

The Sense of Entrapment.

In an abusive relationship, the deep need that a child has for protection becomes an additional source of pain for the child. Abusive caretakers take advantage of childhood's constitutive vulnerability to instate an hegemony of harm.[36] Because the child has no place to go to escape the physical abuse, the abuse perverts the child's natural state of dependency into a condition of entrapment.

We can appreciate the sense of abiding horror that attends this perversion and entrapment by drawing from an interesting passage in Orson Scott Card's *Red Prophet*. A young boy, Alvin, has powers over nature. In this case, he has power over cockroaches and has made an agreement with them: he will take care of them, and they will not climb onto his bed or clothes. But one night his sisters play a trick on Alvin, and he is angry. He decides to tell the cockroaches that there is food in the next room on the bodies of his sleeping sisters. The cockroaches, trusting him, go in to eat, and terrify the girls until the parents come in and kill the cockroaches. While Alvin is gloating, a Native American comes into his room, and undertakes to show him his misuse of power from the perspective of the cockroaches. He shows him

> The picture of his sisters' room as a small weak creature [would see] it. Rushing in, hungering, hungering, looking for the food, certain that the food was there; on the soft body was the promise, climb the body, find the food. But great hands slapped and brushed, and the small creature was thrown onto the floor. The floor shook with giant footfalls, a sudden shadow, the agony of death.
>
> Again and again, each small life, hungering, trusting, and then betrayed, crushed, battered.
>
> Many lived, but they cowered, they scurried, they fled. The sisters' room, the room of death, yes, they fled from there. But better to stay there and die than run into the other room, the room of lies. Not words, there were no words in the small creature's life, there were no thoughts that could be named as thoughts. But the fear of death in the one place was not as strong as another kind of fear, the fear of a world gone crazy, a place where anything could happen, where nothing could be trusted, where nothing was certain. A terrible place.[37]

Unlike the cockroaches in *Red Prophet*, children in abusive homes must return to that room of lies and betrayal of trust, that terrible place.[38] The vulnerability and need for protection that defines childhood is exploited, until childhood itself becomes a trap. Toward the end of *The Prince of Tides*, Pat Conroy's moving novel exploring the consequences of physical abuse, Tom Wingo articulates that same sense of entrapment: "I learned that it's normal for a man to beat his wife, Dad. I learned that it's normal for a man to beat his children, to brutalize his whole family anytime he felt like it, because he was stronger than any of them and because they couldn't fight back and had no place to go."[39]

Adult survivors of abuse have learned, then, to fear and avoid any vulnerability at all because they have learned from childhood that their vulnerability can be used to entrap them. If we are to are to offer any liberation, we might think theologically of such liberation as a kind of resurrection from entombment, a resurrection empowered by a Spirit whose express purpose is to "set the captives free."[40]

Anxiety and Fear.

Studies of infants and caregivers have shown that, in moments of intimacy, the disparity in power between infant and caregiver is irrelevant, and the child is in perfect communion with the parent.[41] We have seen how exploitation of their childhood vulnerability leaves the adult survivor of abuse with a fear of their own vulnerability. Here, we might further this realization by understanding that victims of abuse develop an acute sensitivity to any disparity of power between the self and another.[42] Together with the sense of entrapment, then, comes a constant state of fear and anxiety—fear because of the anticipation of physical attack and anxiety because one never knows when it is going to come or what one can do to prevent it.

In "Consequences" (Part IV of *Spare the Child*), Greven writes of the persistence of anxiety and fear, since the child begins to anticipate the beatings with dread, and that dread becomes part of the child's makeup. But Greven also notes that the arbitrariness of the beatings increases the anxiety in the child. In *The Prince of Tides*, Tom Wingo pointedly reflects on the indeterminacy of the incidents of abuse and the anxiety that arbitrary exercise of authority produced was greater even than the physical attacks.

> Though the beatings were bad enough, it was the irrationality of my father's nature that was even worse. We never knew what would set him off; we could never predict the sea changes of the soul that would set the beast loose in our house. There were no patterns to adhere to, no strategies to improvise. . . . Our childhood was spent waiting for him to attack.[43]

Alice Miller, in her well-known examination of Hitler's abusive childhood, concurs in that analysis of the source of anxiety. She writes, "This was Adolf's function throughout his childhood; he had to accept the fact that at any moment a storm could break over his helpless head without his being able to find any way to avert or escape it."[44]

That anxiety reaches deeper than the normal fear that comes when something foreseeably bad and unavoidable is going to happen. It is more like an existential dread, an *angst* perhaps. That existential angst occurs because, as many studies have discovered and as we have indicated previously, what is being resisted is not the behavior, but the very being of the child. And that existential anxiety is deepened because of the arbitrariness of the exercise of parental authority over the helpless child. An adequate theological account of abuse and redemption then, would not only have elements of justification and empowerment, it would have to grant to the victim that she could live "free from fear,"[45] since "all fear is a fear of punishment. But perfect love casts out fear."[46]

Anger.

As we might expect, such violations of the self induce anger in the one who is assaulted. The nature of that anger is very complex, however. First, the anger might be directed toward the abusive parent or caretaker. But the victim must suppress that anger because the child has no place to go, no independent way of being, if the child repudiates the regime of the parents. Alternatively, the victim suppresses the anger against the abusive parents because the anger is identified with self-will, and demonstrations of self-will only bring more assaults upon the self. Second, the victim's anger might be induced because the victim has appropriated the anger of the abuser, and that also has two attendant forms of suppression. The victim may appropriate the anger against himself simply, in a process similar to replacing his will with the will of the abuser. Thus, his anger is turned against his own very existence. Alternatively, the victim of abuse can marshall the more powerful appropriated anger of the abuser to suppress the anger she would naturally feel at being assaulted.

Those angers are not separable. They overlap and reinforce each other in one great anger. Under any description, however, Alice Miller's studies of abuse accurately reveal that the anger of the abused "does not disappear, but is transformed with time into a more or less conscious hatred directed against either the self or substitute persons. . . ."[47] And Miller claims that the anger of the abused child is the primary source of the practice of violence in adults,[48] violence that expresses the anger against the self and against others. Here I would like to draw our attention to the form of violence that is directed toward the self, especially toward one's own embodiment.

We have already seen several examples of this self-directed anger in this chapter, most notably in the writings of Daniel Paul Schreber.

In extreme cases, the self-destructive anger seeks to eliminate the embodied self altogether through suicide. Again, it is unclear whether suicide is the final result of seeking to punish the self for the unacceptable anger against the abusive parent, or the completion of the appropriated intention to destroy the self and its self-will by finally collaborating in one's own soul murder. In any case, we can agree with Miller that one of the characteristic expressions of anger in the abused is *self-annihilation*. Though anger against the self may be present among others, the dynamic of self-annihilation among the abused is particularly severe since their self-condemnation rests not on anything that they have *done* but simply on the fact that they *exist*.[49] As Tom Wingo reflects about his abusive mother, Lila, in *The Prince of Tides*, he observes, "As her children, she looked upon us inconsistently as both her co-conspirators and her enemies. . . . She looked upon our births as crimes we committed against her."[50] The abused child seeks to rectify this crime by annihilating the self.

As we stated at the beginning of this section, it is expected that assaults against the self should induce anger. It is not the anger but its inversion that causes such difficulties among the victims of abuse. A good theology of redemption for survivors of abuse, then, must provide us with a good account of the proper role and redirection of anger.

Dissociation.

The final characteristic of the abused child is closely allied to self-annihilation, and also already suggested by our earlier discussion of the loss of perspective in the abused child: *dissociation*. Dissociation may take the form of a loss of a sense of time and place. In part, that is due to the very nature of pain, as Emily Dickinson eloquently describes,

> Pain—has an Element of Blank—
> It cannot recollect
> When it began—or if there were
> A time when it was not—
> It has no Future—but itself
> Its Past—enlightened to perceive
> New Periods—of Pain.[51]

Victims of abuse, however, have an even more profound reason for dissociation: it is a strategy for surviving assaults on the embodied self. Greven writes that,

> The ability to disconnect feelings from their contexts and to disconnect one's sense of self from the external world are at the heart of the process of dissociation that underlies so many psychological phenomena. Dissociation is one of the most basic means of survival for many children, who learn early in life to distance themselves, or parts of themselves, from experiences too painful or frightening to bear. Traumas, both physical and emotional, are often coped with by denial and repression of the feelings they generate.[52]

Adult victims of childhood abuse can find this strategy of dissociation often unconsciously evoked in many situations, especially situations involving physical pain, or the possibility of a loss of control, which would make them, in their recapitulative imagination, vulnerable to physical attack again. Such dissociation might be characterized by withdrawal, loss of affect, inattentiveness to loved ones, or an intense need to establish one's dominance over a situation or person.

Greven's entire discussion of dissociation in its many forms is illuminating, but again let us focus on embodiment. Abuse humiliates and shames a child. But because the body is the target of the attack, the shame also becomes embodied, and in a unique way for the abused child, the body itself becomes a locus of pain and shame. Through dissociation the consciousness seeks to withdraw, as it were, from this pain and shame, abandoning the body, its feelings, and especially its vulnerability to being affected by others. Because we are embodied, however, we have inescapable needs: food, protection, touch, intimacy. To continue speaking metaphorically about the truth of dissociation, we might say that if the body through those needs tries to reassert itself in the self's consciousness, it is met with denial, repudiation and, in extreme cases, destruction.

Finally, in trying to understand dissociation, we are once again helped by Scarry's insights, especially on the confusion between body as sufferer and body as instrument of pain:

> Regardless of the setting in which he suffers (home, hospital, or torture room), and regardless of the cause of his suffering

(disease, burns, torture, or malfunctioning of the pain network itself), the person in great pain experiences his own body as the agent of his agony. . . . [It] contains not only the feeling 'my body hurts' but the feeling 'my body hurts me.' . . . it sometimes becomes visible when a young child or an animal in the first moments of acute distress takes maddening flight, fleeing from its own body as though it were a part of the environment that could be left behind.[53]

Seen in that way, dissociation is an attempt to flee the self, the self that exists in time and space. It is an attempt to flee the embodied self and its vulnerability—surely its vulnerability to pain and shame, but in the end an attempt to avoid or escape all the vulnerability of the body, even the body's hunger and need for touch. An appropriate theological anthropology, then, would seem to require not only a robust theology of embodiment, but a strong soteriology for bodies that have been tortured and abused.

Having completed this overview of the characteristics of both child abuse and the proper response it requires, let us turn to the writings of Thomas Aquinas. I believe we can discover there a great sensitivity to the terrible realities of abuse, and construct a therapeutically and theologically sound path toward healing and forgiveness.

INSIGHTS FROM THOMAS AQUINAS.

In this section we will ask Thomas to provide a theological framework for the chief characteristics of child abuse. Any individual request of Thomas's theology, however, must be received in the context of his larger systematic theology. Thus, we will not ask Thomas to address each characteristic of abuse, point for point. Instead, we will first trace and describe his theological ethics, focusing on areas that would prove most fertile for addressing the problems of abuse. In the course of our exploration, we will see that Thomas can and does provide us with a structure for theological reflections on those characteristics of abuse.

Then in the following section, our exploration will concentrate primarily on the *Treatise on the Passions* in Thomas's ethics as presented in the *Summa theologiae*. Of all Thomas's moral reflections on the interaction between the self and the other, the *Treatise* provides us with the best opportunity to study the effects of the *other* upon the self (Thomas calls the other an "agent" in the self's passions) and affords us the best opportunity to glimpse the profound power of the Ultimate Other, God, for healing and empowering survivors of abuse.

In his lectures on the *Nicomachean Ethics*, Thomas has an opportunity to comment on child abuse, since Aristotle mentions it it in Book VII. In Book VII of the *Nicomachean Ethics*, Aristotle is discussing moral weakness (ἀκρασία) and behavior that cannot strictly be called ἀκρασία, such as patterns of behavior that spring from disease or insanity. Then he remarks that other types of unacceptable behavior, "such as pulling out the hair, biting nails, and eating of ashes and dirt," can be acquired by habit (ἔθους) ". . . as is the case with those who have been abused from childhood."[54] The Greek word for "abused" is very strong there: ὑβριζομένος. It is of course etymologically related to ὕβρις ("pride," "a false and destructive sense of one's own superiority") and carries with it the special connotation of the use of a superior power or strength in such a way as to insult, outrage, or maltreat with bodily injury. There, Aristotle seems aware that child abuse can later cause disruptions in normal behavior.

Thomas does not seem to be as attentive to the force of abuse as Aristotle in that passage. That, however, is because of the Latin translation of Aristotle's work. Thomas could not read Greek, and the translation of ὑβριζομένοις ἐκ παίδων ("abused [with the previously-noted connotations] from childhood") was the rather mild *"asuefactis ex pueris"* ("become accustomed to from childhood'). So Thomas comments merely that these aberrational activities

> occur through becoming accustomed to them, perhaps because they have become accustomed to similar things from childhood. And in these things it is similar to those in whom these things occur because of sickness of the body. For destructive activity that has been habituated is like a certain sickness of body and soul.[55]

Later in VII, Aristotle considers how easy it is to pass anger from one generation to the next. He tells the story of a man who is challenged for beating his father. The challenged man replies that "my father used to beat his father, and he used to beat his and this one (indicating his own son) will beat *me* when he is grown. It is genetic (συγγενὲς) with us." In this later passage Aristotle focuses on the point that anger is more readily passed on from father to son than the desire for pleasures. Thomas follows his lead and does not seem to consider that such behavior could be learned.[56] We *can* find, however, an interesting point of agreement here between those two ethicists and modern commentators on abuse: the abuse, as Greven has said, travels "through time inside our bodies, minds and spirits and living on long after our individual deaths through the legacies we bequeath to our children and grandchildren and to future generations throughout the world."

What is important for our discussion here is that both Aristotle and Thomas consider that there can be character flaws in a person which are unlike ἀκρασία. We are familiar with ἀκρασία as a defect in character something akin to a failure of will or courage, when one sees the good, but does not accomplish it. Accounts of virtue ethicists often concentrate on such a classical understanding of virtue, and such a classical understanding of Thomas, and so focus on conscious, individual efforts to overcome weakness and acquire virtue. This is surely correct for a standard account of virtue. But the standard account cannot present us with an adequate ethical description of the abused person's struggle for freedom and empowerment. Nor, I contend, does that account give us a full understanding of Thomas's account of virtue and how his Christian account differs from Aristotle's. Nevertheless, it is important to note that Aristotle here acknowledges that some character flaws occur not through ἀκρασία, but through some early violation of the self through the action of an other. For it is there, in that violation by another, that we wish to locate the abused person's struggle for becoming empowered, for acquiring virtue. The abused person struggles not because he is morally weak, but because he is burdened with primitively appropriated habits of self-defeat and self-destruction.

Though Thomas is not as clear as Aristotle in acknowledging the other-inflicted, non-ἀκρασία character flaws here, we will see that Thomas addresses such a possibility much more fully in his later work. In fact, it is the contention of this chapter that Thomas's theology is much more capable of promising empowerment to survivors of abuse than is Aristotle's philosophy. In the *Nicomachean Ethics*, Aristotle admits that he cannot train a young man who has not been properly formed from his youth. Thomas, however, can rely on the action of an Other whose power to liberate the self reaches deeper even than the formative powers of parents. We should, then, turn to a later work of Thomas, the *Summa theologiae*, to see if we can draw from it a Thomistic framework for understanding abuse, its effects, and its healing.

In the *Summa*, Thomas details the *exitus* and *reditus* of creation from God, to God. The human soul is created by God as a principle of movement, and so the human can move himself. But as a creature, the soul can also *be moved*—in particular by the body,[57] because it is naturally composite with the body. Though the soul is the primary principle of life in the body,[58] the soul is not in the body as its *motor*, but as its *form*.[59] Beginning with his discussion of sensate beings (animals), Thomas says that the fact that a body is ensouled means that animate beings (as opposed to rocks and fire, for example) have the power of *perception*. With this perception comes *choice*. So Thomas sees the three—spirit, sense-perception, and choice—as bound together. Think of a cat stalking a bird. Eyes, nose, ears, whiskers are all engaged in pursuing that goal. Without those, the cat could not stalk and could not even intend to stalk the bird. With its sense-perception, the cat has a certain amount of freedom: the cat can stalk the bird or not; it can stalk this or that bird; it can give up if the bird is unreachable. So when Thomas saw that a creature had sense-perception, he knew that it also had spiritual capabilities, like choice and intention.[60] The reverse is also true. The fact that a physical creature had choice and intention must mean that it also had senses. If the cat's senses were confused (Thomas would say, "not in order") the cat could not stalk the bird. It is important to our discussion to emphasize that disruption of those *physical* senses would mean impairment of the *spiritual* characteristics, like intention and choice.

In sum, God is the unmoved mover of all creation; the human being is a moved mover.[61] The human being's rational soul cannot naturally be said to exist apart from the body. As a spiritual reality, the soul has primacy over the body,[62] but Thomas is quite clear: ". . . although the soul is part of the human body, it is not the whole human being, and my soul is not my [entire] self."[63] Anything predicated of the person, then, must be predicated of the entire composite self, soul and body. Thomas even insists that the soul needs the body in order to know anything at all and, interesting for our discussion, that all of the soul's knowledge is based upon physical contact—upon the sense of *touch*.[64] This theological anthropology allows Thomas to explain, under the rubric of "merit," that how we act (how we *move*) and how we suffer (how we *are moved*) in our embodiment affect the condition of our soul, the nature of our return to God, and the kind of enjoyment of God we will have in heaven.[65]

We can begin to see, then, the advantage of considering child abuse from a Thomistic perspective. We recall from the first section of this chapter that the dichotomy between physical and spiritual in our popular understanding gives us no adequate way to understand why a *bodily* attack on the abused child could have such deleterious effects on her *spiritual* reality (understood, for example, as intention, disposition, and choice). Thomas's rich understanding of the interplay of body and spirit can identify those spiritual realities as characteristics of the *soul (anima)*, but it can also show how the soul can be profoundly disturbed by disorder in the body, especially in the sense of touch. In short, what we do or suffer in the body affects the soul.

In the *Summa*, Thomas indicates another characteristic of the body that is important for appreciating the effects of physical abuse. We have seen several times in the first section how the effects of physical abuse continue through to adulthood, persisting long after the abuse has stopped. Thomas's notion of the soul as embodied allows him to explain this. He writes that "the forms which corporeal material receives, it holds not only while the body is actually acting as informed; [it holds them] *even after direct activity of the forms has ceased.*"[66] That is, the body is the soul's way of existing in space and time. The diachronistic nature of the body explains how the physical effects of abuse can perdure through time, affecting the body and the soul long after the actual attacks by the agent-other had ceased.

Let us attend to one additional point as we begin to develop a Thomistic position on child abuse. In I-II.49, Thomas begins his discussion of *habitus* (broadly, "habit"). He tells us that there can be habit in the body, but primarily habit is in the soul.[67] In I-II.51, he explains that these habits of the soul can be caused by our acts. But when we read that habits are caused by our acts, it is important for our discussion to realize that for Thomas, "action and passion are one act."[68] That is why his subsequent discussion of the nature of habit is so long and careful. In discussing how we can be affected by habit, he reminds us that as human beings, we can have habits that are natural to the species or natural to the individual, and that in human beings there are no natural habits ("habitus naturales"), either of species or of individual, that are wholly the work of nature. Thus, he can say, "There are in humans certain natural habits [particular to the species or to the individual], which exist partly from nature, and partly from an exterior principle."[69]

Thomas is careful to attend to both active and passive dimensions of habit here because he has placed this discussion of *habitus* immediately after the *Treatise on the Passions*. The *Treatise on the Passions* presents us with Thomas's most serious and thoroughgoing discussion of the effect of the *other* upon the self, both body and soul.[70] With respect to passions in the self, he often refers to the other as an agent of those passions.[71] More important, he wants to show in his subsequent discussion of virtue that virtue is grounded in the initiating action of God. Furthermore, Thomas wants to preserve the sense that the ongoing practice of virtue is always maintained by the gifts of God, and finally he wants to show that the fulfillment of the virtues is found in friendship with God. That is why he presents *habitus* as a relational notion in his discussion, telling us

> Thus it is possible for habits to be caused in agents by such acts, not certainly inasmuch as it is a first active principle, but inasmuch as its principle of activity is that of a moved mover. For all which suffers [patitur] and is moved by another is disposed by the action of an agent. Thus there is generated through many acts, a certain quality in the passive and moveable power, which quality we call habit.[72]

Again, we acknowledge that virtues are caused by our own conscious and individual actions. What I want to highlight for our discussion, however, is Thomas's insight that habits of the soul are possible precisely because of our capacity to be *moved by an other*. We will see the importance of Thomas's attention to that capacity again in our discussion of Thomistic remedies for abuse and especially in Thomas's understanding of *hope*. For now, I draw our attention especially to this passive dimension of character formation because it is so germane to our understanding of the effects of abuse. Thomas's attention to embodiment, touch as the most important way of learning, and our openness to being moved by an other, helps us to appreciate the effect parents have on the formation of the child's character[73] and the profoundly disruptive effect that parental abuse would have on the child.

In sum, then, we can understand that the soul is affected through embodiment and learns mainly through the touching of an other.

Habits are in the body, but principally in the soul. These habits of the soul and body are acquired by repeated acts, either through one's own power or through the power of an other. And again, it is that formation of the character in passion that we will be focusing on here.

With these reflections as background, we can turn now to the *Treatise on the Passions* (I-II.22-48),[74] where we hope to find our chief resources for a Thomistic understanding of child abuse, especially because of the passivity of the child before the actions of the parents. It is from the *Treatise* too, that we hope to construct an adequate soteriology for the survivors of child abuse.

THOMAS ON THE EFFECTS OF CHILD ABUSE: AN INTERPRETATION.

Thomas's purpose in the *Treatise on the Passions* is to outline exactly what it would mean for us to be morally responsible for how we are moved—for our passions.[75] In the first question in the *Treatise* Thomas argues against the objection that passions cannot be in the soul because only material (bodily) things can be said to suffer *(pati)*, and the soul is not physical. Thomas responds by recalling the composite nature of the human being and thereby establishes that the passions are in the soul precisely because they are in the body.[76] Thus, just as the body is crucial for Thomas's theological anthropology overall throughout the *Summa*, the body is crucial here for Thomas's account of the passions of the soul.

Thomas does not consider the bodily changes characteristic of the passions (such as trembling, feeling hot or cold, having watery knees) to be second-order effects of mental or spiritual dispositions. Rather those bodily changes are part of the complex of *causes* of a passion, and Thomas calls those bodily changes the *material cause* of passions. Again, and here more explicitly, Thomas enables us to understand why physical assaults can have such a profound effect on the interior life, upon the *soul* of the victim of abuse.

Within the *Treatise*, the discussion that most fits the topic at hand is Thomas's treatment of the passion of *pain (dolor)* and *sorrow (tristitia)* in 35-39. Thomas begins his discussion of sorrow with a discussion of pain *(dolor)*. The objections say that pain *(dolor)* is a sheerly physical thing and therefore cannot be in the soul. Thomas argues that pain is in the soul, since two things are required for pain: conjunction with some evil and perception of that conjunction.[77] The perceiving does not come from the body *qua* body, but from the fact that the body is *ensouled*. Thus pain must be in both. In 35.2ad2, he adds that the soul's awareness of pain is another way in which pain perdures, since "the exterior sense only perceives what is present. The interior cognitive power, however, is able to perceive present, past, and future. Thus sorrow is able to be about present, past, and future."[78]

We can see then, that the human being has a unique ability, in both her body and her soul, to carry pain through time. Thomas summarizes his position best in his reply to the first objection in 35.1. He draws on his already established position that the body and soul are one composite reality to summarize his understanding of the all-encompassing reality of pain. He says, "We speak of pain of the body, because the cause of pain is in the body, perhaps because some injury has been suffered by the body. But the movement of pain is always in the soul, for, as Augustine says, 'The body is not able to suffer pain unless the soul is suffering pain.'"[79] From such a perspective, we can see that the pain of physical abuse deforms the soul as it disfigures the body.

It is important for our topic to note that Thomas begins and grounds his study of the passion of sadness (*tristitia*) with a discussion of pain—a physical reality. In his discussion of sorrow, he is also sensitive to the fear, anxiety, and confusion we have seen as characteristic of victims of child abuse. The fear in bodily pain is caused precisely by the soul's ability to perceive past, present, and future. Although the sorrow is caused by a present pain, the soul's ability to see the future anticipates that such pain will continue or recur. Thus in Thomas, fear is also one of the features of pain.[80] When Thomas speaks of anxiety, he relates it to the sense of entrapment, another of the difficulties for the child that we have already observed. When an exterior force causes sorrow and cannot be escaped, Thomas says, "This is anxiety, which so weighs down the spirit that there does not appear to be any escape to a haven. That is why (*anxietas* [anxiety]) is also called 'being in straits' (*angustia*)."[81]

Though *confusion* is more of an intellectual disturbance, we have already seen how Thomas can account for the confusion of the abused person by drawing on the perdurance of physical disturbance in the victim of abuse. Recalling our example of the cat, we understand that the perduring *physical* disorder characteristic of the victim of abuse can lead to an ongoing confusion of mind, since the spirit, perception, and choice mutually entail each other in Thomas's thought. Later we will see Thomas take up the same themes when he discusses the physical remedies for sorrow. But for now, we can note that in the article we have just quoted, Thomas draws special attention to the loss of the power of speech in sorrow. That physical incapacity is important, he says, "because the voice, more than all other exterior movements, expresses interior thoughts and feelings."[82] Here Thomistic anthropology can encompass what Sáldor Ferenczi characterized as the "overwhelming power and authority of the adults" rendering the children silent, and Scarry's description of torture as "language destroying."

We had commented further that part of the anxiety and confusion of victims of abuse stems from their acute awareness of the disparity of power between the child and caregiver. Although Thomas does not explicitly mention parent and child, he does establish in 36.3 that a desire for unity (which is a "concupiscible passion" for Thomas) causes sorrow, since "the good of each thing requires a kind of unity,"[83] and "we sorrow for the delay, or complete removal, of the good we desire."[84] Again, we see the importance of the other in Thomas's account of the formation of character, and we can surely relate Thomas's desire for unity to the child's natural desire to bond with the caregiver. Then immediately afterward in 36.4, Thomas argues that sorrow is caused by a greater power, since to compel a thing to go against its inclinations requires a stronger power. Even though, as we have said, Thomas does not specifically consider childhood as a category, we can surely apply his notion of sorrow caused by a greater power to the power that parents have over children. It is an especially apt application, too, because of the unity that children naturally desire with their parents, a unity the deprivation of which makes abuse all the more painful. Here, then, Thomas seems finally to be addressing the disparity in power denoted in Aristotle's word for abuse, $\dot{v}\beta\rho\iota\zeta o\mu\acute{\epsilon}\nu o\varsigma$.[85]

When Thomas begins to discuss the effects of sorrow, his description sounds remarkably like a portrait of depression. And because for Thomas sorrow is grounded in physical pain as its material cause, his discussion also sounds remarkably like the psychological difficulties that spring from physical abuse.

For Thomas, sorrow is more harmful to the body than all the other passions, since no other passion so inhibits the natural movement of life.[86] In 37.2, he asks whether the effect of sorrow or pain is to burden the soul. His description there of the effects of sorrow—

even to the point of catatonia—is all too familiar to those who suffer from depression:

> A person is said to be weighed down by that burden which prevents him from the movement which is fitting for him. It is clear from what we have said earlier that sorrow occurs from some evil that is present to us. This evil, from the very fact that it works against the movement of the will, weighs down the soul, inasmuch as it hinders it from enjoying what it wants. And if it happens that this sorrowful (*contristantis*) evil is not so powerful as to preclude the hope of escaping it, then the soul is still depressed, in that it does not have the power in the present to do what it wants. [In such a case] however, it still has the power to repel the injurious evil which is making it sorrowful.[87]

> But if the force of the evil grows so great as to exclude the hope of escaping it, then even the interior motion of the soul is simply constrained, so that the soul is unable to turn this way or that. When that happens, even the exterior motion of the body is inhibited, such that the person is confined, paralyzed, within himself.[88]

For Thomas, then, the most destructive form of sorrow is when the person no longer can escape the thing that is causing the sorrow, when the person is trapped. In *Images of Hope*, a remarkably insightful book on the dynamics of mental illness and recovery, William F. Lynch writes,

> We have seen that in hope there is a principle of adaptability, and that it works. There is a sense of possibility. If a movement to the left fails, a movement to the right is tried, and finally the venturing finds a way out. But in [mental] illness the very opposite is true; nothing works, though everything seems to have been tried. There is a deep sense of entrapment and helplessness.[89]

There, Lynch speaks of a sense of entrapment in mental illness whose features are remarkably similar to those just described by Thomas, and both insights are applicable to the sense of entrapment felt by vicitms of abuse.

Earlier in the *Treatise*, Thomas said that whereas there could be union with good, there could not be real union with evil. That is why joy (the intellectual *appetitus* in union with, and knowing it is in union with, the good) has no real opposing concupiscible passion. He adds, however, that the presence of an evil can give rise to anger.[90] The passion of anger is treated much more completely in Diana Fritz Cates's contribution in this book. Here we can say that, for Thomas, anger occurs when we experience a slight or contempt for our excellence.[91] It is the passion most immediately concerned with justice—especially with the restoration of lost equality and mutuality. In that, anger serves two purposes. First, it alerts us to the fact that an excellence has been threatened or harmed. Most pertinent to our discussion, the anger associated with pain alerts us to the goodness of our nature as embodied creatures. Thomas writes, "In physical pain those two things [the recognition and rejection of evil] attest to the goodness of nature, a goodness by which the senses perceive, and nature escapes, injury, which causes pain."[92] Second, anger serves the previously mentioned desire for unity by restoring the dignity of the self and thus reestablishing the equality necessary for communion. Reading Thomas's treatment of sorrow for a greater understanding of child abuse, we can say that the anger associated with abuse is a valuable tool for restoring the dignity of the individual and for attaining to the unity that the individual seeks.

In our discussion of the anger of the victims of abuse, we mentioned that it was unclear whether the anger occurred as a result of the child's natural resistance to such violations, or because the child had appropriated the anger of the violator toward the child. We can see from the above discussion that Thomas conceives of anger in the first sense. When Thomas wants to consider what we would now call "internalized anger," he does it by showing how the will or intention of a person can be completely overridden by the force of an other. We have heard him speak of that several times, when discussing the person's inability to escape sorrow. In the following article, he explicitly considers this phenomenon.

> But we should know that if the stronger power so weakens [the weaker power] that it changes the contrary inclination into its own inclination, there will be no longer repugnance or violence

> ... such is the result only when the contrary inclination of the *appetitus* remains. And hence Augustine says that the will *resisting* a stronger power, causes sorrow: for if it did not resist, but yielded by feeling along with [the stronger power], the result would be not sorrow but pleasure.[93]

Thus Thomas can give us a structure for understanding the "soul murder" of child abuse, "that it is somehow possible to take possession of another person's soul." He also gives us a structure for understanding how one can even derive a certain pleasure from continuing self-destructive habits.

Last, Thomas also speaks of the *dissociation* characteristic of victims of abuse. For example, Thomas states that pain can deprive a person of the power to learn: it attracts so much of the intention of the soul to itself that the soul cannot place its intention on other things,[94] it sometimes deprives a person of reason altogether.[95] He would say that under conditions of extreme physical pain, the *rationality of the soul* would be obscured, or better, collapsed into the body. That is, extreme physical pain causes the person to lose the "rational" ability to know things beyond the senses—and perhaps beyond mere physical survival. In prayer subsequent to his own confession after torture, Walter Ciszek had to admit, "The act of signing had been prompted by an almost animal-like urge for survival. It had hardly been conscious and surely not deliberate enough to deserve the name human."[96]

Thomas explains dissociation even more profoundly when he tells us that it is the nature of the passion of sorrow to flee or withdraw.[97] That is why it is so inimical to life. The human being is a social animal, and the withdrawing nature of sorrow works against the desire for unity that is fitting for us. Within the individual, too, the withdrawing nature of sorrow attacks the very life principle, which consists of motion. When Thomas imagines sorrow's withdrawing taking place within an individual, he writes,

> As far as the movement of the *appetitus* is concerned, being constricted and being weighed down refer to the same phenomenon, because the soul, through being so weighed down that it cannot pursue outward things freely, *withdraws to itself, as though constricting itself within itself.*[98]

Thus the sufferer would, in Thomistic terminology, lose her rationality. For Thomas, the final abandonment of the body by the soul would result in paralysis of the body (as we have seen in earlier citations). But the intermediate stages of sorrow's withdrawal of the soul can be seen to have all the fear, anxiety, and anger that characterize the victims of abuse.

The image that Thomas presents us with here—of the soul withdrawing from the body—can lead to a speculation on another aspect of physical abuse. In many places in *Spare the Child*, Greven shows how the dynamics of physical abuse can lead to difficulties in sexual self-understandings and practices. We have already seen, for example, his discussion of how the dynamics of sadomasochism are initiated by the fusion of love and abuse in childhood. Suppose we were to consider those sexual difficulties from a Thomistic viewpoint? We might say that the body derives its loveliness principally, though not exclusively, from the presence of the soul. If, through abuse, the soul has withdrawn from the body, then the body is, as it were, left on its own, without confirmation of its own loveliness from the soul. Still staying in Thomistic theological anthropology, we could say that the body, inasmuch as it is created by God and has existence, would still have some loveliness in and of itself. Without the accord of the soul, however, that loveliness would be unconfirmed and ungoverned. The body then would be left to seek assurance of its loveliness from outside, apart from its own soul, the seat of its own identity. If we can say further that the locus of the attractiveness of the body is in its sexuality, then the abused person would find himself on a constant search for affirmation of his physical loveliness (which affirmation his own withdrawn soul cannot provide) through various sexual activities that would be out of character with his true identity. In our counseling of, or friendship with, the victim of abuse, we have perhaps noticed this. We often see a swing between a continence that is really an attempt to be sexless and a fall into practices for which the person is embarrassed and ashamed. Thomistic anthropology, which can understand the soul as fleeing from a body that continually carries the pain and shame of abuse, can help us to understand, accompany, and encourage those who struggle with this painful characteristic of abuse.

Now that we have used Thomas's theology to frame the characteristics of victims of abuse, we can, I believe, also draw on Thomas for a soteriology adequate to redress the pain of abuse and even to lead the survivor to reconciliation.

THOMISTIC REMEDIES FOR THE EFFECTS OF ABUSE.

In the previous section, we relied especially on Thomas's discussion of sorrow in the *Treatise on the Passions* to provide a structure for our reflections on abuse. In this section, we can expect to find a healing of the effects of abuse in his discussion of "Remedies for Sorrow" (I-II.38). We also know that Thomas wants to conclude (in the *tertia pars*) by showing that life in "the body of Christ" is the supreme practice of virtue and the highest form of empowerment. Therefore, we should also consider forgiveness and reconciliation as characteristic of a Christian soteriology from abuse.

At the end of *Spare the Child*, Philip Greven offers us a disappointing conclusion. Now that we know the dangers of abuse, he seems to say, we can make choices about what we will do.[99] This seems, however, to ignore the force of the embodied and ensouled *habit* of abuse, which Greven himself has so well documented. That is, in the face of embodied, internalized, and habitualized self-destruction, a simple choice stands little chance of success. In fact, new habitual relationships must be formed with new others, and those new others must be allowed time and frequency of touch so as to reform and reconfigure the self. Only with such empowerment (and not through knowledge alone) can one become free enough to choose a different path of life. Once again, in other words, we see how crucial receptivity, or passion, is for proper character formation.

Once again, too, we find the theological anthropology of Thomas helpful in our hope for salvation from abuse. Because Thomas's account of the formation of Christian character considers the agency of the other in the self's passion, he can begin to consider that the healing of sorrow can come from an other, as well. In the end, Thomas wants to ground that "hope from the power of another" in God. And that also is helpful in considering the healing of parental abuse, since in Thomas's theology, God is the primary cause, and parents only the secondary causes, of our existence. Thus, it is possible theologically to construe the ongoing action of God as more foundational in the abused person's life than the borne-through-time abuse of the parents.[100] With such a theological vision, we can realistically hope that the action of the ultimate Other can supersede and so dislodge even so fundamental a formation as that of parents.

In 40.1ad1, Thomas says there are two ways in which we can receive hope for escape from sorrow. The first way that we can receive hope *(sperare)* is through our own resources ("per propriam virtutem adipisci"). The second is that we can receive hope through the power of another ("ex auxilio virtutis alienae"). In the latter case, hope is called *expectare*, which Thomas says is derived from "ex alio spectare." In that regard, it counts that we are rational; that, unlike animals, we can know things beyond our senses. The abused person can have hope for experiences of healing from others, even though he himself has had the direct personal experience of physical abuse. Later in the same question, article 7, he states that sometimes "a difficult object becomes possible for us, not through ourselves, but through others."[101]

That is the same discovery that Lynch made in his study of hope and emergence from mental illness:

> The first of these burdens [on hope] . . . would be to declare that hope is a final interior resource, which needs nothing but itself . . . The fact is that hope is a relative ideal. It is always relative to the idea of help. It seeks help. It depends. It looks to the outside world.[102]

Thomas will have this passion of "hope through the power of another" flower in his discussion of the theological virtue of hope.[103] For our discussion it is important to note here that Thomas can accommodate the notion that hope for the abused can (and *de facto* must) come from outside, and that it can finally be rooted in God.

The same capability that the victim of abuse had for appropriating the intention of the violator can work to the good, because the victim can appropriate the intention of an other, and especially of God, for the victim to become well. The crucial difference is that such an intent is in keeping with the original nature of the person: to will the good. Hence, such an intention is not imposed, but more properly *shared*, and the dynamic between the self and the other is love (which is the goal and source of hope). We might add here that the principal Word that gives expression—and through that expression, empowerment—to the victim's suffering is Christ Himself.[104]

Proceeding in his discussion of how sorrow can be healed through the action of another, Thomas reminds us of our common experience, that sorrow is assuaged through the compassion of friends.[105] Here, Thomas says that, even though our friend is in sorrow because of our sorrow, we can see that the sharing comes from love, and that brings us delight. He also says that, because sorrow weighs down,

> when a person in sorrow sees that others are joining him in sorrow, he has a certain imaginative construal that others are bearing the weight with him, striving, as it were, against it, in order to alleviate the burden. Thus the burden of sorrow becomes lighter, the same as if carrying physical weights.[106]

In the next article,[107] Thomas adds that pain and sorrow are assuaged by contemplating the truth. The third objection has argued that this is not possible, since contemplating of the truth is the operation of the intellect, and not the body, and so cannot assuage physical pain. Thomas replies that, because the faculties of the body are in sympathetic vibration (*redundantia*), the delight of contemplating the truth can affect the lower (physical) powers as well.[108] Perhaps we can combine those two articles and state that the friends we approach in our sorrow about abuse have to be knowledgeable and truthful, and that truth has to be contemplated together.[109] With our friends, then, we share the truth of our experience of abuse and become empowered as that sharing alleviates our burden. With our friends, too, we can share the certain knowledge of the Spirit's power to redeem. Since the Spirit raised Jesus from a death by violence, the same Spirit can overcome any of the debilitating effects of physical abuse in our bodies or in our souls.

Therapists remind us of how important it is to attend to the anger that victim has because of her violation. Thomas, we recall, says that the irascible passion of anger is the fitting passion for the violation of our excellence. In fact, Thomas even says that sorrow can be good; if something sorrowful has been done, we should grieve about it especially if we are good persons.[110] We would add, in our discussion of abuse, that sorrow is a fitting passion for the violation of the excellence of the *embodied* self. The healing community would respect the excellence, even the sacredness, of the embodied self, hearing the anger of the abused as an understandable cry for justice at the violation of the sacred. Anger, Thomas says, springs from a concupiscible passion for unity. Our truthful friends can empower us to bear that anger, work for justice, and move toward reconciliation. We could look for that respect and justice even in *charity*, which is interaction with our best friend and best delight, God.[111]

Thomas is, as we have seen, also impressed with the dissociation that is characteristic of sorrow. We say that a person is afflicted with sorrow, and the Latin root for that word means "to be turned away." Combating this withdrawal, then, and returning the victim to rationality, is the basic strategy for the remedy of sorrow. That is another reason that reaching out to friends is a remedy for sorrow, since it works against the withdrawal into isolation that is destructive for a constitutively social being.

We have seen that this withdrawal, or dissociation, takes place even within the self, with the soul withdrawing from the body. In that light, we can see that Thomas's analogy of lifting sorrow to lifting a physical burden in the quote above is not a random one. In general, Thomas says that *all* pleasure is allopathic to sorrow,[112] especially because pleasures would lure the soul back to the body. In 38.2, for example, Thomas asserts that sorrow or pain is mitigated by weeping, "since everything sorrowful that is closed into the interior increases affliction, because more and more of the intent of the soul is absorbed by it. But when we pour it out into the body, then the 'cluster of intent' that the soul has invested in it, is likewise diffused into the exterior."[113] This is a free translation, but it shows the consistency of Thomas's realization of how preoccupying, afflicting, and constricting sorrow is. More and more of the attention of our spirit is drawn to the sorrowful thing, if we keep it in. The body assists in restoring the balance to our intentionality, by drawing the soul back, drawing sorrow away, and diffusing it in tears. In this restoring of the balance of the self, Thomas would see that the confusion of the victims of abuse can be alleviated.

Thomas concludes his discussion of the remedies for sorrow by arguing that pain and sorrow can be assuaged by baths and sleep. Even though the third objection has argued that this emphasis on physical remedies is at odds with Thomas's earlier assertion that (intellective) contemplation of the truth assuages sorrow, Thomas replies again that all the person's powers are in sympathetic vibration (*redundat*) with each other, and so what is good for the exterior self is good for the interior.[114] From this framework, we can see that Thomas would suggest that practices that soothe the body, so perduringly afflicted by abuse, must also be part of the program of healing and empowerment. In that, we should remember that Thomas states that God is the greatest delight for human beings.[115] Thus, when he attends especially to physical remedies, we can include reception of the Eucharist as a powerful means of reuniting the soul with the body, just as the Word of God became flesh.

The ultimate step in the process of healing of the survivor of abuse would be forgiveness of, and reconciliation with, the abusive parent. In a recent article, Michael McCullough and Everett Worthington issued a call to "investigate the psychological effects of traditionally religious behaviors like forgiveness to determine what, if any, psychological benefits they may yield,"[116] admitting that "Clinical research on forgiveness is embarrassingly sketchy."[117] They caution, however, that "Encouraging survivors of brutal offenses to forgive (even if having expressed a desire to do so) may exacerbate feelings of low self-worth that often follow such traumas. Clients may also perceive such encouragement as the minimizaiton of the brutality they incurred. Only after an expression of a desire to forgive *and* the resolution of the more immediate event-related difficulties should forgiving be encouraged with such clients."[118] Marie M. Fortune states that forgiveness is the last step in the process of healing the effects of abuse.[119]

For his part, Thomas would say that reconciliation is the last step of the victim's dealing with the shame, anger, and dissociation that come from abuse. As such, he might see reconciliation as "first in intention, last in execution." In the Thomistic framework, however, that final step of reconciliation must govern all the passions, intentions, and actions in the struggle to heal the effects of abuse. Put another way, because the form of all the virtues is friendship with God in Christ, and because God's love in Christ is one of forgiveness, we might best say that *forgiveness is the form* of all the steps one takes in the healing of abuse. It is precisely there that we need a faithful community to remind us of our final goal. And inasmuch as the final goal is reconciliation, the community must facilitate and support the dimensions of the healing journey that require confrontation with the abuser—with an eye toward repentance, reparation,[120] and reconciliation. Indeed, only through proper community can we rightly attend to such anger, lest the anger become isolating and justifying of an attitude of vengeance, or the reconciliation be another capitulation of the self to the abuser.[121] Christ himself, and the community that embodies Christ, or at least a representative of that community, accompanies us on the journey and celebrates with us its rightful completion. In this, "a difficult object [can become] possible for us, not through ourselves, but through others."[122]

When that anger is properly attended to, when the effects of sorrow are remedied, then this passion, the original cause for sorrow, is clarified and liberated: love's desire for unity, embodied especially in the communion of the Eucharist, the body of Christ. That is why, as Paul Wadell points out in his chapter, Thomas concludes his study of ethics with a study of the sacraments. Precisely in their ongoing celebration of the divine/physical union, the sacraments (and the sacramental community) heal, empower, guide, and strengthen the abused person toward reconciliation. Because of the inherent social nature of the self, that Love gradually reconfigures the self until the abused discovers a love within, a love she can appropriate that, strengthened in the love of Christ, is stronger than the abuser's ability to hurt. It is as though the survivor has received a personal taste of Thomas's deep, identity-grounding ontological attachment to God of which Judith Kay wrote in the first chapter of this volume.

It is from that great Love that authentic resistance to the characteristics of abuse can arise. It is from that Love that forgiveness flows, since "the One who is in you is greater than the one who is in the world."[123] It is by being grounded in that greater power that the abused can safely consider the right way to reconcile, and to be in communion, with the abuser. And when that desire for the right communion of love has been fulfilled, the irascible passion of anger can correctly cease, since it has served its purpose, which is finally the communion of love. For

> ... the irascible is a kind of fighter for, and defender of, the concupiscible powers when it rises up against that which is preventing the concupiscible powers from enjoying what is fitting [for which the concupiscible has *appetitus*], and when it inflicts harm upon that which the concupiscible flees from. That is why all the irascible passions begin in concupiscible passions and terminate in them, *as anger is born to take away sorrow*, and upon bringing about vindication terminates in joy.[124]

NOTES

My sincere thanks go to my brother, Philip Harak, my friends, Bob and Katherine Doolittle, Jim and Carolyn Rusiackas, to John Thiel, Chair of the Department of Religious Studies at Fairfield University, to the members of the Christian Ethics Roundtable in Washington, D.C., and to Jim Buckley, Chair, and the members of the Theology Department at Loyola College in Baltimore for their review of, and helpful comments on, this work. I have learned from all of them. An earlier version of this chapter appeared in *Modern Theology*, 11, no. 3 (July 1995): 315–40.

1. Charles Taylor, *The Ethics of Authenticity* (Cambridge, Mass.: Harvard University Press, 1992), p. 45.
2. Taylor, *Ethics of Authenticity*, p. 49.
3. In our discussion, we will use both the word "victim" and the word "survivor." Though it is not intended as a hard and fast distinction, I will use the term survivor to indicate those who have acknowledged their abuse and have begun some kind of healing journey.
4. In St. Thomas Aquinas, *Summa theologiae* (Blackfriars, 1967). The *Treatise on the Passions*, the longest treatise in the *Summa*, extends through I-II.22–48.
5. See Selwyn M. Smith, "Maltreatment of Children: an Historical Perspective," in *The Battered Child Syndrome* (Boston, Mass.: Butterworths, 1975), pp. 3–20, and Ruth Inglis, "Early Attitudes to Children: Early Cruelties," in *Sins of the Fathers* (New York, N.Y.: St. Martin's Press, Inc., 1978), pp. 14–33. Both give good general histories of cruelties toward children, with the latter concentrating on England and the U.S.
6. Robin E. Clark and Judith Freeman Clark, *The Encyclopedia of Child Abuse* (New York, N.Y.: Facts on File, 1989), p. xv. Much of the Introduction by Richard J. Gelles, author and co-author of numerous books, journal articles, and studies on child abuse, is devoted to this discussion. For discussions of the difficulty of defining abuse, see also David A. Wolfe, *Child Abuse: Implications for Child Development and Psychopathology*. Developmental Clinical Psychology and Psychiatry Series, edited by Alan E. Kazdin, (Newbury Park, Calif.: Sage Publications, 1987) vol. 10, pp. 14–18; Marla R. Brassard, Robert Germain, and Stuart N. Hart, *Psychological Maltreatment of Children and Youth*. Pergamon General Psychology Series, edited by Arnold P. Goldstein and Leonard Krasner. (New York, N.Y.: Pergamon Press, 1987) pp. 5–7. The National Center on Child Abuse and Neglect defines child abuse as: "The physical or mental injury, sexual abuse, negligent treatment, or maltreatment of a child under the age of eighteen by a person who is responsible for the child's welfare under circumstances which indicate that the child's health or welfare is harmed or threatened thereby" (Public Law 93–237 [1974]). For a definition that might ground international discussion of child abuse, see David Finkelhor and J. Korbin, "Child Abuse as an International Issue," *Child Abuse and Neglect: The International Journal*, 12, no. 1 (1988): 3–23.
7. Douglas Barnett, Jody Todd Manly, and Dante Cicchetti, "Defining

Child Maltreatment: The Interface between Policy and Research," in *Child Abuse, Child Development, and Social Policy*, Dante Cicchetti and Sheree L. Toth, eds. Advances in Applied Developmental Psychology Series, Vol. 8, edited by Irving E. Sigel (Norwood, N.J.: Ablex Publishing Corporation, 1993), pp. 7–73. The authors have submitted a comprehensive list of interfacing criteria for evaluating child abuse, including (1) Subtypes (as for example, physical or sexual abuse, or neglect), (2) Severity, (3) Frequency, and (4) Developmental Period of the child (cf. figure #3 on p. 33).

8. Gelles, *The Encyclopedia of Child Abuse*, p. xx.

9. "The Subtype that is most easily documented and the most frequently studied is *Physical Abuse*. This subtype is scored whenever a caregiver inflicts a physical injury to the child by other than accidental means. Whereas extreme forms of physical abuse are generally regarded as maltreatment, the lower boundaries of the category are more controversial because of the acceptance of corporal punishment in this country. Typically, Child Protective Services reports of excessive corporal punishment are not substantiated unless an injury to the child has been sustained." Barnett et al., "Defining Child Maltreatment," p. 35 (emphasis in text). When applying their criterion of "Severity" to the phenomenon, the authors signify a range from #1 (minor marks) to #5 (hospitalizable, permanent, and/or fatal injury), pp. 55–57.

10. Gelles, *The Encyclopedia of Child Abuse*, Introduction, p. xvii. The strong-hearted reader can view the physical effects of abuse in a series of terribly distressing photos in Ray E. Helfer, M.D. and Ruth S. Kempe, M.D., eds., *The Battered Child*, 4th ed. (Chicago, Ill.: University of Chicago Press, 1987).

11. ". . . not all child maltreatment leads to immediately or easily documentable harm. Consequently, basing decisions about maltreatment solely on demonstration of harm would prevent large numbers of children from receiving help before they had been seriously impaired." Barnett et al., "Defining Child Maltreatment," p. 23.

12. To the previously mentioned studies we might add David Finkelhor, Richard J. Gelles, Gerald T. Hotaling, and Murray A. Straus, eds., *The Dark Side of Families: Current Family Violence Research* (Beverly Hills, Calif.: Sage Publications, 1983); Richard J. Gelles, *The Violent Home* (Newbury Park, Calif.: Sage Publications, 1987); Anne L. Horton and Judith A. Williamson, eds., *Abuse and Religion: When Praying Isn't Enough* (Lexington, Mass.: Lexington Books, 1988); Gerald T. Hotaling, David Finkelhor, John T. Kirkpatrick, and Murray A. Straus, eds., *Coping with Family Violence, Research and Policy Perspectives* (Newbury Park, Calif.: Sage Publications, 1990), especially Sharon D. Herzberger and Howard Tennen, "Applying the Label of Physical Abuse," pp. 18–30, for a review of the literature.

13. Morton Schatzman, *Soul Murder: Persecution in the Family. A unique and insightful study of schizophrenia and family psychology, based on the classic memoirs of a famous mental patient and his father's writings on child-rearing.* (New York, N.Y.: Random House, 1973), p. ix. This is also a famous Freudian case study. One of Schatzman's purposes in writing *Soul Murder* is to redress Freud's neglect of the effects of abuse.

14. Principally, Daniel Gottlieb Moritz Schreber's *Education Toward Beauty by Natural and Balanced Furtherance of Normal Body Growth, of Life-Supporting Health, and of Mental Ennoblement, Especially by the Use, if Possible, of Special Educational Means: for Parents, Educators, and Teachers* [*Kallipädie oder Erziehung zur Schönheit durch naturgetreue und gleichmässige Föderung normaler Köperbildung*] (Leipzig: Fleischer, 1858).

15. "At sixty one [Daniel Paul Schreber] published *Memoirs of My Nervous Illness*, a book he compiled from notes about his experiences and thoughts while 'suffering from a nervous illness.'" Schatzman, *Soul Murder*, p. 4.

16. Schreber, *Education Toward Beauty*, pp. 136–7, quoted in Schatzman, *Soul Murder*, p. 24 (emphasis in *Soul Murder*, not in *Education Toward Beauty*). Cf. also *Education Toward Beauty*, p. 60, quoted from *Soul Murder*, p. 29: "'One must look at the moods of the little ones that are announced by screaming without reason and crying. . . . If one has convinced oneself that no real need, no disturbing or painful condition, no sickness is present, one can be assured that the screaming is only and simply the expression of a mood, a whim, the first appearance of self-will. . . . One has to step forward in a positive manner: by quick distraction of the attention, stern words, threatening gestures, rapping against the bed. . . . or, when all this is of no avail; by moderate, intermittent, bodily admonishments consistently repeated until the child calms down or falls asleep. . . .'"

17. Schreber, *Memoirs*, p. 131, quoted in Schatzman, *Soul Murder*, p. 40. The point of Schatzman's work is to "propose (as Freud did) that the author of the *Memoirs* transfigured the father of his childhood into the God of his 'nervous illness.' Throughout this book I display links between the father's probable behavior toward his son and the son's strange relations with God" (pp. 18–19). It would be fascinating, but beyond the scope of this chapter, to discuss the abused children's images of God. Philip Greven, *Spare the Child, The Religious Roots of Punishment and Psychological Impact of Physical Abuse* (New York, N.Y.: Alfred A. Knopf, 1991), cf. pp. 13, 15, 35, 47ff., 62, 72, 88–89, also briefly touches on this.

18. Schreber, *Memoirs*, p. 145, quoted in Schatzman, *Soul Murder*, p. 41.

19. Schreber, *Memoirs*, p. 133, quoted in Schatzman, *Soul Murder*, p. 46.

20. Schreber, *Memoirs*, p. 164, quoted in Schatzman, *Soul Murder*, p. 51.

21. Schatzman, *Soul Murder*, p. 52. Of such "reenactment," Gelles writes, "Theories and students of violence posit that the family serves as an agent of socialization in teaching violent behavior. Not only does the family expose individuals to violence and techniques of violence, the family teaches approval for the use of violence. Bakan asserts that every time a child is punished by violence he is being taught that violence is a proper mode of behavior" (*Violent Home*, p. 171).

22. Greven, *Spare the Child*, p. 7, cf. p. 10. See also Inglis, *Sins of the Fathers*: "'At the moment of bashing,' Professor Kempe told me, 'they abreact to their own childhood. They themselves have experienced severe corporal punishment and have had an imprinting of violence at a very early age'." Greven also indicates how the effects of abuse might even continue after our

death: "The impact of physical punishment is like this, traveling through time inside our bodies, minds and spirits and living on long after our individual deaths through the legacies we bequeath to our children and grandchildren and to future generations throughout the world" (p. 5). We should mention that the reactions and legacies do not always include that the abused become abusive parents themselves. Carol J. Adams provides an excellent refutation and constructive reply to the assertion that battered children grow up to batter, in *Restoring Holiness: An Ecofeminist Analysis of Violence in the Home* (unpubl. ms.).

23. In the first chapter of my *Virtuous Passions: The Formation of Christian Character* (Mahwah, N.J.: Paulist Press, 1993).

24. Melvin Konner, *The Tangled Wing: Biological Constraints on the Human Spirit* (New York, N.Y.: Holt, Rinehard and Winston, 1982), p. 61. Cf. also H. F. Harlow and M. K. Harlow, "Social Deprivation in Monkeys," *Scientific American* 207 (1962): 136–46. Greven also writes that "the body and the brain probably encode such pain" (*Spare the Child*, p. 19), but does not give a scientific basis for such a claim. For a fuller discussion of this entire phenomenon, see chapter One, "The Body," in my *Virtuous Passions*.

25. Schatzman, *Soul Murder*, p. 30.

26. Tracy Nagurski, "To Daddy," in Toni A. H. McNaron and Yarrow Morgan, eds., in *Voices in the Night: Women Speaking About Incest*, (Pittsburgh, Pa.: Cleis, 1982), pp. 157–8. See also the more popular Suzanne Somers, *Wednesday's Children: Adult Survivors of Abuse Speak Out* (New York, N.Y.: Jove Books, 1992). We should note that incest is a particularly intense form of physical abuse. In fact, its effects are so extreme and profound that I tend to consider it a different species of abuse.

27. Schreber, *Memoirs*, p. 55, quoted in Schatzman, *Soul Murder*, p. 37.

28. Schatzman, *Soul Murder*, p. 55. Note again his comment, "It occurred to me only much later, in fact only while writing this essay did it become quite clear to me that God Himself must have known of the plan, if indeed he was not the instigator, to commit soul murder on me. . . ." (Schreber, *Memoirs*, p. 77, quoted in Schatzman, *Soul Murder*, pp. 37–8). My brother Philip Harak points out that this training in surrender of the soul to another probably accounts for why abuse victims need to meld with powerful figures in adulthood.

29. Quoted in Greven, *Spare the Child*, pp. 65–66.

30. Quoted in Greven, *Spare the Child*, p. 66. We cannot help but notice the use of the impersonal pronoun in Mrs. Wesley's statement.

31. Sáldor Ferenczi, "Confusion of Tongues Between Adults and the Child," Jeffrey M. Masson and Marianne Loring, trans., in Jeffrey M. Masson, *The Assault on Truth: Freud's Suppression of the Seduction Theory* (New York, N.Y.: Penguin, 1985), p. 298.

32. Elaine Scarry, *The Body in Pain: The Making and Unmaking of the World* (New York, N.Y.: Oxford University Press, 1985), p. 19.

33. Scarry, *The Body in Pain*, p. 4.

34. Scarry, *The Body in Pain*, p. 20.

35. Scarry, *The Body in Pain*, p. 50.

36. Elaine Scarry writes of a similar perversion of authority in her study of torture. She writes that the infliction of pain "can be separated from the sufferer and referred to power, broken off from the body and attached instead to the regime. [I]t is not the pain but the regime that is incontestably real, not the pain but the regime that is total, not the pain but the regime that is able to eclipse all else, not the pain but the regime that is able to dissolve the world" (*The Body in Pain*, p. 56).

37. Orson Scott Card, *Red Prophet* (New York, N.Y.: Tom Doherty Associates, Inc., 1988), pp. 91–92. Interesting also in this regard is Arthur Kopit, *End of the World* (New York, N.Y.: Hill and Wang, 1984). In this play, Philip Stone has commissioned Michael Trent to write a play about the end of the world through nuclear annihilation. Trent finally discovers that the reason he has been chosen is because he had a terrifying experience of absolute destructive power over his newborn son (pp. 94–95).

38. Scarry also discusses the terrifying significance of the *room itself* for the victim of torture because so many objects in the room have been used to harm the tortured person (*The Body in Pain*, pp. 40–41).

39. Pat Conroy, *The Prince of Tides* (Boston, Mass.: Houghton Mifflin [Bantam], 1986), p. 577. Richard Gelles writes, "When violence takes place in the home, there is often no place to go, and to leave the scene means leaving one's possessions, one's children, and one's home territory. Thus, when violence occurs between family members, [there is] often no place to which the victim or offender can retreat" (*Violent Home*, pp. 93–94). See the discussion of psychological entrapment, and especially "learned helplessness" in Michael J. Strube, "The Decision to Leave an Abusive Relationship," *Coping*, pp. 100–102. Lewis Okun discusses economic dependency in "Termination or Resumption of Cohabitation in Woman Battering Relationships: A Statistical Study," *Coping*, pp. 107–119.

40. Is 61:2; cf. Lk 4:18.

41. Cf. Colwyn Trevarthen, "Emotions in Infancy: Regulators of Contact and Relationship between Persons," Chapter 6 in *Approaches to Emotion* (Hillsdale, N.J.: Lawrence Erlbaum Associates, Inc., 1984), pp. 129–157.

42. David Finkelhor, assistant director of the Family Violence Research Program at the University of New Hampshire, writes, "Family abuse is more precisely the abuse of power," and then adds, "[T]he most common patterns in family abuse are not merely for the more powerful to abuse the less powerful, but for the most powerful to abuse the least. This is an interesting commonality: Abuse tends to gravitate toward the relationships of greatest power differential." *Dark Side*, Introduction, p. 18. Ginny McCarthy writes, "Together they [emotional and physical abuse] are powerful ways to control another person, and that control is the fundamental drive of the abusive person," in "Building Self-Esteem: Overcoming Barriers to Recovery," *Abuse and Religion*, p. 114. Greven discusses this characteristic under the rubric of "Authoritarianism" in *Spare the Child*, pp. 198–204.

43. Conroy, *The Prince of Tides*, p. 157. The outcome of such anxiety may very well also be obsessiveness and rigidity. See Greven, *Spare the Child*, pp. 135–41.

44. Alice Miller, "Adolph Hitler's Childhood: From Hidden to Manifest Horror." Reprinted in Roger S. Gottlieb, ed., *Thinking the Unthinkable: Meanings of the Holocaust* (New York, N.Y.: Paulist Press, 1990). The provocative point in Miller's work is that Hitler recreated his early childhood's "poisonous pedagogy" in his formation of the Nazi state, with the Jewish people playing the scapegoat role of the young Adolf. ". . . a man wearing an SA [sic] armband attacks him; this man has the right to do anything to the Jew he wants, anything his fantasy happens to dictate and that his unconscious craves at the moment. The Jew can do nothing to alter this; he is in the same position as little Adolf once was" (pp. 96–97).

45. Lk 1:74.

46. 1Jn 4:18.

47. Alice Miller, *For Your Own Good: Hidden Cruelty in Child-Rearing and the Roots of Violence*, Hildegarde Hannum and Hunter Hannum, trans. (Toronto, Ont.: Collins Publishers, 1989; [1st ed. Frankfurt am Main: Suhrkamp Verlag, 1980]), pp. 61ff.

48. In using the word "primary," I am being cautious. There are times in reading Miller's corpus when one might be convinced that abuse is the *sole* cause of adult violence, though Miller never explicitly states this.

49. For this discussion see Miller, *For Your Own Good*, "The War of Annihilation against the Self," pp. 107–41. We should note that, in defense against such self-annihilation, the children often settle on a particular fault in their nature, and names *that* as the reason they have been beaten. Deflecting the condemnation away from the entire self and onto this fault can save a child from self-annihilation.

50. Conroy, *The Prince of Tides*, p. 251. Note also in *Sins of the Fathers*, "The baby does not have to *do* anything; just to *be* is enough to put him in the parental firing line" (p. 72). "In physical pain, then, suicide and murder converge, for one feels acted upon, annihilated, by inside and outside alike" (Scarry, *The Body in Pain*, p. 53).

51. *The Poems of Emily Dickinson*, vol. II., Thomas H. Johnson, ed. (Cambridge, Mass.: The Belknap Press of Harvard University Press, 1979), pp. 501–2.

52. Greven, *Spare the Child*, p. 148.

53. Scarry, *The Body in Pain*, p. 47.

54. VII.v.3; (1148b). Translation mine. He also mentions men who are attracted to men as though to women. I believe he means traumatic homosexuality here.

55. ". . . accidunt ex consuetudine, puta quia consueverunt ad huiusmodi a pueritia. Et simile est de his qui in hoc incidunt ex aegritudine corporali. Nam prava consuetudo est quasi quaedam aegritudo animalis." Lect. V on Book VII, 1374. Note that the Latin adjective *animali* can draw its meaning from either *anima* or *animal*. I believe this indefiniteness is intended by Thomas

at this point to refer to both the spiritual and physical disruptions that such behaviors betray.

56. "Unde pronitas ad iram de facili propagatur a patre in filium, quasi consequens naturalem complexionem." He concludes with "Sic ergo quia ira naturalior est, minus turpis est incontinens irae" (Lect. VI on Book VII, 1392).

57. I.75.1ad1; 75.2.

58. I.75.1.

59. I.76.6; cf. also I.76.7.

60. I took this excellent example of a cat stalking a bird from G. E. M. Anscombe, *Intention* (Oxford: Basil Blackwell, 1958), pp. 85–86. She writes, "Thus the possession of sensible discrimination and that of volition are inseparable; one cannot describe a creature as having the power of sensation without also describing it as doing things in accordance with perceived sensible differences" (p. 67). Also cf. the *Summa theologiae*, I-II.40.3. Henceforth, all references will be to the *Summa theologiae* unless otherwised noted.

61. I.80.2. Cf. also Aristotle's *De Anima*, III.10, 433b16; and his *Metaphysics*, XI.7, 1072a26.

62. In "Aquinas's Concept of the Body and Out of Body Situations." *The Heythrop Journal* 34, no. 4 (Oct. 1993): 387–400, Patrick Quinn shows that Thomas shares with Aristotle the view that body and senses are indispensible for the production of knowledge. He states that for Thomas, however, ". . . in order to understand God's essence, we must dispense with any kind of knowledge that is mediated through the senses and the body's capacity to interfere with the intellect at this highest level of cognition must consequently be curbed. This view emerges in those parts of Aquinas's writings where he discusses rapture, which he maintains is a living state in which God's essence can be known, and also when he writes about the knowledge of God that is available to the beatified soul both when separated from the body by death and when reunited with it in the state of resurrection" (p. 387). Diana Fritz Cates has offered correction along similar lines to my positions on embodiment in Thomas's theology, pointing out that "there are, for example, neo-Platonic elements in Thomas's understanding of the 'higher' and 'lower' appetites" (Cates, Diana Fritz, review of *Virtuous Passions: The Formation of Christian Character*, by G. Simon Harak, S. J., *Soundings*. LXXVII, no. 3–4, [Fall/Winter 1994]: 487–89).

Except for extraordinary circumstances, however, like rapture (which Aquinas interestingly refers to as "contra naturam elevatum," in *De Veritate* 13.1) and death (and again, Thomas states that the lasting separation of soul and body is not natural, for example, in *Summa contra Gentiles* IV.79), Thomas states that the natural and appropriate way of human knowing is through the body and the senses (*ST* I.89.1).

63. "Anima autem cum sit pars corporis hominis, non est totus homo, et anima mea non est ego." *In I Ad Cor.* XV, lect. 2. Cf. I.76.8, and I.75.2ad3: "Corpus requiritur ad actionem intellectus, non sicut organum quo talis actio exerceatur, sed ratione objecti." Cf. I.75.7ad3 and I.76.7ad3.

64. I.75.6; see also I.84.2; I.84.7; I.84.8. It is interesting, then, to watch Aquinas struggle with the problem of the life of the soul after death, and

before the "general resurrection" when the soul receives its new, spiritual body, in this question, and in I.89.1.

65. See I-II.5.2sc, and the entire article; also art. 7, and I-II.21.4.

66. "Materia corporalis formas quas recipit non solum tenet dum per eas agit in actu, sed etiam postquam agere per eas cessaverit" (I.79.6, emphasis mine).

67. I-II.50.

68. "Actio et passio sunt unus actus." Aquinas, *In Physic.*, lect. 8. Cf. Aristotle, *Physics*, V.4. 228a20.

69. "Sunt ergo in hominibus aliqui habitus naturales, tamquam partim a natura existentes et partim ab exteriori principio" (I-II.51.1).

70. Thomas means this "otherness" in its broadest sense. We are moved by everything, from gravity to hunger to friends and enemies to God.

71. He begins by stating, "Nam pati dicitur ex eo quod aliquid trahitur ad agentem . . ." (22.1). Cf. also, 22.2: ". . . nomine passionis importatur quod patiens trahatur ad id quod est agentis." We find this usage throughout the *Treatise*. Paul Wadell makes several insightful statements in this regard, noting that the virtues are "anchored" in the passions, so that they "gradually prepare us to rely on an agency other than our own" (Paul Wadell, *Friendship and the Moral Life* [Notre Dame, Ind.: University of Notre Dame Press, 1989], p. 169). That necessity for relying on the agency of an other is especially visible in Aquinas's treatment of the irascible passion of "spes" (I-II.40). The reader should also pay attention to Aquinas's considered use of the passive voice throughout the *Treatise*.

72. "Unde ex talibus actibus possunt in agentibus aliqui habitus causari, non quidem quantum ad primum activum principium, sed quantum ad principium actus quod movet motum. Nam omne quod patitur et movetur ab alio, disponitur per actum agentis; unde ex multiplicatis actibus generatur quaedam qualitus in potentia passiva et mota, quae nominatur habitus." Emphasis mine. Cf. also ad1 in the same article, I-II.51.

73. One of the most satisfying features of Sara Ruddick's study of child rearing is her attention to bodily reality. She writes, for example, that "Maternal practice begins with a double vision—seeing the fact of biological vulnerability as socially significant and as demanding care" (Sara Ruddick, *Maternal Thinking: Toward a Politics of Peace* [New York, N.Y: Ballantine, 1989], p. 18). On page 136, she writes of nonviolence, "This requires specific oppositional comparisons between particular concepts and values of caring labor and their counterparts in dominant, abstractly masculine ways of knowing— for example, comparisons of maternal and military concepts of the body and of control." Cf. also pp. 48–49, 130, and all of chapter Eight, "Histories of Human Flesh," pp. 185–218.

74. Since most subsequent quotes will be taken from the *Treatise on the Passions*, I will only give the reference beginning with the Question.

75. I refer the reader to my discussion of the importance of the *body* in Thomas's account of the passions, in "The Passions, the Virtues and Agency: Modern Research and Thomistic Reflection" *Logos*, 8 (March 1987): 31–44.

76. I-II.22.1.

77. ". . . ita etiam ad dolorem duo requiruntur: scilicet conjunctio alicuius mali (quod ea ratione est malum, quia privat aliquod bonum); et perceptio huiusmodi conjunctionis" (35.1). (I use the somewhat awkward word "conjunction" in translation because it is not possible, in Thomistic anthropology, to be "in union with" evil.) The evil must be present, and it must be resisted by the person. If the evil is *future*, the passion is *fear*. We will see this taken up again later.

78. ". . . sensus exterior non percipit nisi praesens: vis autem cognitiva interior potest percipere praesens, praeteritum et futurum. Et ideo tristitia potest esse de praesenti, praeterito et futuro . . ." We would not expect Thomas to explain the temporal perdurance of the effects of pain *solely* in terms of the body.

79. ". . . dolor dicitur esse corporis, quia causa doloris est in corpore: puta cum patimur aliquod nocivum corpori. Sed motus doloris semper est in anima: nam 'corpus non potest dolere nisi dolente anima,' ut Augustinus dicit *(Super Psalm.* lxxxvii.4)."

80. 35.2ad2.

81. ". . . et sic est anxietas, quae sic aggravat animum ut non appareat aliquod refugium; unde alio nomine dicitur angustia" (35.8).

82. "Ideo autem, specialiter acedia dicitur vocem amputare, quia vox inter omnes exteriores motus magis exprimit interiorem conceptum et affectum . . ." (35.8).

83. ". . . etiam appetitus unitatis vel amor causa doloris ponendus est. Bonum enim unius cujusque rei in quadam unitate consistit, prout scilicet unaquaeque res habet in se unita illa ex quibus consistit ejus perfectio . . ." (36.3).

84. "Et sic per consequens concupiscentia fit causa tristitiae, inquantum de retardatione boni concupiti, vel totali ablatione, tristamur" (36.2).

85. It seems also possible to consider that Thomas could analyze confusion that stems from the "fusion of love and abuse" (see note 30) as a confusion of concupiscible and irascible passions, though he never makes such a move anywhere in the *Summa*.

86. He later states again that passions such as fear and hopelessness also harm the body, but "prae omnibus tristitia, quae aggravat animum ex malo praesenti, cujus est fortior impressio quam futuri" (37.4).

87. It is impossible adequately to translate the force of the *con-* here and in *contristantis* above. Thomas's constant emphasis throughout the *Treatise* is that passion is both interactive between the self and the other, and characteristic of the entire organic unity of the person. Thus, we encounter the use of the prefix *con-* here and with many other words throughout the *Treatise* where we would otherwise not expect them.

88. "Dicitur enim homo aggravari, ex eo quod aliquo pondere impeditur a proprio motu. Manifestum est autem ex praedictis quod tristitia contingit ex aliquo malo praesenti. Quod quidem, ex hoc ipso quod repugnat motui voluntatis, aggravat animum, inquantum impedit ipsum ne fruatur eo quod vult. Et si quidem non sit tanta vis mali contristantis ut auferat spem evadendi,

licet animus aggravetur quantum ad hoc, quod in praesenti non potitur eo quod vult; remanet tamen motus ad repellendum nocivum contristans. Si vero superexcrescat vis mali intantum ut spem evasionis excludat, tunc simpliciter impeditur etiam interior motus animi angustiati, ut neque hac neque illac divertere valeat. Et quandoque etiam impeditur exterior motus corporis, ita quod remaneat homo stupidus in seipso."

Thomas makes a similar observation of the "paralysis" of sorrow in 35.8: "Proprius autem effectus tristitiae consistit in quadam fuga appetitus. Unde extraneum circa effectum tristitiae, potest accipi quantum ad alterum tantum, quia scilicet tollitur fuga: et sic est anxietas quae aggravat animum, ut non appareat aliquod refugium: Unde alio nomine dicitur angustia. Si vero intantum procedat talis aggravatio, ut etiam exteriora membra immobilitet ab opere, quod pertinet ad acediam; sic erit extraneum quantum ad utrumque, quia nec est fuga, nec est in appetitu . . ."

89. William F. Lynch, S. J., *Images of Hope* (Notre Dame, Ind.: University of Notre Dame Press, 1974), p. 63. The whole chapter, "Hopelessness as Entrapment," pp. 63–80, is illuminating in this regard, as is his next chapter on perplexity, "Hopelessness and Confusion," pp. 81–104.

90. 23.4.

91. 47.2.

92. "Quae quidem duo in dolore corporali attestantur bonitati naturae, ex qua provenit quod sensus sentit, et natura refugit laesivum, quod causat dolorem" (39.2). Cf. also 39.1ad1: ". . . Nam sensus et recusatio mali corporalis attestatur naturae bonae."

93. "Sed sciendum est quod, si potestas fortior intantum invalescat quod mutet contrariam inclinationem in inclinationem propriam, iam non erit aliqua repugnantia vel violentia . . . Sic igitur si aliqua potestas major intantum invalescat quod auferat inclinationem voluntatis vel appetitus sensitivi, ex ea non sequitur dolor vel tristitia: sed tunc solum sequitur, quando remanet inclinatio appetitus in contrarium. Et inde est quod Augustinus dicit quod voluntas resistens potestati fortiori, causat dolorem: si enim non resisteret, sed cederet consentiendo, non sequeretur dolor, sed delectatio."

94. 37.1.

95. 37.4ad3.

96. Walter J. Ciszek, S. J., with Daniel Flaherty, S. J., *He Leadeth Me* (Garden City, N.Y.: Image Books, 1975), p. 78.

97. 35.8.

98. ". . . quantum ad motum appetitivum pertinet, ad idem refertur constrictio et aggravatio. Ex hoc enim quod aggravatur animus ut ad exteriora libere progredi non possit ad seipsum retrahitur, quasi in seipso constrictus" (37.2ad2, emphasis added).

99. Greven, *Spare the Child*, pp. 215–22.

100. I put this colloquially to the survivors I pray with as, "They may have marred you, but they did not make you."

101. ". . . arduum objectum fit possibile nobis, non per nos, sed per alios." This hope in another's agency is rooted in the hope for salvation

through God, as the Blackfriars translator, Reid, points out in his note. The entire article is instructive for understanding reliance on another's agency for the granting of our own agency.

102. Lynch, *Images of Hope*, p. 31. The entire work is still the best examination of this important dimension of "hope through another." Again, we are reminded of Scarry's account of the Amnesty International's hope: "to present regimes that torture with a deluge of letters and telegrams, a deluge of voices speaking on behalf of, voices speaking in the voice of, the person silenced . . ." (p. 50).

103. II-II.17–22.

104. In all his works, Paul Wadell has pointed out that friendship with God in Christ is the form of all the virtues in Thomas's *Summa*.

105. 38.3.

106. "Cum ergo aliquis videt de sua tristitia alios contristantos, fit ei quasi quaedam imaginatio quod illud onus alii cum ipso ferant, quasi conantes ad ipsum, ab onere alleviandum, et ideo levius fert tristitiae onus, sicut etiam in portandis oneribus corporalibus contingit" (38.3).

107. 38.4.

108. 38.4ad3.

109. According to Susan Forward, psychotherapist and author of a popular book on the treatment of abusive families, one of the most profound and liberating truths to be appropriated is that the victim is not responsible for the abuse. Susan Forward with Craig Buck, *Toxic Parents, Overcoming their Hurtful Legacy and Reclaiming your Life* (New York, N.Y.: Bantam, 1989).

110. 39.1&2.

111. For example, we might contemplate together on the scourging of Jesus, emphasizing that He is sharing—and redeeming—the pain of the abused person.

112. 38.1.

113. ". . . quia omne nocivum interius clausum magis affligit, quia magis multiplicatur intentio animae circa ipsum; sed quando ad exteriora diffunditur, tunc animae intentio ad exteriora quodammodo disgregatur, et sic interior dolor minuitur" (38.2).

114. 38.5ad3. Cf. also 35.1ad1; 37.1 and especially 45.2, where the "warming of the heart" "repellet timorem et causat spem."

115. 34.3.

116. Michael E. McCullough and Everett L. Worthington, Jr., "Encouraging Clients to Forgive People Who Have Hurt Them: Review, Critique, and Research Prospectus," *Journal of Psychology and Theology*, 22, no. 1 (Spring 1994): 4. For a review of recent literature, see J. Gartner, D. B. Larson and G. D. Allen, "Religious commitment and mental health: A review of the empirical literature," *Journal of Psychology and Theology* 19 (1991): 6–25.

117. McCullough and Worthington, "Encouraging Clients," p. 11.

118. McCullough and Worthington, "Encouraging Clients," p. 8.

119. Marie M. Fortune, "Forgiveness: The Last Step." In Horton and Williamson, *Abuse and Religion*, pp. 208–20. See also Forward, *Toxic Parents*, "People *can* forgive toxic parents, but they should do it at the conclusion—

not at the beginning—of their emotional house-cleaning. People need to get angry about what happened to them. They need to grieve over the fact that they never had the parental love they yearned for [see my note 61]. They need to stop diminishing or discounting the damage that was done to them. Too often, 'forgive and forget' means 'pretend it didn't happen'" (p. 191).

120. I do not rule out that submission to the legal system of the state may be part of this confrontation and reparation.

121. In the seeking of justice, Susan Forward in *Toxic Parents* makes an important—and I believe Thomistic—distinction. She "divides forgiveness into two areas: giving up the need for revenge, and absolving someone of his rightful responsibility" (p. 188). We must achieve the first and avoid the second. Thomas for his part would distinguish between hatred and anger, saying that hatred is worse than anger because hatred implies the application of evil to evil, whereas anger denotes application of good to evil. ". . . odium est per applicationem mali ad malum; ira autem per applicationem boni ad malum" (I-II.46.7; cf. also 46.2).

122. Though McCullough and Worthington indicate that forgiveness has a value as a practice, even for nonbelievers, it is important for the person of faith to recognize the active, participatory role that both Jesus and the community play in the victim's recovery.

123. 1Jn 4:4.

124. "Patet etiam ex hoc, quod irascibilis est quasi propugnatrix et defensatrix concupiscibilis dum insurgit contra ea quae impediunt convenientia quae concupiscibilis appetit et ingerunt nociva quae concupiscibilis refugit. Et propter hoc omnes passiones irascibilis incipiunt a passionibus concupiscibilis et in eas terminat, sicut ira nascitur ex illata tristitia, et vindicatam inferens in laetitiam terminatur" (I.81.2, emphasis added).

Growing Together in the Divine Love: The Role of Charity in the Moral Theology of Thomas Aquinas

Paul J. Wadell, C. P.

Friendship is a most crucial practice of the moral life; indeed, it ought to be a central way of forming, guiding, and empowering our everyday lives. But it is not at the forefront of our thinking about morality, especially the relationship between morality and our ordinary lives. Most of us associate the moral life not with virtuous relationships in which character is developed and holiness secured, but with moral quandaries and dilemmas of conscience. We search for universal principles to guide us through the thickets of contemporary life because we are convinced the heart of morality is grappling with issues not easily resolved. Friendships are comforting, but they are hardly essential for successfully negotiating the tasks and challenges of morality. We cherish our friends and we know our life would be impoverished without them, but we do not think the moral life depends on them.

But Thomas Aquinas did. For Aquinas, everyday moral life was called to be an ever-deepening friendship with God and all those God loves, sinners and saints, angels as well as enemies. Like Charles Taylor, who argued that one of the distinctive characteristics of morality since the Reformation is the belief that the fullness of the Christian moral and spiritual life can be achieved within the structures and activities of ordinary life,[1] Aquinas too was convinced that the most extraordinary possibilities of the life of grace could be practiced and embodied in the framework of ordinary life.

Aquinas called this life of friendship *charity*, and for him it was not only important for an authentically worthwhile life, but also what ordinary and everyday Christian morality essentially involved. For Aquinas, our moral and spiritual life was charity, a friendship "begun here in this life by grace" and "perfected in the future life by glory."[2] Aquinas knew that charity is more than kindness and certainly more than that most contemporary of virtues: being nice to everybody. Rather, charity is the most godlike life possible because through it we are transformed and transfigured in the goodness and holiness of God, and this godlike life is something we are to live each day. If the purpose of the Christian life is to be drawn into God in order to enjoy God's goodness and happiness, such intimacy and beatitude can only be achieved through charity, the lifelong friendship that makes us enough like God to find happiness with God. For Thomas, to be Christian is to live each day in friendship with God and to consider this extraordinary possibility the ordinary way of understanding our lives. We are to love God as friend because God's goodness is our happiness and God's life is our peace.[3]

This sounds wonderful but quaint. We live in a culture that often misunderstands, trivializes, and sometimes even subverts friendship. How can we build the moral life on friendship when much in our culture encourages us to use others, claiming them as friends when they are advantageous, abandoning them when they are not? Friendship today is sentimentalized. We associate friendship with cordial relations and passing acquaintances. But we seldom think of friendship substantively. We seldom envision it as a moral enterprise important for our everyday lives, namely the relationship in which we become good in company with others who want to be good too.[4] Even in Christianity friendship is often not understood or appreciated because we fail to see, as Aquinas realized, that the only true friendship is one guided and informed by our ultimate good; indeed, friends are those who help one another seek and share in the life and holiness of God in the most intimate and enduring way.[5]

What I want to explore in this chapter is exactly what Aquinas means when he describes the ordinary moral life of Christians as friendship with God, suggesting that for him charity comprises a transformative and challenging way of life constituted by distinctive virtues such as forbearance, compassion, justice, forgiveness, and peace. Put more strongly, I will argue that charity must be seen not so much as an individual virtue, but as a communal and ecclesial practice characteristic of those striving each day to practice the ways of God in the world. To substantiate these claims, four points will be considered: (1) what in our culture serves to trivialize and undermine authentic friendship; (2) Aristotle's understanding of friendship and its role in the moral life; (3) Aquinas's description of charity as friendship with God and what the life of charity entails; and (4) why for Aquinas friendship with God is inseparable from Christ.

CULTURAL IMPEDIMENTS TO FRIENDSHIP

Morality requires friendships of depth, substance, and endurance, but it is exactly these kinds of relationships that cannot be presumed today. Many people lack such relationships or else have no idea what they would possibly mean or how they could be nurtured and sustained. Furthermore, what passes for friendships in our culture may not be friendships at all; indeed, they may be relatively superficial acquaintances, passing relationships, or worse, manipulative, unhealthy partnerships in which persons are diminished and sometimes destroyed. Friendship is a moral skill that demands at least minimal generosity and thoughtfulness, a capacity to care, and at least sufficient justice to recognize how we are obliged to respond to the needs and well-being of others. A true friendship also is always a relationship capable of bettering the self, and such relationships can be hard to find.

Rodney Clapp addresses this in his article "The Celebration of Friendship." Clapp argues that "friendship has become a difficult, even counter-cultural practice" because of a variety of social and cultural forces that sabotage the good and abiding relationships we need for the moral and spiritual life.[6] One of those social forces is consumerism. We live in a culture that is aggressively materialistic, urging us to believe we need things more than we need people. This cultural narrative tells us that we are liberated through what we own, not through friendship, and our identity is measured by our possessions, not by the richness of our loves. People formed by a consumerist society can lose the deeper spiritual resources necessary for friendship, particularly justice, generosity, compassion, and availability. If we believe what we own matters more than whom we love, we will hardly be unselfish enough to seek the good of another for her own sake or to find joy in spending ourselves for her well-being, exactly what good friendships require.

In a consumer society, friends can become just another commodity to pick up or dispose of as we see fit, novelties that are quickly displaced when something new and more interesting comes along. If our identity is primarily formed by the consumerist narrative of our culture, we will lack the qualities and dispositions necessary to relate to others on a deeper level or to be friends in a truly life-giving and meaningful way. Even more tragic, we will be blind to our need for others because we will have been duped by the fantasy that our salvation lies in the clutter of our possessions, rather than in the joy that comes from loving and being loved.

Second, friendship is jeopardized by an Enlightenment understanding of the self that sees us not as social and relational beings, but as essentially solitary and autonomous. In this view, the true self is the inner self, the self one comes to not through friendship and love but by turning inward.[7] Here the self is pictured as isolated, self-sufficient, and fundamentally private.[8] We come to know ourself not through relationships with God and others, not through friendships in which we are challenged, grow, and develop, but by disengaging ourself from others in order truly to know ourself. Who we really are is not how God and others see us, but how we know ourself in the deepest recesses of our being; and yet, it is a self *only* we can know because it is essentially mysterious and unsharable. Bluntly put, if charity calls us outside ourself toward others, this modern understanding urges disengagement and introspection because it is only in moving "from society to solitude" that we discover who we really are.[9] The truth, however, is that introspection is vulnerable to self-deception and delusion; thus, we often come to know ourself not by turning inward, but through the care and goodness of friends who not only remind us of our best self, but nurture it.

In this modern account, which is buttressed by consumerism and extreme individualism, selfhood and identity not only precede community, but also exist apart from community. In this view, we do not need others to be; in fact, because the self is basically asocial, others are more likely to take life from us than give it. In its most extreme form, this suggests that community and relationships come at the expense of the self; we are more likely to be impeded and restricted by others than enlivened and freed. Obviously, in such a view deep friendships have little value and may even be seen as dangers to avoid.

This is very different from a social and communal understanding of the self that argues that the most basic quality of human beings is to live in communion with others.[10] We can speak of our need to live in communion by saying that human nature is relational, or we can talk about the essential sociality of the self. No matter how we express it, this means we are and can be human only in and through friendships with others that draw us to life and lead to communion with them. From this perspective, we discover who we are not by turning away from others to some isolated inner self, but through the generosity, care, and justice that draw us out of isolation and into the lives of others through friendship. Here the true self is not an unsharable mystery, but something that comes to life and is illumined as we love our friends and are loved by them.

Far from being isolated, self-sufficient, and private, the self lives only as it loves, and it loves only as it learns the skills of good friendships. The most basic law of our nature is that we exist, have a self, and achieve identity and personality only insofar as we are intimately and consistently engaged in friendships with others, and most certainly with God. We are not essentially asocial and self-absorbed because the only way to have a self, especially an interesting and appealing self, is through the enchanting rigors of friendship-love. Contrary to the Enlightenment understanding of the self, the friendship model argues that "the 'we' is prior to the 'I.'"[11] Thus, our identity does not pre-exist our friendships, but is made possible by them. It is not the case that we first have a fully formed identity and then decide, if we like, to enter friendships with others, but that our identity is a reflection of how we have been known and loved by our friends.

Thus, friendship is not superfluous to the moral life but its absolute condition. The starting point for understanding our humanity is our friendship with God, other people, and the world. And this means not only that we can be human only insofar as we live in friendship with others, but also that the depth and quality of life possible to us is a measure of the depth and quality of our friendships. As Mounier puts it, "One might almost say that I have no existence, save in so far as I exist for others, and that to be is, in the final analysis, to love."[12]

Third, friendship will be impossible, and not even desired, if the self is understood to find life not through *caritas*, charity's friendship-love, but through *dominium*, sovereignty or dominion over others. In *Theology and Social Theory*, John Milbank argues convincingly that since the Enlightenment and the rise of capitalism there has been a radical shift in our understanding of the self that has critical repercussions for friendship. Instead of believing that selfhood and identity are established through love, both the Enlightenment and capitalism, Milbank suggests, have contributed to the view that they are constituted through owning and controlling, but here ownership and control are extended beyond possessions to persons.[13] In this view friendship has no place because people are seen more as competitors and adversaries than friends. Self-identity is not determined by our relationship with God and our neighbors, but by what and who we are able to dominate and control; in short, our identity is proportionate to our power, but here power is understood not in terms of service, justice, or love, but in terms of mastery over one's self, one's possessions, and others. We thrive not when we are friends, but when we manipulate and control.

There is something brutal and inescapably violent in this understanding of the self because it fundamentally argues that identity requires oppression. It is a vision of life that sees human beings locked in ceaseless competitive struggle as everyone seeks to dominate everybody else. It is a world in which people come to life through self-love and self-assertion, not gentleness, mercy, and sacrifice. Here we grow not when we endorse others, raise them up, and love them in joyful self-forgetfulness, but when we are able to manipulate, maneuver, and exploit. This is not a world in which friendship is possible or even desired because the otherness of people is seen as something to overcome or control, not as something we are blessed to receive. It is also not a world in which people can live together in the kind of harmony and peace necessary for friendship because there is too much violence and division to achieve anything more than the false and shaky peace that comes when the strong subdue the weak. This is the world not of blessed and saving friendship-love, but of the barbaric nihilism that inevitably marks a culture in which power is the ultimate idol.[14]

No wonder so many people live shoulder-to-shoulder, but their lives hardly touch. No wonder that for many there is physical proximity, but no spiritual connectedness, no mingling of souls or unity of spirit. For many people today life, in Ignace Lepp's haunting phrase, is nothing more than "a mere juxtaposition of solitudes."[15] This should not astonish us. To the degree that we are shaped by and submit to the cultural ideologies of consumerism and materialism, radical individualism, and dynamics of self-assertion and domination, we will lose the art of friendship and forget what friendship, in the richest and most promising sense, entails.

Our understanding of friendship, as well as its possibilities, is intrinsically connected to our understanding of self. What we lack today is a philosophy of self adequate for a healthy and flourishing moral life. I want to suggest not only that friendship is a much more promising understanding of the self for the moral life, but more strongly, that it is absolutely essential. In this view, morality is not something other than friendship, but is what happens to us through the best and most enduring relationships of our lives, with God to be sure, but also with family, spouses, communities, or lifelong companions. It is in these friendships that our character takes shape and we are transformed in the good.

In order to sustain an argument for friendship as central and constitutive to the moral life, we must, I think, adopt a richer and far more promising understanding of the self than one governed by consumerism, individualism, and domination. This is exactly what Aquinas's understanding of *caritas* provides because it incorporates us into a distinctive way of life constituted by ongoing friendship with God and neighbor, and characterized by love, joy, justice, and peace. Before considering what Aquinas means by *caritas* and how it functions in the Christian moral life, however, we need to examine Aristotle's understanding of friendship and its role in the life of virtue because it is in Aristotle that much of Aquinas's treatment of charity's friendship, however different, is rooted.

ARISTOTLE'S UNDERSTANDING OF FRIENDSHIP AND ITS ROLE IN THE MORAL LIFE

Aristotle identified three kinds of friendship, each distinguished by whatever goods or purposes bring the friends together and explain the life of the friendship. There are friendships of usefulness or advantage, friendships of pleasure, and friendships of character or virtue.[16]

A friendship of usefulness or advantage is one in which relationships are formed around common tasks or projects. For instance, we work together with others. They are useful to us because we depend on their talents and need their expertise; in fact, we know we cannot do the job well without them. Aristotle calls these friendships of usefulness or advantage because the relationships are formed around activities in which each person is useful to the other. It is the shared project that brings them together and identifies or explains the friendship. These are not exploitative relationships because each person is aware of the role they play for the other.

An example of a friendship of usefulness would be relationships we have with people with whom we work every day. We may spend a lot of time with them on a job but do not necessarily spend time with them outside our work. We may know them well from the time we share with them, but the point of the relationship is not so much getting to know them better but working on something in which both of us are invested and need one another. There are clear limits to the relationship and well-defined expectations. Each person knows what his or her role is in the relationship and does not look for anything more from the other person than what he or she contributes to the common task. Both recognize the friendship as useful but do not expect it to be pivotal to their lives.

These relationships are not always long lasting because they often end as soon as the task or project is completed. Since the purpose of the relationship was to help one another on a shared project, once the project is finished the relationship ends unless people choose to remain friends for some other reason, which can easily happen because through working with others we discover more about them that makes us want to continue to spend time with them. A different kind of friendship can emerge from a friendship of usefulness, but for this to happen the friends must choose to develop their relationship for other reasons. Their friendship may continue, but if it does it is no longer a friendship of usefulness; rather, it has become a friendship of pleasure or even a friendship of virtue.

The second type of friendship is a friendship of pleasure. These are relationships we have with people whose company we enjoy. There is something about them that appeals to us, something in their personality that attracts us and makes being with them a joy. Perhaps there are things we enjoy doing with them: going to a play or a movie, dining together, sharing hobbies or other activities.

Are friendships of usefulness and friendships of pleasure genuine friendships? Yes and no. Aristotle believed we have many relationships in our lives, each of which contributes something to who we are. He saw friendships of usefulness and friendships of pleasure as two different types of friendship and very important ones, but he did not consider them to be friendships in the complete sense of the word, as he did friendships of character or virtue; he spoke of them as friendships "only incidentally."[17] Only friendships of virtue pass the test of friendship in every way because they are formed around the best of all goods and the most perfecting of activities, namely, a love of virtue and a desire to seek a life of virtue in company with others.

What makes virtue friendships most praiseworthy is the object of their benevolence. The explicit purpose of virtue friendships is to work for the moral well-being of one's friend, and for Aristotle this was to love her or him truly.[18] By contrast, in friendships of usefulness or pleasure we may implicitly wish for another's moral well-being and certainly would not hinder it, but her or his character is not the explicit focus of the relationship. It is not ruled out in these friendships, but neither is it their purpose.

What all friendships have in common is benevolence, mutuality, and a shared good.[19] This is true whether they are friendships of usefulness, friendships of pleasure, or friendships of virtue. No matter which type, each is characterized by one person wanting what is good for another for his or her own sake. What this good is will vary according to the type of friendship, but for a relationship to count as friendship at all, mutual benevolence must be part of it.[20] Thus, what distinguishes friendships is not mutual benevolence itself, but the *object* of benevolence, which will be one thing in friendships of usefulness, another in friendships of pleasure, and a third in friendships of character or virtue.[21] Aristotle has to make benevolence a quality of friendships of usefulness and friendships of pleasure if they are not to be self-serving and exploitative relationships. They would be exploitative if each person aimed solely at his or her own pleasure or advantage, and had no regard for the well-being of the other; however, if that were the case they would not be friendships at all.

It is important to focus not on how friendships of usefulness and friendships of pleasure fall short of friendships of virtue, but on what they contribute to our everyday lives and why we cannot do without them. We should appreciate their positive value and important contribution to a good and flourishing life—what Aristotle calls *eudaimonia*. The fact that Aristotle identifies three kinds of friendship suggests that a good and balanced life must include all three. Although character friendships are the best and most important, it is also true that not every friendship needs to be, can be, or even should be this most perfect type. Our nature is such that we need more than one kind of relationship in our lives. We need a variety and blend of relationships because we have a variety of needs and possibilities, but also limitations.

There is an intensity, commitment, availability, and permanence demanded of virtue friendships that is not only impossible, but would be overwhelming and exhausting if attempted in every relationship. Just as our health would be damaged if we ate a gourmet meal every time we sat down at table, so would our emotional and psychological well-being be damaged if we attempted virtue friendships in all our relationships. Character friendships may be best, and indeed Aristotle says we cannot have a truly human life without them, but they are also most costly and demanding, which is why Aristotle insists the number of such intimate friendships any person can have is limited.[22] Friendships of virtue take time, indeed they take years to develop. They require an extraordinary investment of self. Friendships that are useful or pleasurable may not have the moral excellence of one based on virtue, but they are still morally important because they contribute to the variety and blend of relationships that make a balanced and healthy life possible.

Nonetheless, despite their positive value and important contribution, friendships of usefulness and pleasure are lesser forms of friendship that are easily corrupted unless they are pursued by people of good character.[23] In order to operate well and to be morally upbuilding, they must be accompanied by friendships of virtue; otherwise they can degenerate into manipulative or hedonistic relationships. Friendships of advantage and pleasure are necessary for a good life but not sufficient. They are part of the life of the virtuous person for whom character friendships remain central and definitive.

In other words, friendships of advantage and pleasure are secondary and derivative. If the more fundamental friendship of virtue is lacking, the lesser types of friendship will be much more difficult to sustain because the friends will lack the character necessary for benevolence. Even friendships of usefulness and pleasure demand a person of character adequate enough to show respect for others, to care for their well-being, and to act justly toward them. Thus, Aristotle's positive evaluation of the lesser types of friendship presumes the presence of virtue friendships as the relationships in which one develops the character and skills necessary for friendship at all.

Clearly for Aristotle the most excellent and indispensable friendship is a friendship based on character and virtue. It is the friendship of the highest moral value; in fact, it is so qualitatively superior that it alone is friendship in the most "perfect and complete sense."[24] Character friendship's moral excellence is derived from the good or purpose that constitutes and identifies the friendship. In friendships of character, the center of the relationship is a mutual love for virtue and a mutual desire to become good. Aristotle argues that friendships of character are the deepest and most permanent and worthiest because they are constituted by the best and most excellent of goods, namely a shared desire to develop the qualities of character and virtue that are most perfecting of human beings.[25] Since Aristotle believed there was nothing more humanizing than goodness and nothing more perfecting than the virtues, these relationships will be the most crucial and indispensable for the moral life. They are the friendships in which people who want to be good can become good.

Describing virtue friendships as "perfect" can make them sound beyond our reach, admirable but impossible, good but too ideal to be real. Aristotle's account of the moral superiority of virtue friendships can be disheartening if we read it to imply that most people, who are a mix of good and bad qualities, would be excluded from the kind of friendship most crucial for the moral life.[26] Friendships of moral goodness cannot be the preserve solely of those who have already become virtuous, but must also be the relationships in which people who want to be good can become good. If by perfect Aristotle means virtue friendships can be enjoyed only by those already completely virtuous, we are left with the depressing conclusion that the moral life, indeed a genuinely human life, is possible only for a select few; in other words, Aristotle's ethic is limited to a moral elite.[27]

The problem is avoided if we understand that Aristotle calls these relationships perfect not as a description of the moral excellence of the friends, but as a description of the moral possibilities of the friendship. It is not the friends who are perfect, but the friendship that can be perfecting. Aristotle calls our attention not to the friends, but to the moral power of the relationship. Since the life of every friendship is defined through the goods and purposes that join the friends, virtue friendships are perfecting because their distinctive activity and unique power is to be the relationship through which the goodness and virtue of the friends are developed and enhanced. Such relationships are not the sole preserve of people who are already good, but of people who want to be good and see their friendships as the means to achieving this.[28]

But how exactly do character friendships figure in Aristotle's overall account of the moral life? To answer this question we must recall how Aristotle envisioned the moral project. Aristotle believed there was a purpose or goal given to human life that we must strive to accomplish if our lives were not to be judged failures. This goal, or *telos*, represented the goods and activities in which each of us is perfected.[29] At the heart of any teleological ethic is the conviction that life is given with something to achieve. There is some understanding of human wholeness and completion to which we are to direct our energies and devote our lives, for it is in striving for this that we grow into our humanity. In a teleological ethic, we develop and perfect ourselves to the degree that we come to embody the goods and practices in which human fullness resides. On the other hand, to neglect these goods and practices is to diminish, and to ignore them completely is to lead an ultimately dehumanizing life.

The whole point of the moral life for Aristotle was for one to achieve the highest possible human excellence and perfection. Aristotle described this complete well-being as *eudaimonia*, a word commonly translated as happiness, but whose meaning is far richer. *Eudaimonia* is the best possible life, a life utterly worthwhile and lacking in nothing. It describes a whole way of life that is "finally" or "completely" good because it gathers and arranges all worthwhile goods into an integrated way of living.[30] *Eudaimonia* is a life in which we are lacking nothing essential to the development and prospering of our nature. It is not a single good, but embraces all the goods and activities necessary for living well.

Of course, for Aristotle, the virtues were at the heart of *eudaimonia* because collectively they are the activities that bring us to our optimum development as human beings. Put more exactly, *eudaimonia is the virtuous life* because through the virtues we develop our human nature in the most fitting and complete way. Aristotle captures this by saying "happiness [*eudaimonia*] is some kind of activity of the soul in conformity with virtue."[31] What he suggests is that *eudaimonia* and the virtues are one—they are internally connected—not only because the virtues are the most intrinsically worthwhile activities, but also because they are the most distinctively human activities in which each of us must be involved if we are to become who we, as human beings, are meant to be. For Aristotle, to be human is to be virtuous.

But how do we connect the life of virtue and the life of friendship? L. Gregory Jones rightly suggests that happiness, the life of virtue, and good friendships are inextricably connected in Aristotle's ethics. "The supremely happy person is the good person, and in order to be both good and happy one needs and desires the presence of friends."[32] Moreover, good friendships are not only instrumental to happiness and virtue for Aristotle, but intrinsically necessary.[33] As regards the first, friends are instrumentally necessary because they strengthen us in the moral life through their encouragement and support, the example of their goodness, their counsel and wisdom, and by offering opportunities for cultivating and exercising virtue.[34] As to the second, friends are intrinsically necessary because they provide "the very form and mode of life," Nancy Sherman writes, "within which an agent can best realize her virtue and achieve happiness."[35]

For Aristotle the moral life is unavoidably a cooperative enterprise, "a jointly pursued life,"[36] because we need others to create a way of life in which growth in virtue and development of character are possible.[37] Friendship is constitutive of the virtuous life for Aristotle precisely because the virtues are shared activities. They are not disconnected pieces of behavior, isolated acts that occasionally engage us, but constitute an ongoing way of life in which people joined in a partnership of the good come to understand what the virtues are and how they need to be expressed. Contrary to our dominant cultural understandings, Aristotle could never conceive of happiness or a good life as something we could achieve on our own; rather, by their very nature as shared activities, the virtues require "a life in companionship with others."[38]

And so Aristotle is saying much more than friendship makes the virtues more interesting and pleasant; he is claiming that friendship makes the life of virtue *possible*. He agrees that we need friends "only to provide what we are unable to provide ourselves,"[39] but exactly his point is that the one thing we cannot offer ourselves is virtue. Virtue friendships are more than conveniences; they are indispensable moral enterprises because the only way for us to come in touch with the good is through lasting relationships with people who share our love for the good and are committed to helping us grow in it.

Virtue comes to us in friendships with good people. It is this mutual, communal seeking of the good that makes us good; in fact, it is truer to say in this mutual, communal seeking of the good we make one another good because at least to some extent virtue is mediated through the love and life exchanged among friends. By seeking goodness for one another and encouraging each other in virtue, the friends are transfigured in goodness themselves. It is not surprising then that by the end of the *Nicomachean Ethics*, friendship has emerged as the crucial context for acquiring, exercising, and flourishing in the virtues. It is the ordinary moral community in which those who love the good come together in a shared life so they may actually become good.[40]

If virtue friendships figure so significantly in the moral life, then certainly such persons must be chosen carefully and wisely. As Nancy

Sherman observes, "in choosing a character friend, we select 'another self,'[41] who shares a sense of our commitments and ends, and a sense of what we take to be ultimately 'good and pleasant' in living. We choose another to be a partner in the joint pursuit of these ends."[42] Such a person cannot be chosen haphazardly because his or her impact on our character and moral development will be profound. We are looking for someone whose values and concerns are fundamentally in agreement with our own, someone who shares our ideals, aspirations, and principles, and especially someone who agrees with us on what a truly good and worthwhile life involves. Even to discover who might be best suited for this kind of relationship requires time, testing, much reflection, and prudence.[43]

Once chosen, the friend makes one's moral life a partnership, a joint adventure in which the friends mutually deliberate about what their life together means and how it can best be pursued.[44] Their life is truly defined by a common good because not only do they strive to develop shared purposes, but they also seek to coordinate their choices and actions so that they serve both the interests and activities they share in common, and the interests and activities that might be unique to the friend. As Nancy Sherman comments, "In choosing a friend, one chooses to make that person a part of one's life and to arrange one's life with that person's flourishing (as well as one's own) in mind. One takes on, if you like, the project of a shared conception of *eudaimonia*."[45] Practically this means that each friend, as an abiding expression of benevolence, ought to promote the special interests and concerns of the other; indeed, each is especially equipped to do so because he or she knows the other and what is best and most pleasing for them in a way no one else does.[46]

This lengthy analysis of Aristotle's ethics may seem far removed from Aquinas's vision of the Christian moral life, but actually they are closely connected. In many respects, Aristotle provides the foundation on which Aquinas constructs his account of the moral life. For instance, like Aristotle, Aquinas has a normative understanding of the good life and a normative understanding of a good person. In addition, transformation is at the heart of the moral life for Aquinas, as it is for his Athenian predecessor. Both believe morality involves change and growth through the virtues; indeed, it is a way of life shaped to take us beyond already achieved levels of goodness and, for Aquinas, of holiness. And both insist that this transformation of the self in virtue is not something we could possibly achieve alone, but something attempted in the crucible of virtue friendships; in short, Aristotle, like Aquinas, sees friendship not to be exceptional, but central and indispensable for our ordinary moral lives.

Nonetheless, for all their similarities, there are considerable and important differences. Aristotle gives a privileged place to friendship in his schema of the moral life, but ironically only the privileged could partake of it. As Aristotle sees it, the best and most necessary of friendships are possible only for politically free men; women, children, and slaves are excluded, and in this respect are neither able to partake of the moral life nor judged capable of virtue. And while Aristotle does not believe human beings can be friends with the gods because the gods are too unlike us, Aquinas argues that without friendship with God we cannot truly be human at all. Where Aristotle sees irremediable disparity between the gods and human beings, Aquinas claims that God is not only the most fitting *(conveniens)* Being for us to love, but also that friendship with God *(caritas)* is our most perfecting possibility and key to our beatitude.

Thus, for Aquinas, Aristotle is useful but limited. As we shall see, Aquinas radically re-envisions what the moral life is about. In his account of charity as friendship with God, he explodes the boundaries Aristotle puts on what the best of friendships might be, what they are seeking, and who could enjoy them. For as Aquinas sees it, the most crucial and blessed of friendships is not with politically free men, but with God, and it is seeking happiness not in Athens, but in the kingdom of God in fellowship with the saints. And most important, unlike Aristotle, Aquinas believes it is a happiness open to all.

CHARITY AS FRIENDSHIP WITH GOD: WHAT IT MEANS AND WHAT ITS LIFE ENTAILS

God wants to share with us his life and his happiness. This is why we who are children of God are called to be the friends of God. Such is Aquinas's vision of the moral life and it stands behind his claim that charity is not just love for God, but specifically friendship with God.[47] God wants to love us as friends, abiding in our lives each day as keenly and deeply as possible, loving us, cherishing us, doing everything for our good. But friendship is reciprocal, so we too are called to love God as friend, working on God's behalf, seeking God's will, delighting in God's good, and through the life of this friendship finding union with the One who is our peace and our joy.

Charity is friendship with God, and it is what the Christian life of grace is all about. It is something more than kindness, and it is certainly something more than being nice or occasionally thoughtful; indeed, it is sharing in the very life and goodness of God so intimately that through our ordinary lives we become lovers of God in all things.[48] Friendship with God is the vocation all share; however, far from being a cozy, complacent relationship, it is the daunting challenge to be transformed in order to live God's life now. Charity is friendship with God, and that friendship is a life of never-ending conversion and deep change of heart, a metamorphosis so complete that those who enter charity go from being sinners to saints. Charity contains both the great hope and the great challenge of the Christian life. Charity's hope is that through grace and love we can enjoy a life together with God now, a kinship of hearts so intimate that we can become for God who God has always been for us, a friend, a lover, a source of happiness and delight. Charity's challenge is that the only way for us to enter the life of God is by undergoing a radical reconstruction of ourself, the thorough *ascesis* required for rising to new life through repentance, contrition, forgiveness, and virtue.[49]

But why is charity the cornerstone of Thomistic ethics? Aquinas begins his investigation of the moral life with the simple reflection that people are inclined to whatever they think is good and will set up their lives to possess whatever goods they most desire.[50] We are drawn to whatever attracts us, to whatever fascinates and intrigues, and we use our intelligence, freedom, and imagination to move toward all the things we think will bring us life, peace, and satisfaction. For Aquinas, human beings are creatures of powerful needs and desires. We hunger for wholeness and completion, we strategize how to possess all the goods we hope will bring peace to our souls. Our moral life begins in indigence because we know we lack something crucial to our well-being. We are poignantly aware of our incompleteness, constantly reminded that we are far from whole. But we also know we lack within ourselves whatever is necessary for fullness of life. As we live we search for a goodness to do for us what we cannot do for ourselves. Our history of loves, blessed as well as mistaken, is testimony enough of our ceaseless and necessary search for completion in something outside of ourselves.[51]

Our life is bent on wholeness, but the trick lies in discovering what is genuinely fulfilling and what is not. Everybody is after happiness, but not everybody knows what happiness is. Aquinas argues that "happiness is our true good,"[52] "our proper and complete good,"[53] and concludes that the only perfect and lasting happiness will be found in God because God alone has the goodness and holiness and life necessary to satisfy and perfect us.[54] Like Aristotle, Aquinas believes that goodness and happiness are inseparable because goodness alone can fulfill our quest for happiness and achieve the utmost possible development of our humanity; however, unlike Aristotle, Aquinas gives this goodness a name.[55] Goodness is God and human beings are happy in the measure that they share in, imitate, and are transformed by the goodness of God.

Furthermore, like Aristotle, Aquinas believes we are happy when we do what is good for us, and, like Aristotle, suggests there is some appropriate activity or function by which this goodness is achieved that is unique to human beings and sets us apart from other creatures. Both stress that what is good for us hinges on who we *essentially* are, focusing not on what we share in common with other creatures, but on what makes us different. This essential difference is defined through our unique and particular function, a distinctive activity that makes us what we are and not something else. The key to happiness is discovering what this proper function is and perfecting it. As Davies comments, "With this point in mind, Aquinas maintains that to see what fulfils people, which means to see what is good for them, we have to consider what marks them out from other things in the world. What is it that they are which other things are not? Aquinas thinks that in noting the answer to this question we will see what really fulfils them."[56]

What distinguishes us from other things is that we can know and love God. This is why the ultimate good for Aquinas is not Aristotle's *eudaimonia*, a life of well-being and flourishing constituted by human goods and activities, but *beatitudo*, a word that for Aquinas connotes the particularly relational dimension of reflecting on, and partaking of, the goodness, beauty, and holiness of God.[57] Aquinas does not disparage the value and importance of created goods and human activities; indeed, they are an integral part of a good and happy life and, even more important, are intimations of the goodness and loveliness of God. But he does say the happiness and well-being these goods offer us is limited, essential but nonetheless falling infinitely short of the goodness for which we are made and in which we find peace and perfection.[58] For Aquinas, *beatitudo* is nothing else but friendship with God and, consequently, everything God loves.

In the quest for perfection and peace, only in God do we find the life and goodness necessary to end our restlessness, and the reason is that neither we nor our world is the answer to our happiness. We are not made for this world or for our own sakes; rather, we are "destined for an end beyond" ourselves, destined to find happiness by participating in the lovelife of God.[59] From the perspective of faith, Aristotle's *eudaimonia* pales before Aquinas's *beatitudo*, for whatever flourishing the goods and virtues of the world offer is tragically insufficient for what the human heart seeks. For Aquinas, nothing short of uniting our minds and hearts with God will make us who we are meant to be and bring us the wholeness marked out for us.[60]

Aquinas believed that God called us to share in the life of the Trinity in this world now and in the reign of God to come.[61] He saw us not primarily as fallen, but summoned—creatures who, despite whatever frailty and wickedness, were relentlessly and ingeniously loved by God and called to union with God. Aquinas interpreted the whole of history as an endless chronicle of God reaching out to us in love and friendship, healing and restoring and empowering us through grace, leading and redeeming us in Christ, sanctifying and strengthening us in the Spirit. God's foremost desire, Aquinas believed, is to share with us his happiness and perfection, and to do so by drawing us into his life each day. Yes, God loves all things, but he loves us uniquely and passionately with the special love marked out for friends. Yes, God loves everything that is, Aquinas reasoned, but he loves us as friends, wanting for us all the goodness and happiness that is himself.[62] The message of charity is that God is in love with us, making us his friends.

This life of intimate friendship with God that is charity begins when God shares with us his very happiness and life. Aquinas captures this by saying our friendship with God begins when God "communicates beatitude," imparting to us the love, life, and happiness shared between Father, Son, and Spirit. "Now there is a sharing of man with God by his sharing his happiness with us," Thomas writes, "and it is on this that a friendship is based."[63]

Friendship is possible only when there is something we have in common with another. But what do we have in common with God? Left to ourselves, weakened by sin, Aquinas says we are too unlike God to be friends with God. Left to our own resources, friendship with God is utterly beyond our reach because God's goodness is completely disproportionate to our own. We cannot reach God unless

God reaches out to us first. The only way friendship with God is possible is if God loves us first, befriending us with the love and grace that enables us to love God in return. In short, we have something in common with God sufficient for friendship only because God has gifted us, only because God has first shared with us the friendship life of God we call Trinity, the everlasting community in which love offered is love wholly received and wholly returned.[64] Friendships are possible only when something is shared. What makes friendship with God possible, and indeed sustains its life, are the manifold gifts God offers: the grace in which charity begins, Christ in whom charity is deepened, and the Spirit in whom charity is perfected.

The gifts of charity are radically transformative; indeed, they make us a new creation. Through charity fallen ones "become God's adopted sons and daughters, intimate members of God's family."[65] As Mary Ann Fatula remarks, for Aquinas charity means "*We* belong to the God who loves us; but even more radically, through love, *God* truly belongs to us. The love that is ours in the Holy Spirit allows us to *possess* the divine persons who give themselves to us precisely so that they will 'belong' to us in love."[66] With the gift of charity, poured forth into every heart, "the Holy Spirit makes us God's home, and through this same Spirit, the triune God becomes our home."[67] Charity means God dwells in us continually and seeks with every human being an intimate communion of life and love. To live in charity is to deepen in love for the God who is literally sealed to our hearts. In other words, to be ourselves is to be in love with God.

The gifts of charity also work a healing. Whatever capacity we might have had for friendship with God was lost, and continues to be damaged, by sin. Sin describes the state of disorder and alienation between God and ourselves, between ourselves and others, and between ourselves and the rest of creation. Sin is disharmony where there is meant to be peace, estrangement where there is meant to be unity and love. For Aquinas, original sin represents the disorder inflicted on our whole human nature as a consequence of the loss of original justice. In the paradisal state of innocence our relationship with God, one another, and all other creatures was rightly ordered; however, with the Fall, and apart from grace, we find ourselves, in Aquinas's graphic phrase, under "the thraldom of sin."[68]

The power of original sin is cripplingly pervasive, constituting a disordering of all dimensions of our nature. Nothing escapes it, everything is affected by it. Aquinas calls it a "congenital habit" corrupting our entire being, a disintegration of self that spreads throughout our nature.[69] It is not just that original sin leaves us feeble in one or other aspect of our being, but that in its power we are infirm throughout. If prior to the Fall our nature was healthy, after the Fall we suffer a sickness only God's grace can heal. Aquinas speaks of the wounds inflicted on us by sin. There is the wound of ignorance by which our desire for truth is lessened, leaving us often wanting darkness instead of the light; the wound of malice by which we turn away from the good and sometimes delight in evil; the wound of weakness through which we fall into sin when doing the good is difficult; and the wound of concupiscence by which we lose our freedom and dignity to base pleasures.[70] Collectively these wounds express the deterioration and corruption of a life in rebellion against God. This is hardly the stance from which to become God's friends.

Thus, the grace that makes friendship with God possible must initially heal, restore, and rehabilitate a nature living more at enmity with God than in friendship. Aquinas describes this succinctly by saying grace is "a certain habitual gift, by which spoiled human nature is healed, and once healed, is raised up to perform works which merit eternal life."[71] That is quite a turnabout, the transition from living in enmity to living in God, the dazzling change from being powerless in sin to being gloriously empowered in divine goodness through grace. Describing grace as a *habitual* gift captures well that grace is essentially new life, indeed, a radically transformed and powerfully liberating life constituted by grace and forgiveness, and deepened and nurtured through the virtues and the sacraments, particularly baptism, the Eucharist, confirmation, and reconciliation.[72] Through grace we are reconciled to God and become sharers in God's life, companions of the Trinity, but the effects of grace should not stop there. On the contrary, if grace is a gift it is also a *habitus*, a new way of life constituted by distinctive practices. Those practices must be learned, indeed they require considerable training, but their transformative effects are stunning. As Thomas puts it, through the *habitus* of grace, erstwhile sinners find themselves "performing works which merit eternal life."

More than anything, the life of charity is characterized by a deep and heartfelt longing for God. The Spirit of God poured forth into our hearts is the gift of charity, and the power of this gift is not only to heal hearts wounded by sin, but also to nurture in us a steadfast and ever-deepening yearning for God. Charity turns our hearts to

God, it is the foundational grace by which we are supernaturally inclined to hunger and thirst for God as the supreme good of our lives. Put more strongly, charity *revives* us because with charity God dwells in our hearts each day, ever present to us as the love in which we are fulfilled. As Mary Ann Fatula writes, "Through charity, therefore, the Spirit heals our wounds and gives us ease and joy in loving God, inclining us from within the depths of our heart to the very goal which will totally satisfy our heart."[73] In a beautiful passage, she elaborates:

> Lavished on us by the risen Lord, the Holy Spirit now lives in us, gently drawing and "goading" us to love the triune God in return. Even our very desire for God, Thomas tells us, comes from God. The Holy Spirit within us strongly, gently inclines us to God, filling us with desire for the Trinity as the God of our heart. Through grace, therefore, the Spirit of love dwells in us, inspiring and protecting us, drawing us into loving relationship with the triune God.[74]

Furthermore, the grace of charity ought to make a concrete, discernible difference in our lives; indeed, we misunderstand the purpose of this grace if we receive it and remain unchanged, or if we think it calls for exactly the same patterns of living we knew when we were fallen. Grace not only reconciles us to God, but, as a *habitus*, a distinctive way of life, works through the virtues and the sacraments to empower us to live, however incompletely, a godlike life now.[75] To understand the effects of grace rightly and what they entail for friendship with God, we must envision our healing and reconciliation with God as a summons to cross over to a new kind of life, a life no longer under the death-dealing tyranny of sin, but a life that is essentially a resurrection to new and better possibilities. This does not mean that a life of friendship with God takes us out of the world, but it does mean that through charity we are called to live in the world differently, acting according to who we truly are, fallen ones who thanks to love are sharers in God's life.

As a *habitus*, grace takes the form of charity, and charity is not only a single virtue, but also a comprehensive way of life that seeks God in all things. Aquinas expresses this when he speaks of charity as the "form" of all the other virtues.[76] What he means is that through charity everything we do in our ordinary, everyday lives is directed to God and by God so that all our thoughts, words, feelings, and actions might be pleasing to God; with charity love for God permeates every aspect of our daily lives. Aquinas captures this by speaking of charity as the "mother" of all the other virtues because just as a mother gives birth to her child, charity gives birth to a way of life that gives glory to God in every way.[77] As Jean Porter observes, "It follows that for Thomas, charity functions as the supreme organizing principle in the personality of the justified, by which not only all of their actions, but all their desires and impulses, are directed to God (2a2ae 23.3,7). Through charity, the individual is enabled to participate in the very mind and will of God, . . . to grasp intuitively what God's will for that individual is in any given situation (2a2ae 45.1,2)."[78]

The new life of charity is no solitary enterprise; indeed, it is inescapably a *shared* life, first with God and then with all those loved by God, family, friends, and neighbors in this world, angels and saints in the next.[79] All friendship is shared life. Aristotle commented that "nothing characterizes friends as much as living in each other's company"[80] because friends find being together delightful; they not only enjoy the same things, but especially enjoy doing them together.[81] Charity is no different. Charity is a shared life with God, it is living in company with God each day not out of duty or duress, but because we find keeping company with God delightful. In his *Commentary on the Sentences of Peter Lombard*, Thomas speaks of friendship in general as a certain society or partnership of the lover and beloved in love, and then refers specifically to charity as the friendship we have with God in which God loves us and we love God, and the mutual exchange of love creates a society or partnership between God and ourselves.[82]

In this respect, the shared life of charity, rooted in grace and pursued through the sacraments and the virtues, is like an ongoing conversation with God in the ways of God. But this ongoing conversation is essentially a never-ending conversion because it is impossible to live in friendship with God without being changed by God. The special grace and distinctive hope of charity is that by living in friendship with God each day we gradually take on the ways of God. In every friendship we take on the ways of our friends; we cannot love them or be loved by them and remain the same. Neither can we love God nor be loved by God and be unchanged, for in the partnership of charity we become godly.[83] This is precisely why Aquinas was able to affirm the value of ordinary life and insist that we could reach the fullness of the Christian life within it.

But charity is also a shared life with others. As we saw with Aristotle, the virtuous life requires the company of friends. These friends sought each other's good, encouraged and supported one another, and contributed to one another's moral development. The life of charity is similar except for one crucial difference: in charity the friends are united in God and are seeking the fullness of virtues that will bring them likeness to God. The goal of charity is not fellowship in Athens, but kinship with the saints in the kingdom of God.

For Aquinas, it is a quest we pursue *together*. Charity is a cooperative enterprise by which people seeking ever greater union with God and with one another help one another grow in friendship with God, in divine goodness, and in all the virtues that mark those who hunger for holiness. Charity is a life of communion with God that cannot be separated from a life of communion with others. It is, like Aristotle's virtue friendships, a jointly pursued life clustered around a common project, but the common project of charity is ultimately a transfigured life, a life that shines with the goodness we see in the saints. In the special friendship of charity, the friends work for one another's well-being by helping one another seek the things of God and grow in discipleship with Christ. They challenge one another to imitate Christ and to practice gospel virtues. They encourage one another, support one another, and together seek the utmost perfection of their lives in love. Charity is the highest form of friendship because it is founded on, and seeks the fullness of, the best of all goods: the love and happiness of God. It is the distinctive moral community by which people united together in God seek to love like God in all things. And it is the most perfecting of friendships because through it we participate not only in a good human life, but also in the divine life; in short, friendships founded in charity lead to beatitude.

The distinctive life of charity cannot be sustained without cultivating special practices or virtues. Aquinas calls these the acts or effects of charity and names them joy, peace, mercy, kindness, almsgiving, and fraternal correction.[84] Far from being accidental, these are the virtues that must be developed if the shared project of charity, instead of being undone by anger, dissension, selfishness, or dishonesty, is to deepen. Aquinas's choice of these virtues is deliberate because their opposites are precisely the vices by which this highest form of friendship is corrupted. People who are ill-tempered, divisive, begrudging, stingy, joyless, and unwilling to be honest with us not only lack the character necessary for charity's friendship, but also are not capable of truly seeking our good in this most graced of relationships. Just as not everyone was fit for Aristotle's friendships of virtue, neither is everyone capable of the shared life of charity without developing a certain kind of character, especially when charity is seen not only as a grace, but also as the particular moral community through which we grow together in the love of God. In the friendship of charity we entrust ourselves to those committed to helping us grow in divine goodness. As with Aristotle's friendships of virtue, this requires a special person, specifically someone who will persevere in what is best and who is willing to do all that is necessary to help us achieve the greatest of possible goods.

Friends joined in charity ought to make everyone around them better. Their friendship exists not solely for their own perfection, but ultimately for the perfection and sanctification of the world. There is a mission and ministry to charity, namely to remind others of who they truly are, people who have been loved and befriended by God, and who are called to enjoy the highest possible happiness in God. The truth of charity is that God loves everybody, even our most persistent enemies. Through charity everyone is enfolded in the divine love, even those who seem furthest from God, and everyone is desired by God. Charity means everyone belongs to God and is meant for God; thus, the most urgent responsibility of the friends of God is to invite others to the way of life that allows them to share in the love of God in the deepest possible way.

For this to happen there must be a community committed to practicing, embodying, and witnessing friendship with God each day. There must be a people whose very way of life is an invitation to others to live the fullness of grace. This is why charity is ultimately an ecclesial practice, a communal way of life that may often be at odds with the dominant practices of society, but whose very difference is a summons to something eminently better. If the life of charity is a witness of joy, peace, mercy, kindness, generosity, and truthfulness, then the community of faith we call the church must show in its very being that these practices constitute life's greatest possibilities and most promising activities. In their life together, Christians should demonstrate that violence is not inevitable, that joyful life together is possible, that selfishness can be overcome by forbearance and generosity, and that nothing is more life-giving than kindness, compassion, and care. The church exercises the life-giving ministry of charity when it gives the world a hint of what is possible when we take God's love to heart.

But if the church is to witness friendship with God, it must understand clearly what the love of charity entails. It needs examples to which to point, flesh and blood instances from which it can learn what friendship with God involves and how it might be lived every day. Charity cannot remain an abstraction, an inspiring but unreachable ideal; rather, it demands a history, a specific form of life with concrete practices by which it can be embodied and pursued within our ordinary lives.[85] The Christian community finds examples of such friendship in the lives of the saints, but each of those lives, for all their distinctiveness, was patterned on the life of Christ. The saints learned the life of charity through the grammar of discipleship; it was by seeing their lives as an imitation of Christ that they plumbed the depths of friendship with God. They knew, as Aquinas did, that Christ is the exemplar of charity, the one in whom friendship with God is normatively displayed. They knew, as Aquinas did, that the life of charity is always also life in Christ because it is in and through Christ that we grow together in friendship with God. The life of charity is inseparable from Christ. Aquinas knew this, and it is why any study of his account of charity is incomplete without examining his Christology.

WHY FRIENDSHIP WITH GOD IS INSEPARABLE FROM CHRIST

In the *terita pars*, the third and final part of his *Summa theologiae*, Aquinas turns his attention to Christ and the sacraments. Although studies of Thomistic ethics seldom note the connection between Aquinas's treatise on human action, the virtues, and other elements of morality outlined in the second part of the *Summa*, and his Christology and sacramental theology outlined in the third part, Gerald Vann is right in arguing that the *terita pars*, "far from being a mere appendage" to Aquinas's ethics, "is in fact the conclusion, the completion" of his ethics.[86] Aquinas makes this very clear. The whole thrust of his massive *Summa theologiae* is to show how we who have come from God can return to God. In the third part of the *Summa*, Aquinas illustrates how we make our way back to God through Christ and the sacraments. He speaks of Christ as the "path" to blessedness, the way to fullness of life in God.[87] The point is clear: our union with God in charity is inseparable from a life in Christ, and life in Christ means the life of the sacraments, especially the Eucharist, in the community we call church.

If Aquinas's account of the moral life in the second part of the *Summa* is read not independently of the *terita pars* but in connection with it, it is clear that a life of friendship with God is intrinsically related to life in Christ, and life in Christ is inescapably sacramental. Christ is intrinsic to the life of charity first of all because "the Incarnation, the life, and the death of Jesus are acts of God the Word's deepest friendship with us,"[88] the most perfect expression of God's absolute benevolence. Jesus is God's "intimate friendship with us in person,"[89] the one through whom God takes everything about us into himself and gives us all that he has and loves.[90] In Jesus God comes to be the best of all possible friends, the one who is for us and with us at every moment.[91] But Christ is also intrinsic to the life of charity because Christ is the most perfect manifestation for us of what a life of friendship with God is. In his example, his attitudes and virtues, especially his total openness to God's will, Jesus shows us what friendship with God entails. Thus, because charity is definitively displayed in Christ, our friendship with God is possible only through participation in and conformity to the life of Christ.[92]

Christ makes friendship with God possible. Aquinas develops this in two ways. He speaks of Jesus as mediator and exemplar. A mediator, Aquinas observes, is someone who brings two sides together, often reuniting those who have been separated or estranged. This is the role of Christ "through whom men are reconciled with God: 'God was in Christ reconciling the world with himself.' It follows," Aquinas concludes, "that Christ is the self-sufficient mediator of God and men by reason of his having reconciled through his death, the human race with God."[93] In this first sense, Christ is integral to charity by being the one who mends and restores our relationship with God broken by sin. Christ reconnects us to God through his Cross, healing the breach between God and ourselves. As L. Gregory Jones writes, "The claim Thomas makes is that although in our sinfulness we have lost the gifts of God's friendship, God makes an overture of friendship to us in Jesus Christ."[94] In other words, Jones concludes, "Christology is central for Thomas's understanding of friendship with God" because it "is precisely because of God, who became flesh that we might be reconciled to Him, that participation in divine happiness is possible."[95]

Second, Jesus is the exemplar or model for creation, the one who represents the ideal and perfection of what God created us to be. Aquinas speaks of God the creator as a "craftsman" and of Jesus as the model God uses in crafting and fashioning us. Every craftsman creates with something in mind, a picture or image of what he is trying to make, and, Aquinas reasons, when God created us he had the forgiveness, strength, healing, mercy, compassion, justice, and love of Jesus in mind as the most fitting expression of who we are meant to be. Because of our fall from grace and our life in sin, however, what God fashioned was damaged and had to be repaired. In restoring us, Aquinas says, God the craftsman again looked to Christ as the model or blueprint for who we are to be.[96] Thus, in every possible way Jesus is the fulfillment of our nature.

We are restored to friendship with God through Christ. But friendship with God develops over time. It is something into which we grow as we come to know more of God and what it means to be God's friend, and as we become habituated in the ways of God. Intimate relationships do not begin instantly, at least ones that last do not. They require a history, years spent knowing one another and learning from one another, long times together in which trust is developed and love expressed. Aquinas taught that our friendship with God develops through our life in Christ, and our life in Christ is displayed through the sacraments. It is through a life of discipleship begun in Baptism and sustained and deepened through the Eucharist, confirmation, and the sacrament of reconciliation that we come to know the ways of God and are able to live the life of God. It is by watching, following, and practicing the example of Jesus that we deepen in friendship with God. The life of charity is an *imitatio Christi* because it is only by conformity to Christ that we have friendship with God.

Aquinas expressed this by saying that we reach the perfection of charity "through a participation in the Word of God, even as the pupil makes progress by receiving the teacher's word."[97] The comment is telling because it suggests friendship with God requires a life of following, learning from, and imitating Christ. Charity demands "taking the Word" to heart. It demands that we see the life of Christ as the normative example of friendship with God and set ourselves to making Christ's life a model for our own. There is then a direct correspondence between discipleship and charity. To participate in God's word is to adopt Christ's life as the one to which our own must conform. Aquinas's point is that it is only by having our life directed by Christ that we grow in friendship with God or even know what it means. We make progress in charity by patterning our life on the life of Christ. We learn the *habitus* of charity only insofar as we apprentice ourselves each day to the one who mastered friendship with God. The two are internally connected, absolutely inseparable: Friendship with God demands a discipleship life with Christ.

Our primary participation in the Word is through the sacraments, particularly the Eucharist. In the *terita pars* Aquinas comments, "Baptism is required in order to begin this spiritual life; the Eucharist is necessary in order to bring it to its culmination."[98] The Incarnation continues through the sacraments because they are the means God uses to reach out to us in Christ; through each of them God befriends us now and into the future, inviting us to share the divine life.[99] And through the sacraments, especially the Eucharist where Christ is *really present* to us and becomes our contemporary, we live as though we were his contemporaries, listening to him, conversing with him, learning from him, and rejoicing with him. Christ lives in us and we in him; indeed, our daily life is a friendship, a holy companionship with Christ.[100]

This is why Aquinas spoke of the Eucharist as the central sacrament. If Baptism is the sacrament of faith, Aquinas said, the Eucharist is the sacrament of charity, the means by which we are brought "to spiritual perfection" by "being closely united to Christ who suffered for us."[101] The Eucharist is the sacrament of friendship with God because through a life patterned on Christ we are brought to union with God. The Eucharist is the perfect symbol of the form our life should take if we are to enjoy the happiness God wants for us. The Eucharist reveals that the best possible life, indeed the only truly fulfilling one, is a life spent in intimate friendship with God through Christ. That is the kind of life that brings us to our utmost possible development as human beings, which is exactly what Aquinas's ethics seeks. For Aquinas, our highest possible excellence is the life of *caritas*, the life of being loved by God and loving God, the life of seeking God's good and delighting in God's beauty just as God seeks our good and delights in us. The image here is of mutual indwelling through Christ, God living in us and we living in God, the fellowship of which is beatitude. If Aquinas was right to describe friendship as a society of lover and beloved in love, then the Eucharist indeed is the sacrament of charity, the means by which we who love God live intimately together with the God who has always loved us. Thus, Brian Davies is certainly right when he says that the Eucharist is "the ultimate sign of what people are meant to be."[102]

Living together with God in Christ changes us; ultimately it makes us saints. Aquinas captures the nature of this change by drawing an analogy between food for our bodies and food for our souls. He says "this sacrament does for the life of the spirit all that material food and drink does for the life of the body, by sustaining, building up, restoring, and contenting."[103] But there is a crucial difference between food for the body and food for the soul. When we eat a meal, Aquinas observes, the food we consume is digested and assimilated into our bodies to nourish and strengthen us. It is not we who are changed according to the food, but the food that is changed according to us. But spiritual food is different. When we eat the Body and drink the Blood of Christ, it is not Christ who is changed according to us, but we who are changed according to Christ. As Aquinas puts it, "Spiritual food changes man into itself. This is the teaching of Augustine in his *Confessions*. He heard, as it were, the voice of Christ saying to him, 'You will not change me into yourself as you would the food of your flesh; but you will be changed into me.'"[104]

We become God's friends by eating Christ. We grow in charity by feeding on the one who is perfect friendship with God. "So it is that as we were reborn in Christ through Baptism," Aquinas writes, "we eat Christ through the Eucharist."[105] Aquinas does not flinch at this graphic description. He wants it to be clear that we acquire the self necessary for charity by *eating* the life of Christ, by absorbing everything about him into our ordinary lives. When we eat the Body and drink the Blood of Christ we consume Christ entirely, his attitudes, his outlook, his values, his example, and we allow him to transform and challenge our ordinary lives. To feed on Christ is to take Christ to heart, it is to allow Christ to affect every dimension of who we are. As Aquinas commented, food is of no use unless it is consumed, and the same is true with the food of Christ. It is of no use unless it is wholly consumed, completely taken to heart, so that our unredeemed life can be made over into his own.

The Eucharist is central to a life of friendship with God because to eat Christ is to become like Christ, and it is exactly the radical, total conformity of the self to Christ that is the perfection of friendship with God. To eat Christ is gradually to lose one kind of self in order to become another kind of self, a self capable of intimacy and union with God, a self who wants nothing more than to give God glory, as God has given us his Son, and all other things besides, that we might be glorified. To eat Christ is a transfiguration, the acquisition of a new and redeemed self, and one fit to partake of the beatitude God, from the beginning, has wanted to share with us.

CONCLUSION

In this chapter we have argued not only that friendship, particularly the special friendship of charity, is indispensable for the Christian moral life, but also that it is central for connecting morality to our ordinary lives; indeed, the friendship of charity is the crucial practice for forming, guiding, and empowering our everyday lives. This is not the friendship of cordial relationships or passing acquaintances, but the friendship that is a moral enterprise of pursuing the life of grace together. This is not easily attempted in a culture that often misunderstands and minimizes friendship, and lacks any consensus on the substantive goods that constitute the virtuous life. In fact, in a society marked by consumerism and individualism, and one in which the self is sometimes defined against others instead of in need of them, any friendship model for the moral life, especially the model of friendship with God, can almost appear countercultural. Why friendship is important for the moral life became clear when we examined Aristotle's ethics, especially his central argument that a good and flourishing life—indeed, the only genuinely human life—is a life of virtue, and why for him a life of virtue can only be pursued in company with good friends.

But Aquinas radicalizes Aristotle's treatment of friendship through charity, for Aquinas saw the Christian moral life as an ongoing and ever-deepening friendship not with Athenian free men, but with God and everything God has made and loves. For Aquinas, having first healed and restored us through grace, God revives, empowers, and, most perfectly, befriends us through charity. Through charity Aquinas affirms the moral and spiritual value of ordinary lives because he truly believes both that everyone is called to the life of charity— it is the one vocation everyone shares—and that it is indeed the most godlike life possible, the life through which erstwhile sinners begin to shine in the goodness of God. The transformation brought about through charity is always achieved in company with others. Charity is a shared life, a communal and ecclesial practice by which the friends of God imitate Christ, grow in holiness, and seek the love and happiness of God. It is also a life of witness and mission by which the friends of God, through the example of their lives, call others to their highest possible goodness and happiness. There is no more promising and adventuresome account of friendship than to see it, as Aquinas does, not only as a moral enterprise, but also as a crucible for holiness and as a gospel witness to a world that so desperately needs to hear good news.

We become friends of God through Christ. If the Christian moral life is constituted by friendship with God, it is also inextricably connected to discipleship-friendship with Christ. If charity is to be more than a formal abstraction, it has to be definitively displayed. And if it is a way of life to be practiced and pursued now, we must know concretely what living as friends of God means. We learn this from Christ. Jesus is our means of passage to God, the One in whom and with whom we return to God, because Jesus shows us both the fullness of charity—in his life, death, and resurrection we see the perfection of friendship with God—and the virtues and practices we need to master if we are to acquire the character of God's friends.

That is the task of a lifetime, but it is also a task worth pursuing, one infinitely promising and exciting, and one that we should never deprive ourself. At first glance, Aquinas's description of charity and the life that flows from it may sound appealing but utopian, too far removed from life as we know it to be within our reach. But we should take a second look. If our yearnings for friendships of grace and blessedness are often frustrated, it may be because our notions of friendship lack the substantive goods necessary to make life with others truly worthwhile. What Aquinas offers us is the most compelling account of friendship possible because he makes our relationships with others also relationships with God by which we, in the context of our ordinary lives, learn to love God and everything God loves, and thus achieve the fullest possible development of our spirits.

Charity means God is in love with us *now* and empowers us to share in his life *now*. Charity means a genuinely godlike life is possible for us in company with others who seek God too. Most of all, in its commitment to mercy, justice, peace, forgiveness, and compassion, charity means the reign of God need not be completely postponed. Its fullness may be in the future, but its beginnings are now in those who live God's peace and know God's joy through charity.

NOTES

1. Charles Taylor, *Sources of the Self: The Making of the Modern Identity* (Cambridge, Mass.: Harvard University Press, 1989), p. 218.
2. Thomas Aquinas, *Summa theologiae*, I-II.65.5. "Haec autem societas hominis ad Deum, quae est quaedam familiaris conversatio cum ipso, inchoatur quidem his in praesenti per gratiam, perficietur autem in futuro per gloriam; quorum utrumque fide et spe tenetur." The text of the *Summa theologiae* is the Blackfriar's edition (New York: McGraw-Hill, 1963–1969). References will be to the *Summa theologiae* unless otherwise noted.
3. See Paul J. Wadell, *Friendship and the Moral Life* (Notre Dame, Ind.: University of Notre Dame Press, 1989), p. 141.
4. Wadell, *Friendship and the Moral Life*, pp. 1–8.
5. I am grateful to Reinhard Hutter for this insight.
6. Rodney Clapp, "The Celebration of Friendship," *Reformed Journal* 39 (1989): 11–13, at 11.
7. Ann Hartle, *The Modern Self in Rousseau's* Confessions: *A Reply to St. Augustine* (Notre Dame, Ind.: University of Notre Dame Press, 1983), p. 2. See also Taylor, *Sources of the Self*, pp. 127–76.
8. Hartle, *The Modern Self*, p. 6.
9. Hartle, *The Modern Self*, p. 144.
10. Emmanuel Mounier, *Personalism*, Philip Mairet, trans. (Notre Dame, Ind.: University of Notre Dame Press, 1952), pp. 17–32. See also Ignace Lepp, *The Ways of Friendship*, Bernard Murchland, trans. (New York, N.Y.: Macmillan, 1966).
11. Mounier, *Personalism*, p. 20.
12. Mounier, *Personalism*, p. 20.
13. John Milbank, *Theology and Social Theory: Beyond Secular Reason* (Oxford: Basil Blackwell, 1990), pp. 12–13.
14. For a fuller treatment of this argument, see Milbank's *Theology and Social Theory*, pp. 326–434.
15. Lepp, *The Ways of Friendship*, p. 15.
16. John M. Cooper, "Aristotle on Friendship," in *Essays on Aristotle's Ethics*, Amélie Oksenberg Rorty, ed. (Berkeley, Calif.: University of California Press, 1980), p. 303.
17. Aristotle, *Nicomachean Ethics*, Martin Ostwald, trans. (Indianapolis, Ind.: Bobbs-Merrill, 1962), 1156a17.
18. *NE*, 1156b6–25.
19. *NE*, 1156a3–5.
20. Cooper, "Aristotle on Friendship," p. 309.
21. Martha C. Nussbaum, *The Fragility of Goodness* (Cambridge: Cambridge University Press, 1986), pp. 355–6.
22. *NE*, 1171a10–15.
23. I am grateful to Reinhard Hutter for this important qualification.
24. *NE*, 1157b33.
25. *NE*, 1056b24.

26. Cooper, "Aristotle on Friendship," p. 304.
27. Cooper, "Aristotle on Friendship," p. 305. See also Wadell, *Friendship and the Moral Life*, p. 54.
28. Cooper, "Aristotle on Friendship," p. 308.
29. For a fuller treatment see Wadell, *Friendship and the Moral Life*, pp. 27–45.
30. For an excellent account of Aristotle's understanding of *eudaimonia*, see J. L. Ackrill, "Aristotle on *Eudaimonia*," in Cooper, ed., *Essays on Aristotle's Ethics*, especially pp. 21–28.
31. *NE*, 1099b25.
32. L. Gregory Jones, "The Theological Transformation of Aristotelian Friendship in the Thought of St. Thomas Aquinas," *New Scholasticism* 61, no. 4 (1987): 374.
33. Nancy Sherman, *The Fabric of Character: Aristotle's Theory of Virtue* (Oxford: Clarendon Press, 1989), p. 125.
34. Sherman, *The Fabric of Character*, p. 126.
35. Sherman, *The Fabric of Character*, p. 127.
36. Sherman, *The Fabric of Character*, p. 131.
37. Aristotle captures this when he writes that friendship "is some sort of excellence or virtue, or involves virtue, and it is, moreover, most indispensable for life" (*NE*, 1155a3–4). And again, "We may also get some sort of training in virtue or excellence from living together with good men, as Theognis says" (*NE*, 1170a11–12).
38. Sherman, *The Fabric of Character*, p. 127.
39. *NE*, 1169b8.
40. See Wadell, *Friendship and the Moral Life*, p. 63.
41. *NE*, 1170b6–7.
42. Sherman, *The Fabric of Character*, pp. 131–2.
43. Sherman, *The Fabric of Character*, p. 132.
44. Sherman, *The Fabric of Character*, p. 135.
45. Sherman, *The Fabric of Character*, pp. 132–3.
46. Sherman, *The Fabric of Character*, p. 139.
47. II-II.23.1.
48. Mary Ann Fatula, *Thomas Aquinas, Preacher and Friend* (Collegeville, Minn.: Liturgical Press, 1993), p. 109.
49. For a fuller treatment of charity as friendship with God see Paul J. Wadell, *The Primacy of Love: An Introduction to the Ethics of Thomas Aquinas* (New York, N.Y.: Paulist Press, 1992), pp. 63–78, and Paul J. Wadell, *Friends of God: Virtues and Gifts in Aquinas* (New York, N.Y.: Peter Lang, 1991), pp. 1–49.
50. I-II.1.1–8.
51. Wadell, *The Primacy of Love*, pp. 29–43.
52. "Beatitudo est verum hominis bonum" (I-II.2.3).
53. "Beatitudo autem est proprium et perfectum hominis bonum" (I-II.2.4).
54. I-II.3.8.

55. Brian Davies, *The Thought of Thomas Aquinas* (Oxford: Clarendon Press, 1992), pp. 227–31.
56. Davies, *The Thought of Thomas Aquinas*, p. 229.
57. I-II.2.8.
58. I-II.2.8.
59. "Manifestum est autem quod homo ordinatur ad aliquid sicut ad finem: non enim homo est summum bonum" (I-II.2.5).
60. Davies, *The Thought of Thomas Aquinas*, p. 230.
61. Davies, *The Thought of Thomas Aquinas*, p. 207.
62. I-II.110.1.
63. "Cum igitur sit aliqua communicatio hominis ad Deum secundum quod nobis suam beatitudinem communicat, super hac communicatione oportet aliquam amicitiam fundari. . . . Unde manifestum est quod caritas amicitia quaedam est hominis ad Deum" (II-II.23.1).
64. See Wadell, *Friendship and the Moral Life*, pp. 121–30.
65. Fatula, *Thomas Aquinas, Preacher and Friend*, p. 112.
66. Fatula, *Thomas Aquinas, Preacher and Friend*, p. 111.
67. Fatula, *Thomas Aquinas, Preacher and Friend*, p. 109.
68. "Quinto, ad liberandum hominem a servitute" (III.1.2.).
69. "Nec debet dici quod peccatum originale sit habitus infusus aut acquisitus per actum (nisi primi parentis, non autem hujus personae), sed per vitiatam originem innatus" (I-II.82.1).
70. I-II.85.3.
71. "Dicendum quod, sicut supra dictum est, homo ad recte vivendum dupliciter auxilio Dei indiget. Uno quidem modo quantum ad aliquod habituale donum, per quod natura humana corrupta sanetur, et etiam sanata elevetur ad operanda opera meritoria vitae aeternae, quae excedunt proportionem naturae" (I-II.109.9).
72. I am grateful to Stanley Hauerwas for this insight and for many other helpful suggestions for this essay.
73. Fatula, *Thomas Aquinas, Preacher and Friend*, p. 157.
74. Fatula, *Thomas Aquinas, Preacher and Friend*, p. 110.
75. See Brian Davies, *The Thought of Thomas Aquinas*, pp. 271–72.
76. "Manifestum est autem secundum praedicta, quod per caritatem ordinantur actus omnium aliarum virtutum ad ultimum finem. Et secundum hoc ipsa dat formam actibus omnium aliarum virtutum. Et pro tanto dicitur esse forma virtutum, nam et ipsae virtutes dicuntur in ordine ad actus formatos" (II-II.23.8).
77. See Wadell, *The Primacy of Love*, pp. 126–8.
78. II-II.42.1.2. Jean Porter, "*De Ordine Caritatis*: Charity, Friendship, and Justice in Thomas Aquinas' *Summa theologiae*," *Thomist* 53, no. 2 (1989): 204.
79. II-II.25.1–10.
80. *NE*, 1157b20.
81. Joseph Bobik, "Aquinas on Friendship with God," *The New Scholasticism* 60, no. 3 (1986): 261.

82. Aquinas, *Scriptum Super Sententiis Magistri Petri Lombardi* (Paris: P. Lethielleux, 1933), III, d.27, q.2, a.1.
83. Wadell, *Friendship and the Moral Life*, pp. 135–7.
84. II-II.28–33.
85. Jones, "The Theological Transformation of Aristotelian Friendship," p. 387.
86. Gerald Vann, *St. Thomas Aquinas* (New York, N.Y.: Benziger, 1947), p. 145.
87. "Quia Salvator noster Dominus Jesus Christus, teste angelo, 'populum suum salvum faciens a peccatis eorum,' viam veritatis nobis in seipso demonstravit, per quam ad beatitudinem immortalis vitae resurgendo pervenire possimus" (ST III, Foreword to the *tertia pars*).
88. Fatula, *Thomas Aquinas, Preacher and Friend*, p. 60.
89. Fatula, *Thomas Aquinas, Preacher and Friend*, p. 61.
90. Fatula, *Thomas Aquinas, Preacher and Friend*, p. 62.
91. Fatula, *Thomas Aquinas, Preacher and Friend*, p. 70.
92. On this point see R. Bernard, "La Vertu Acquise et La Vertu Infuse," *La Vie Spirituelle* 42 (1935), p. 48. C. A. J. Van Ouwerkerk, *Caritas et Ratio* (Nigmegen: Drukkerij Gebr. Janssen, 1956), p. 88; and Dom Odon Lottin, *Morale Fondamentale* (Tournai: Desclee et Cie, 1954), p. 30.
93. "Dicendum quod mediatoris officium proprie est conjungere eos inter quos est mediator, nam extrema uniuntur in medio. Unire autem homines Deo perfective quidem convenit Christo, per quem homines sunt reconciliati Deo, secundum illud II ad Cor., 'Deus erat in Christo mundum reconcilians sibi.' Et ideo solus Christus est perfectus Dei et hominum mediator, inquantum per suam mortem humanum genus Deo reconciliavit" (III.26.1).
94. Jones, "The Theological Transformation of Aristotelian Friendship," p. 386.
95. Jones, "The Theological Transformation of Aristotelian Friendship," p. 387.
96. "Ipsius autem personae Filii, qui est Verbum Dei, attenditur uno quidem modo communis convenientia ad totam creaturam. Quia verbum artificis, idest conceptus ejus, est similitudo exemplaris eorum quae ab artifice fiunt. Unde Verbum Dei, quod est aeternus conceptus ejus, est similitudo exemplaris totius creaturae. Et ideo, sicut per participationem hujus similitudinis creaturae sunt in propriis speciebus institutae sed mobiliter, ita per unionem Verbi ad creaturam non participativam sed personalem conveniens fuit reparari creaturam in ordine ad aeternam et immobilem perfectionem. Nam et artifex per formam artis conceptam qua artificiatum condidit, ipsum, si collapsum fuerit, restaurat" (III.3.8). See also Davies, *The Thought of Thomas Aquinas*, p. 307.
97. "Et ideo homo per hoc in sapientia proficit, quae est propria ejus perfectio prout est rationalis, quod participat Verbum Dei; sicut discipulus instruitur per hoc quod recipit verbum magistri" (III.3.8).
98. "Et ideo perceptio Baptismi est necessaria ad inchoandam spiritualem vitam, perceptio autem Eucharistiae est necessaria ad consummandam ipsam. . . " (III.73.3).

99. Davies, *The Thought of Thomas Aquinas*, p. 350.
100. Davies, *The Thought of Thomas Aquinas*, p. 350.
101. "Sed Eucharistia est sacramentum passionis Christi prout homo perficitur in unione ad Christum passum. Unde, sicut baptismus dicitur 'sacramentum fidei,' quae est fundamentum spiritualis vitae; ita Eucharistia dicitur 'sacramentum caritatis' quae est 'vinculum perfectionis,' ut dicitur Coloss. 3" (III.73.3).
102. Davies, *The Thought of Thomas Aquinas*, p. 362.
103. "Et ideo omnem effectum quem cibus et potus materialis facit quantum ad vitam corporalem, quod scilicet sustentat, auget, reparat et delectat, hoc totum facit hoc sacramentum quantum ad vitam spiritualem" (III.79.1).
104. "Sed alimentum spirituale convertit hominem in seipsum: secundum illud quod Augustinus dicit, quod quasi audivit vocem Christi dicentis, 'Nec tu me mutabis in te, sicut cibum carnis tuae, sed tu mutaberis in me'" (III.73.3).
105. "Unde et sicut per baptismum regeneramur in Christo, ita per Eucharistiam manducamus Christum" (III.73.5).

Epieikeia *and the Accomplishment of the Just*

ROMANUS CESSARIO, O. P.

With only some few exceptions, *epieikeia* no longer figures prominently on the list of topics that engage the interest of moral theologians.[1] Given the influence that the concept once exercised on Christian moral reasoning, such inattention should signal a certain alarm. As part of an effort to restore *epieikeia* to its proper place in moral discourse, this essay presents a historical-doctrinal study of the notion. The study aims principally to present the doctrine of St. Thomas Aquinas, especially as it appears in his mature systematic works, namely, the *Summa theologiae* and the *Sententia libri Ethicorum*. After a short overview of the reasons that account for the eclipse of *epieikeia*, I intend to establish that, during the course of his theological career, Aquinas developed an original and highly constructive account of *epieikeia*. We should not conclude from the current lack of attention paid to *epieikeia* that this virtuous disposition no longer forms an important part of the Christian moral life. For by following Aquinas's lead, we will come to appreciate not only that *epieikeia* enables an agent to make the right choice in moral matters whose determinateness is not immediately manifest, but also that it shapes his or her emotional life so that the energies of the whole person are put at the service of accomplishing the just thing.

The general purpose of this book is to argue that the moral teaching of Thomas Aquinas contributes in a significant way to an authentic Christian vision of empowerment. The present essay advances this central thesis to the extent that it enlarges on the notion that justice signifies a virtue of character. As a virtuous disposition associated with justice, *epieikeia* ensures that the just man or woman is able to come up with the best moral solution in particular cases. This represents Aquinas's clear teaching in *Summa theologiae* II-II.120.1. If theologians have let *epieikeia* slip out of their discourse, philosophers are beginning again to recognize its importance. In his study on *phronesis* and *technē* in modern and ancient philosophy, Joseph Dunne reminds us that Aristotle draws on the builder's trade in order to illustrate *epieikeia*: "when the thing is indefinite the rule is also indefinite, like the lead rule used in making the Lesbian moulding; the rule adapts itself to the shape of the stone and is not rigid."[2] The author goes on to argue that, on Aristotle's account, *technē* can respond to the subtleties of making in the same way that phronesis, or practical reasonableness, is able to respond to the subtleties of action. Because Aquinas's teaching on *epieikeia* helps the theologian deal with the subtleties of human behavior, it merits careful and serious consideration. But moral theologians have not always recognized *epieikeia* as a true virtue of character.

In the period of casuist moral theology, which flourished from about the mid-sixteenth century until the Second Vatican Council, theologians mainly developed the notion of *epieikeia* within a tightly wrought juridical framework.[3] Thus, in an article published in 1913, L. Godefroy could easily make the generalization that all moral theologians treat *epieikeia* under the heading of laws; and Godefroy himself presents *epieikeia* as a part of the casuist structure based on positive and divine law, moral obligation, and the conscientious fulfillment of duties.[4] After World War I, the legal perspective dominates even the construal that a Dominican moralist such as Dominicus Prümmer puts on the concept: *Epieikeia*, he explains, denotes a benign and equitable interpretation not of the law itself, but of the mind of the lawgiver.[5] Indeed, the English term equity still possesses a special meaning in jurisprudence, where it signifies the recourse to general principles of justice (the *naturalis æquitas* of the Roman jurists) to correct or supplement the provisions of the law.

If we are to heed the conciliar plea for a moral theology that takes its bearings first of all from the biblical witnesses, then the contemporary moralist must return to the notion of *epieikeia* with New Testament in hand. Fortunately, there exists warrant for a biblically based conception of *epieikeia*. In his *Lexique théologique du Nouveau Testament*, the French exegete Ceslas Spicq includes the term ἐπιείκεια and documents the evolution of its meaning from "an epithet for justice[6] and for the divine government[7] that treats humankind with mercy"[8] to the New Testament meanings of measure and moderation, but also of goodness, courtesy, and generosity. He further points out that *epieikeia* and its various forms can carry the meaning of a certain graciousness and good grace, and even of the "forbearance"[9] that should characterize all those who "rejoice in the Lord."[10] Spicq then associates the term *epieikeia* with themes that suggest the theological notion of grace: a *habitus* or permanent disposition in one who enjoys divine favor, so that he or she stands ready to accomplish the full righteousness of the new law.

This essay, as I have said, principally examines relevant texts from the works of Thomas Aquinas. Chronology is important. For in order to appreciate the theological creativity that marks Aquinas's later works, it is important to examine the texts that form the basis for Aquinas's reflections on *epieikeia* as a virtue. These are three in number: first, Aristotle's doctrine, especially as found in the *Nicomachean Ethics*, where the Philosopher sets out a moral stance for conduct in defect of specific legislation; second, the commentary of St. Albert the Great, who was among the first to provide a thorough commentary on Aristotle's texts; and third, Thomas's own first effort at incorporating *epieikeia* into a theory of justice in his *Commentary on the Sentences*. Through a careful examination of Thomas's texts, this study arrives at situating the virtue of *epieikeia* within the larger arena of cardinal justice, where *epieikeia* in its own distinctive way accomplishes what is naturally and essentially just.

THE FOUNDATION IN ARISTOTLE

Aristotle's doctrine of *epieikeia* addresses a problem that vexed developing Hellenic jurisprudence: the inadequacy of human positive law to regulate all instances of human interaction. Aware of this problem, the tragic poets had already formulated a distinction between *dikē* (δίκη), the regulative force of human institution, and *epieikeia* (ἐπιείκεια), a superior sort of justice, often divine in origin and identified with *suggnomē* (συγγνώμη), or indulgence mitigating the stern force of positive law.[11] *Epieikeia* occupies much the same place in Plato's account of the less-than-ideal social and political order in *Laws*.[12] Common to both is the view that *epieikeia* is an extra-legal instrument for relaxing the rigor of the justice imposed by positive law. Within its own sphere, the latter sort of justice enjoys an absolute claim; *epieikeia*, by contrast, is introduced as an extrinsic factor, brought to bear upon the regulatory sphere from outside that sphere itself.

What Aristotle himself means by *epieikeia* is by no means simple and uniform in all the instances in which he uses the word. In some texts, for example, *epieikeia* merely signifies comprehensive moral excellence and is synonymous with *aretē*.[13] In others, when it is used as an adjectival substantive (*to epieikes*), it designates the objective at which moral excellence aims and is therefore synonymous with the good.[14] In still other instances, *epieikeia* is a development of character attendant upon and perfective of *aretē*, the comprehensively good character of the morally good man.[15] Finally, we can recognize a transitional phase in Aristotle's use of *epieikeia* in his *Rhetoric*. There, alongside the traditional view of *epieikeia* as an unwritten basis for claiming an indulgent mitigation of the strict requirements of positive law,[16] Aristotle suggests an original opinion about *epieikeia*. According to this explanation, *epieikeia* appeals to the law of nature, superior to written law, as the basis for adjudication. This appeal no longer implies something alien to the sphere of justice itself but to a deeper ground for all claims of justice.[17]

In his *Magna Moralia*, Aristotle defines *epieikeia* in this latter sense, but gives it a narrow and rather negative interpretation.[18] It is the excellence of persons who do not promote their claims beyond what is legally determined, that is, of those ready "to take less than their just right." Mindful of the incapacity of the lawgiver to envisage all possible cases in framing what is legally just, such persons instead cede that part of their claim in excess of the legally determined just. Still, Aristotle insists that *epieikeia* is not merely epiphenomenal to the sphere of the just (τὸ δίκαιον); this is the reason why it cannot operate in such a way as to entail abdication of the claims of absolute justice: "what is naturally and essentially just, he does not waive, but only such legal claims as the lawgiver was obliged to leave unqualified." Here, *epieikeia*'s function is limited to the cession of claims that exceed a foundation in positive law because the lawgiver failed to provide for each and every instance of the just. *Epieikeia* is thus no longer considered as an indulgent court of last resort; rather, as the inner resource of a just party, it is a regulating factor within human interaction.

Aristotle expands this original notion of *epieikeia* in *Nicomachean Ethics* V, 10 (1137a31-1138a4), where he introduces the topic to round off his discussion of the resources of character that mark the just person. *Epieikeia* is a feature of the equitable person—that is, it has its seat in a certain sort of developed human character and springs from an inner resource or pattern of operation. It is not an abstract principle. In his treatment, Aristotle sets himself three questions. The first of these concerns the relation of the equitable to the just. For a dilemma arises from popular usage in which the former is simply synonymous with a better course of action, while the equitable is taken as opposed to the just in its connotation of indulgence. Aristotle solves this dilemma by implicit resort to his theory of homonymy or of "things said manifoldly but according to priority and posteriority." The just (τὸ δίκαιον) is then viewed as such a semantic case, whose meaning cannot be compressed to a single instance of the just, namely, to legal justice. For while the equitable is opposed to legal justice, it is not to justice absolutely. Rather both agree in the just, but they agree according to a certain order by reason of which the equitable enjoys a privileged claim to be "the just" over the legally just.

This precision introduced, Aristotle proceeds to answer the second question: in what field does *epieikeia* come into play? What is legally just is determined by the lawgiver in framing laws that take into account and regulate the ordinary course of human interaction. But the very ordinariness or universality that underlies this determination renders it potentially defective as well, inasmuch as the just person must act justly in a concrete field that may include extraordinary factors for which the lawmaker could not provide. If the just person's inventory of moral cultivation includes *epieikeia*, he or she can correct such a deficiency of the merely legally determined just in the face of the particularities of a given field of interaction by supplying "what the legislator himself would have said had he been present and would have put into his law if he had known."[19] *Epieikeia* is, therefore, an acquired genius for realizing the truly just in the concrete. And, since Aristotle himself remarks (at 1137b19) that human conduct is always in a concrete field of action, *epieikeia* appears as an indispensable property of the truly just character.

What then is the characteristic activity of the equitable person? In broad terms, Aristotle provides an initial answer to the third of his questions. The equitable person aims at a superior justice, at an intensification of the just, beyond the legally required just; moreover, he or she does so because of an excellence at or superior attunement to what is concretely just. When Aristotle tries to specify further this mode of conduct, however, the innate conservatism of the Greek polity asserts itself, urging a restricted place of operation sketched in negative terms (such as we have already remarked in the *Magna Moralia*). The equitable person is one who—in the interests of a higher justice—sets aside or tempers claims of his own that are binding on the basis of legal justice. For this reason, the equitable person remains eminently suited for the task of rendering judgments about conduct in the concrete.[20]

We can summarize in five points the doctrine of *epieikeia* in Aristotle's ethical theory as it would be transmitted to medieval ethicians. First of all, although *epieikeia* is opposed to the legally determined just, it remains a species of justice taken absolutely, and does so with a certain preeminence over legal justice. Second, it is not a principle of conduct but an inner resource of a certain type of conduct; it is a virtue or trait of character. Third, the situation in which it operates is one in which legal specification is lacking; the cause of this defect is that the law cannot account for extraordinary situations—positive law is universal precisely because it is framed in terms of the ordinary course of life. Fourth, *epieikeia*'s distinctive activity consists in settling for less than the letter of the law would grant. Last, Aristotle leaves unsettled the question of the exercise of this virtue: does it preeminently represent the virtue of the individual citizen or of civil judges? That is, what is at issue in the exercise of *epieikeia*—individual action or normative interpretation? Or if it is both, what is the relationship between them?

The notion of *epieikeia* developed by Aristotle did not enter Christian moral discourse until the second millennium.[21] Prior to the twelfth century, the *auctoritates* of Christian ethical wisdom were almost exclusively patristic: John Cassian, St. Augustine, and St. Gregory the Great in particular. By way of exception, two figures of non-Christian antiquity did have a kind of quasi-authentic status: the Stoic Seneca and the philosophically eclectic Cicero.[22] Aristotle's ethical wisdom, however, was scarcely known in Western Christendom prior to the translations of significant portions of the *Nicomachean Ethics* into Latin, a process spanning the period from about 1160 to 1260.[23] If allowance is made for a reasonable period for the dispersion of two of the most significant translations, namely, of Herman the German and, especially, of Robert Grosseteste, any knowledge of or effective influence by Aristotle's doctrine of *epieikeia* upon ethical theory in the Latin West must be dated after 1245.[24]

EPIEIKEIA *IN ALBERT THE GREAT*

It is to Albert the Great that we owe the first truly original analysis of Aristotle's notion of *epieikeia* in the Latin West.[25] He was the first to exploit the riches of Aristotle's ethical theory that had been made available by his predecessors' projects of translation. Only once in his career did Albert give the doctrine of *epieikeia* any considerable attention and extended exposition. This came in the course of his commentary upon the *Nicomachean Ethics*, composed during Albert's second stay in Cologne (1248-1252); if William of Tocco's evidence is accepted, the commentary dates from the period of 1250 to 1252.[26] The importance of this work for the present inquiry cannot be stressed too much, for it was precisely during this period that Thomas Aquinas was Albert's pupil in Cologne.

In accord with the procedure Aristotle adopts, Albert situates his own discussion of *epieikeia* in the context of the virtue of justice. The descriptive definition of justice that Albert espouses is "a certain right order on the basis of equality, which is observed in damages and in payments."[27] From this definition he proceeds to deduce a threefold division of justice. For the right order in question may be considered in two ways: either with respect to a definite sort of object, or as an abstract right order, which would prescind from any determined *aliquid rectum*. In the first case, if the matter concerns damages and payments, then it is a question of justice properly so called (which, for Albert, is opposed to the vice of greed). If, on the other hand, one simply considers the notion of right order (prescinding from concrete details and situation), a further twofold distinction is possible. If the right order be considered in its own essence as simply a "right order on the basis of equality," then equality itself may be termed justice. If this abstract right order be taken in relation to some other regulating factor—namely, law—then the justice in question is legal justice.[28]

Thus, the right order proper to legal justice is constituted precisely by its conformity to what the law establishes.[29] For Albert, it belongs to law to "determine and order all that men do in terms of the common weal."[30] Law, then, has as its end the well-being of the social whole.[31] To the extent that law aims at the common good and marshals the activities of citizens to that good, law must be framed in universal terms. But, Albert notes, this universality is of a special kind:

> Essential universality is not certain in human conduct, and so the universality of the law cannot be of this sort. But there is also a universality of occasions, and this is the sort of universality

that applies to human acts; thus, the universality of law is a material universality. But since the occasions of human conduct would be numberless, the skill of giving guidance in them must gather these into some finite collection. For what is infinite cannot be known. For this reason law cannot cover every occasion, but includes them under a general prescription.[32]

Since law cannot enumerate and therefore explicitly apply to all occasions and situations of human conduct in community, this sort of universality is the reason for the deficiency of law as well.[33]

In all of this, Albert shows himself to remain thoroughly the disciple of Aristotle. For Albert asserts that those situations in which positive law is defective in its application by reason of its universal phrasing are precisely the context in which *epieikeia* comes into play.[34] Albert attempts a definition of *epieikeia*, first on etymological grounds:

> "Epieikeia" derives from "epi," which means "above," and from "dicaion," which means "justice." "Epieikeia" means "that which surpasses justice" after a fashion; the force of this word is that epieikeia is "that which is a sort of justice on its own grounds."[35]

As a supplement to this etymological definition, Albert offers a more proper one: *epieikeia* is a "guiding of law in those matters in which law is defective because of its universality."[36] That Albert considers *epieikeia* to be a virtue can be demonstrated on two grounds. In the first place, he adopts Aristotle's characterization of it as a *habitus* without reservation[37] and in his own right calls it a *disposito*.[38] Second, Albert asserts that the act of *epieikeia* comes about *per seipsum* in the one who exercises it.[39] The force of the phrase *per seipsum* is clearly that, when the external guidance afforded by law is lacking, the person possessed of *epieikeia* can rely on some inner resource to act in accord with right order.

In the matter of what is the proper act of the virtue of *epieikeia*, a certain ambiguity enters Albert's account—perhaps a tension between the letter of Aristotle's text itself and Albert's own development upon it. For, on the one hand, he follows Aristotle in deeming the lessening of penalties the characteristic activity of *epieikeia*.[40] On the other hand, however, Albert seems to grant a broader scope to *epieikeia* as he conceives it. In this connection, he remarks that "the man possessed of *epieikeia* acts in accord with right order of himself and supplies the deficiency."[41] That Albert envisages the act of *epieikeia* on a broader scale than simply the diminution of punishments also seems to be supported by the example that he annexes to the description just cited: *epieikeia* involves acting in a manner different than that prescribed by the law that governs goods held in trust, as in the case of a sword held in trust and now demanded by a madman.[42] Here he is not talking about the mitigation of a punishment. Rather, he is pointing out that certain circumstances call for a course of action other than what the letter of the law generally mandates.

If we examine his articulation of the relationship of *epieikeia* to justice and legal justice, our understanding of Albert's conception of *epieikeia* will gain clarity. General legal justice comprises two specific notes: (1) it regulates human conduct in community in accord with the prescriptions of law, and (2) it accomplishes this for the purpose of seeking and promoting the welfare of the community. Legal justice therefore is concerned with both a *quid* and a *propter quid*.[43] Albert's usual practice, however, as we noted, is to consider the material constitution of legal justice the quasi-generality of the matters of its interest.

A question arises, however, as to the status of *epieikeia* as a sort of justice (albeit a surpassing sort). For its concern is neither with the exchange of goods as in the case of special justice (justice in its most proper and concrete sense), nor with the whole of virtuous conduct commanded by law as in the case of legal justice. By what charter then can *epieikeia* be considered as justice?

Albert clearly asserts that *epieikeia* belongs to the genus of justice.[44] The remote reason for his assertion is to be sought in his earlier remarks on the possibility of abstracting the *ratio justitiae* from a link with any specified matter, commercial or legal. Therefore, insofar as this abstract *ratio* is a constituent of *epieikeia*, the latter is entitled to be considered a sort of justice. This account would be flawed, however, without an effort to square the justice of *epieikeia* with legal justice. For if both agree in a common abstract *ratio justitiae*, in what do they differ?[45]

Distinguishing and relating the two requires an argument that develops under four headings. First of all, Albert states that the genus of justice has an analogical (*secundum ambitum*) range. Nevertheless, he immediately switches ground and addresses himself to legal justice as the prime analogate.[46] Legal justice pursues the same objective as law itself: "the sorts of conduct mandated by law and the goal it pursues through such types of conduct as law mandates—namely, the well being of the civil community."[47] On the basis of this twofold criterion, even if legal justice is taken as the prime analogate of justice, the *ratio justitiae* belongs to *epieikeia* as well. For the latter shares the *ratio* of legal justice at least inasmuch as it shares the common good as its objective. Thus, Albert concludes that, although *epieikeia* is not justice in exactly the same way legal justice is (where *both* criteria are satisfied), nevertheless it is justice analogically by reason of its having one of those criteria in common with legal justice.[48] As a corollary Albert proposes that the opposition of legal justice to *epieikeia* is not absolute but relative.[49]

The second front on which Albert's argument moves comes in his reply to an objection about Aristotle's example of the use of the lead ruler in the fashioning of Lesbian moulding. In this connection, he distinguishes between an ideal or essential right order, which must be rigorous and unchanging, and an "existential" right order, which must possess a flexibility sufficient to apply the universal right order to each particular thing to be so ordered.[50] The implication to be drawn here is that *epieikeia* is precisely such an "existentializing" application of the universal norms of law, to which legal justice cleaves in their literal inflexibility.[51]

When he comes to the third front of his argument, Albert moves in another direction and sketches the relationship between *epieikeia* and legal justice in dynamic terms. The central issue is the directing role assigned to *epieikeia* over legal justice. This directing role can be considered in two ways. Generally speaking, certain things are *essentially* directive of others because they possess in a prior and simpler fashion the nature of the thing to be regulated; in this way natural justice is directive of legal justice. There is, however, another directive class; this is directive of others existentially or actually. The directing role of this class consists in fleshing out what the universal nature lacks when it must be applied to particulars. Whatever exercises a directing role of this sort will be more concrete than and posterior to that which is essentially directive, as in the case of *epieikeia*, which then exercises direction over legal justice.[52]

This leads to the fourth point in Albert's exposition of the relationship of *epieikeia* to legal justice. The objection could be raised that if *epieikeia* is directive of the universality of legal justice, then it must itself enjoy a prior universality. This objection affords Albert a final opportunity to clarify the relationship in question. To this end Albert appears to fall back on a principle he had previously stated, namely, that in cases of human interaction in which there is no relevant legal prescription (e.g., a father dealing with a son, a master with a slave, or one with oneself), the justice obtaining is not full-fledged justice, but a justice by similitude.[53] In a comparable situation in which the guidance of law is lacking, that *epieikeia* directs legal justice does not entail that the former enjoy a prior universality over the latter. Rather, the universality of *epieikeia* is only an imitation of the true universality of law that legal justice has for its objective.[54] The universality of legal justice is both a material universality in accord with legal precept and a universality in terms of goal. *Epieikeia* imitates only the latter aspect of universality: the universal purpose to which law addresses itself, the well-being of the civil community.[55]

It seems fair to conclude that Albert's account of *epieikeia* represents an advance over Aristotle's doctrine for two main reasons. First of all, Albert broadens the scope of epieikiac activity to include not only a negative settling for less but also positive activity in promotion of the common good. Second, much of what is obscure and ambiguous in Aristotle's account is clarified by Albert's painstaking attempts to render a thorough and precise account of the relationship between *epieikeia* and legal justice.

AQUINAS'S DOCTRINE OF EPIEIKEIA[56]

Epieikeia and its cognates occur ninety times in the works of Aquinas.[57] Apart from a few instances in which Aquinas merely reproduces the occurrence of the word in a citation from the Latin translation of *Nicomachean Ethics* or the *Politics* (then always in an adjectival form and with the general meaning "virtuous"), his treatment of *epieikeia* is limited to three works: the *Scriptum super Sententias*, the *Sententiae libri Ethicorum*, and the *Summa theologiae II-II*. As the first mentioned work dates from an early period in Aquinas's career and the latter two, which are roughly contemporaneous, date from the period of his mature development, a separate treatment of the first and of the latter two will be instructive.[58] Such a procedure can serve to illuminate the developmental and original aspects of Thomas's doctrine of *epieikeia*.

The *Scriptum super Sententias* is the fruit of Thomas's teaching and research during his four years (1252-1256) as a *baccalaureus sententi-*

arius at Paris. The work was edited and given basically its published form during the months when Aquinas became a *magister regens* (spring 1256); it was certainly completed by the end of 1256. The French theologian J-P Torrell reminds us that Thomas apparently regarded this as a provisional text; in fact, Thomas considered revising it some ten years later for the benefit of the students at the Dominican studium in Rome.[59]

Thomas's exposition suffers from the limitations imposed by the text of Peter Lombard upon which he was required to comment—limitations that seem to affect his treatment of *epieikeia* as well. The first of these limitations derives from the text of the *Sentences* that was the object of exposition. The treatment of virtuous human conduct develops in a somewhat artificial context in the Lombard's discussion of the graces and virtues of Christ. Moreover, Peter Lombard's discussion of the four cardinal virtues (book Three, distinction 33) consists, in the main, of one lengthy quote from Augustine's *De Trinitate*. This quote itself further complicates matters by tending to identify the cardinal virtue of justice with Gospel righteousness.

The second limitation is that Thomas's analysis of the text must proceed by way of an established tradition held to be normative—namely, the *auctoritates*. These are often at variance with one another and even with the object of the text that they are invoked to illuminate. This convention could not, however, be dismissed in the theological enterprise of that time, for it was viewed as a vital link (*continuatio doctrinalis*) with the true meaning (*sententia*) of the text. Rather, the established tradition was to be "reverently exposed," after the fashion of dialectical inquiry, seeking to redefine problems so as to reconcile diverging *auctoritates*. At this early stage in his career, one might argue, Thomas's reverence seems too sedulous and is occasionally a restriction upon any original rethinking of the tradition. One can see the difficulty with this sort of theological procedure in Thomas's discussion of the virtue of justice and its parts (*III Sent*, d. 33, a. 4). There Thomas undertakes a reverential exposition of the conflicting catalogues of the ornaments of justice as proposed by Cicero (q^{ula} 1), Macrobius (q^{ula} 2), and Andronicus of Rhodes (q^{ula} 4) before addressing himself to that proposed by the newcomer Aristotle.

Within the confines imposed by these factors, however, Aquinas's mature theory of the virtues appears in the broad outline of this early account. Since the natural powers are not determined by themselves to produce full and complete good human acts, some determining factor is required; these formative determinations are the *habitus*.[60] Although *habitus* and *virtutes* are broadly identical, properly speaking the latter operates in the sphere of *human* powers: "Human virtue will be that factor which perfects a human power in the direction of a good act and one that will be the best."[61] Such *habitus* are what they are and are distinguished one from another by reference to the distinctive activities flowing from them; moreover, these activities themselves are ultimately distinguished by the distinct objectives at which they aim.[62] Within the ambit of certain sorts of objectives, however, further specifications can be introduced; these relationships between overall and restricted objectives can be formalized on the model of the relationships between parts and wholes. Depending on the model of wholeness employed, a virtue may include either integral, subjective, or potential parts.[63] Finally, those virtues the objectives of which encompass those of more restricted interest and that are more basic to the broader structures of virtuous conduct are titled *principal* and *cardinal* virtues.

Justice is one such virtue. It is defined as a "right order in exchanges with another."[64] Thomas proposes its objective in a comprehensive fashion (embracing both the *formale quod* and the *formale quo* of later terminology): it is the regulation of external conduct to the extent that it bears upon other members of community; the regulation *ad alterum* consists in rendering to that person what is owed to him or her and how much is owed to him or her.[65] This interest in regulating external conduct distinguishes justice from other virtues, as much as justice must attain not merely to the *medium rationis*, but to the *medium rei* as well.[66] The possibility or impossibility of such an attainment to the *medium rei* in rendering to another what is owed him provides Thomas with the grounds on which to divide the virtues allied to justice into those that are subjective parts of justice (i.e., commutative and distributive justice)[67] and those that are only potential parts because they diverge from the model of strict justice ("reddere quod et quantum debitum").[68] Aquinas does not address the question of the integral parts of the virtue of justice. One additional distinction is invoked by Thomas, that of *special* (or particular) justice and *general* justice. The former bears directly upon one's dealings with other persons and designates the cardinal virtue of justice; the latter bears upon those dealings only indirectly and insofar as they are prescribed by law.[69] Thus, for Thomas in the *Scriptum super Sententias*, legal or general justice lies outside the proper ambit of justice itself. It shares with the latter a field of operation, but only *per accidens* and by a direction extrinsically imposed by law. Thomas does not invoke Albert's notion of an abstract *ratio justitiae*, on the basis of which legal justice would be true justice; he seems to consider the link between the *ratio formalis* and the *materia propia* to be impossible to sever.

This view of legal justice should be carefully noted for an accurate reading of his notion of *epieikeia* at this stage of his career, for it forms the basis for his development in the latter. He sets out his doctrine of *epieikeia* in the most concise fashion. Thomas defines *epieikeia* in this way: *epieikeia* is that moral quality[70] which permits its possessor to follow the intention of the law-giver while not adhering to the letter of the law.[71] Legal justice and *epieikeia* have a common field of interest, namely, that specific interest prescribed by the law.[72] They differ, however, because *epieikeia* follows the intention of the lawgiver when faced with matters to which the law does not explicitly address itself.[73] While the intention of the lawgiver provides the basis for a decision of *epieikeia* about affairs regulated by law, legal justice proceeds on the basis of the written form of the law in those instances that it covers.[74] Although this is the main line of Thomas's doctrine of *epieikeia* in the *Scriptum super Sententias*, traces of the archaic view that *epieikeia* is indulgence are inherited from Aristotle; in that instance, *epieikeia* is equated with clemency.[75] Once again, Thomas refuses to sever formal from material aspects as Albert did. Whereas for Albert *epieikeia* shared with legal justice the *intentio legis* but not the *opera legis*, Thomas insists that *epieikeia* concerns the latter as well. Legal justice need attend only to the written terms of the law and not to the intention of the lawgiver—which is characteristic only of *epieikeia*. It is worth noting that, where Albert speaks of an *intentio legis*, Thomas speaks of an *intentio legislatoris*. On the basis of *Scriptum super Sententias* alone, it is difficult to say what, if any, significance this difference might have. What is clear, however, is that Thomas is by no means following Albert in the essentials of his doctrine of *epieikeia*.

Thomas does not attempt to formalize the relationship between *epieikeia* and the cardinal virtue of justice in explicit fashion. As much as *epieikeia* shares a field of interest with legal justice (". . . circa eadem est"), which regards the objective of justice from the perspective of the explicit or putative direction of the lawgiver, it might be inferred that Thomas considered them to have an equivalent relation to the cardinal virtue of justice. Indeed, the excellence that Aristotle seems to accord *epieikeia* over justice simply, Thomas restricts to an excellence over legal justice.[76] Concerning the relation of *epieikeia* to legal justice, Thomas remarks that the former is a sort of annex ("adjungitur") and supplement to legal justice and even presupposes legal justice,[77] at least insofar as legal justice supplies the matter upon which *epieikeia* bears. And, like legal or general justice, *epieikeia* can be viewed as identical with the virtuous conduct of any kind insofar as all virtuous activity incarnates an order that promotes the well-being of humankind.[78]

Epieikeia also bears a special relationship to the quasi-potential part of the virtue of prudence called *gnōmē*; but the precise formulation of that relationship eludes Thomas at this stage of his career. He is merely content with a statement of such a connection.[79] *Gnōmē* is a sort of intellectual flair for making right judgments about the same matters with which *epieikeia* is concerned and under the direction of the latter. Perhaps what we see in this text is a condensed psychological account of the relationship between a certain excellence of practical reason vis-à-vis a particularly cultivated will. For as a part of prudence, *gnōmē* represents a development of the practical reason, whereas *epieikeia* remains a virtuous disposition of the rational appetite.

What is especially surprising, in view of Albert's well-reasoned account, is that Thomas proposes no reason for the deficiency of law in his *Scriptum super Sententias*. One text from this work, however, is often cited as an indication of how Thomas viewed the characteristic activity of *epieikeia*:

> If a person does not observe a regulation in a situation in which it may be believed with probability that the lawgiver would not want to bind him, were he present, such a person is not to be considered a violator of the law.[80]

First of all, the absence of any explicit mention of *epieikeia* in this sentence and in its immediate context should be remarked. Second, the overwhelmingly negative character of the act should be noted. What is at issue is simply an omission or a nonobservance of a precept, not the service of a higher justice. The basis for nonobservance is not an inclination for the true justice of the lawgiver's intention, but merely a probable disposition of his will in this case. Nonobservance of this sort is for purely personal benefit. Last, the result of nonobservance is not the praise of virtue but only escape from the infamy of being a scofflaw. However, a final verdict as to whether this is in fact an account of how *epieikeia* operates in the moral life must be postponed until this text can be compared with similar passages from the *Summa theologiae*.

As to Albert's influence on Thomas's doctrine of *epieikeia* in the *Scriptum super Sententias*, our conclusions must be negative. On crucial issues Thomas's doctrine diverges from Albert's. Moreover, Thomas's analysis seems sketchy by comparison with Albert's more thorough and sophisticated one. While this latter deficiency may be partially explained by the nature of the task at hand in exposing the *Sentences*, the divergences in explicit doctrine cannot be so explained. Nonetheless, we know that, while in Cologne, Thomas in all likelihood followed Albert's lectures on the *Nicomachean Ethics*.

Because of its greater development and completeness, the discussion of *epieikeia* in the works of Thomas's maturity, the *Sententia libri Ethicorum* and especially the *Summa theologiae*, proves more satisfying. Nevertheless, these later accounts are by no means without their own difficulties. Chief among these is the difference between the tasks that Thomas sets himself in each of the two works. In the *Summa* Thomas was not fettered by a prescribed organizational structure nor by the topics of *auctoritates*; rather, the themes and organization of the *Summa* were wholly of his own choosing and shaping. As his principal creative work, the *Summa* focuses upon the very intelligibility of the matter itself, its inner logic. In his commentaries upon Aristotle, by contrast, creativity was at least partially subordinated to the objective at hand: the exposition of the text itself in its own right. Although Thomas does not hesitate to register a criticism when Aristotle's doctrine seems susceptible of an interpretation offensive to Christian faith, his principal concern was that the text itself be allowed to speak interpretatively. So devout was this concern that it left unaltered the Philosopher's doctrinal divergences from Thomas's personal positions in the *Summa*. We can expect, therefore, that the *Summa* will provide a fuller account of Thomas' precise position on the nature of *epieikeia*.[81]

For Aquinas, all law is an ordination of practical reason[82] that aims at promoting the good of a community.[83] It promotes that good by being a rule and measure of conduct, by which members of the community are induced to act or restrained from acting.[84] Human positive law must be grounded in the law of nature insofar as the latter is illuminated in human reason;[85] but this ground provides only certain basic directions and general principles according to which particular legislative determinations must be made.[86]

Human actions, of which law is intended to be the rule and measure, have this peculiarity about them: they "are composed of contingent particulars and are numberless in their diversity."[87] Although human intelligence in its speculative enterprise can frame true and certain universal propositions about states of affairs governed by necessity,[88] such is not the case with matters of human conduct—and this for three reasons. First of all, human acts, as they are posited in the concrete, are characterized not by necessity but by contingency rooted in freedom.[89] Second, to this contingency corresponds a diminished universality, one that is confined to what occurs in the ordinary course and for the most part.[90] Third, because human acts will be as diverse as the concrete elements that are ingredient in them, human intelligence cannot embrace the infinity of these elements and of the acts thus determined.[91] From this Thomas concludes that "because the stuff of human activity is indeterminate, it follows that its norm, namely, law, must be indeterminate in the sense that it is not absolutely rigid."[92]

In this context (i.e., when the legislative universal fails to take some particular case into account) the virtue[93] of *epieikeia* has its distinctive contribution to make.

> If the law were to be applied to certain cases it would frustrate the equality of justice (*æqualitatem justitiae*) and be injurious to the common good, which is what the law has in view. . . . In cases of this sort, observing the law is wrong, and setting the letter of the law aside and following the dictates of justice and the common good are right.[94]

This provides a heuristic definition of *epieikeia* as Thomas conceives of it. As a species of justice (to be determined below), it has as its generic objective the equality (*æqualitas*) to which justice is directed.[95] More specifically, it is directed toward the attainment of the common good in those cases in which the common good would be impeded by the letter of the law. Its generic quest for the equality of justice is not, therefore, directed to some private benefit. Nor does *epieikeia* consist in passing judgment on a given law (such would be the province of a duly authorized judge); rather it operates on the basis of an assessment about the case at hand *sub ratione boni communis*.[96] Nor does its activity consist in interpreting the law; for interpretation of law belongs to the author of law and is needed only when there is reason for some doubt as to its author's intention. *Epieikeia*, on the contrary, operates on the basis of clear and certain practical conviction of the truly (*simpliciter*) just in a given case.[97]

A proper definition of a *habitus* should include some reference to its proper objective. Here the exegesis of Thomas runs up against an ambiguity. As a distinct virtue,[98] *epieikeia* should have a distinct objective at which it aims. In his *Sententia libri Ethicorum*, however, Thomas denies that *epieikeia* is a *habitus* distinct from legal justice and with its own proper object.[99] This apparent ambiguity may be resolved, however, by recalling our earlier remarks about the two different projects Thomas undertook in the *Summa* and in his Aristotelian commentaries. In this instance, Thomas merely restricts himself to the terms of Aristotle's text.[100]

Perhaps the best approach to determining the object of *epieikeia* consists in comparing it with legal justice and its object. For Thomas, general[101] or legal justice has for its objective the achievement of a "harmony with the law which directs all virtuous conduct to the common good."[102] It exists principally in the lawgiver, but secondarily and administratively in his subjects.[103] Thus, both *epieikeia* and legal justice regard the common good. If legal justice be strictly construed as the promotion of the common good *sub ratione legis scriptae*, however, the objective of *epieikeia* is viewed as distinct because *epieikeia* seeks to promote the common good *sub ratione intentionis legislatoris* when the letter of the law does not meet the exigencies of justice in a particular case.[104] This is certainly what Thomas means by his notice in the *Sententia libri Ethicorum* that "what is equitable [the object of *epieikeia*] is better than what is legally just but is contained under the naturally just."[105] If legal justice be broadly defined so as to include the promotion of the common good by the observance of the law, not merely in its letter, but also in the intention of the lawgiver, then *epieikeia* coincides with legal justice and is the same.[106] When legal justice is strictly defined, it agrees materially with *epieikeia*, i.e., as guiding conduct toward the common good; however, the precise formality that engages its interest differs. When legal justice is broadly defined, on the other hand, the virtue remains materially *and* formally the same as *epieikeia*.

A comparison with Albert's view would seem to be worthwhile at this juncture. The broad definition of legal justice that Thomas has in mind would seem to be similar to Albert's view. The admission of such a broad definition represents an advance upon Thomas's position in the *Scriptum super Sententias*. Nevertheless, Thomas's account seems more sophisticated than Albert's. For the latter, the common good forms a part of the *ratio formalis* of legal justice, a part that is shared by *epieikeia* as well; *epieikeia* is then formally distinct from legal justice on the basis of another part of the formal constitution of legal justice. Thomas, on the contrary, perceives that, on the basis of a broad definition of legal justice, *epieikeia* and legal justice cannot differ on the basis of a common formality. In proposing a strict definition of legal justice, Thomas is able to coordinate as material and formal elements what Albert merely juxtaposed as equally formal elements, namely, the end that legal justice seeks to achieve (the common good) and the specific basis on which it seeks to achieve this (the letter of the law).

As a species of justice (of what sort remains to be seen), *epieikeia* must have its seat in the intellectual appetite or will. There it is a certain keenness for and readiness of action in matters touching the common good in defect of the written law; *epieikeia* inwardly shapes the will to elicit a certain sort of just response. That response flows from *gnōmē* or a right assessment of "matters of exception to the law";[107] but that the just be *accomplished* remains the concern of the will "sensitized" by *epieikeia*. The synergy of *gnōmē* and *epieikeia* results in a practical certitude about the right order of a course of action in promoting the common good. In this way, the deficiency of written law as a guide to concrete action and as conducive to virtue does not leave the virtuous person adrift and rudderless; rather, operating out of the inner resources of a certain sort of cultivated character, the virtuous person achieves the concrete good of the community in some specific case where the law falls short. As one contemporary commentator summarizes,

> the need for a special virtue of epieikeia is the need to supplement the willingness to honor the written law [i.e., legal justice], by a willingness to act in the exceptional case for the good to which the law itself is matched. The exception, however, implies no exemption from the ordinary dynamics of the virtuous act. By pointing to a personal responsibility to judge the individual situation (art. 1ad2&3) and then to act for the intention of the law, for a higher form of justice, the meaning of epieikeia thereby points to the fact that in every case the just person acts intending the good, with the law as an interiorly accepted rule of action towards the good intended by the law and the regulator.[108]

An individual's capacity to act in this way exemplifies a quality of character that is marked by justice in the most profound sense of the term. Origen grasps this conception of *epieikeia* when he explains that the generosity of the Virgin Mary on the occasion of her visit to Elizabeth reveals that Mary was "full of delicacy (ἐπιεικής) toward every being."[109] Later theology will describe the embodiment of New Testament rectitude in terms of the grace of the immaculate conception.

Thomas's understanding of the virtue of *epieikeia* can be brought into clearer focus if we examine the relationships he draws between *epieikeia* and particular justice on the one hand, and general or legal justice on the other. At first sight, the precise relationship he intends is obscured for two reasons. The first of these is a purely material and organizational factor—namely, that Thomas treats *epieikeia* at the end of his catalogue of the *potential* parts of justice[110] and, therefore, would appear to include *epieikeia* among these. But material arrangement alone cannot be taken as finally determinative of Thomas's formal doctrine. Of greater perplexity is the apparent discrepancy between his doctrine in Summa theologiae II-II.80.1ad5 (where he states that "epieikeia is annexed, not to particular but to legal justice")[111] and in II-II.120.2ad1 (where Thomas maintains that "epieikeia is a part not of legal justice but of justice in its general acceptation, and is condivided with legal justice, as exceeding it").[112] This discrepancy will yield to solution, however, if one attends to the precise meaning of the relevant terms as they are used in each text. In the first text, the overall genus of justice is being divided into *two* species on the basis of two distinct *ordines ad alterum*. In one of these *ordines* the order is the social whole, the community and its interests (legal justice). In the other case, the other is the individual (particular justice), either in exchanges with other persons (commutative justice) or as the recipient of a share of the goods of a society (distributive justice). Moreover, in this context, legal justice is being taken, in point of contrast with particular justice, in that broad signification that we remarked previously: a sort of comprehensive concern for the common good in keeping with the expressed prescriptions or the intention of the lawgiver.

In the second text (II-II.120.2), the division of justice proceeds along different lines. The *ratio justitae* consists in the right regulation of external conduct as bearing upon some other so that what is due him or her may be rendered.[113] The other to whom the *debitum* must be rendered may be: (1) the social whole and its well-being, served principally by the lawgiver and instrumentally by those subject to his laws; (2) another individual or corporate person; or (3) authorized distributors and recipients in the apportioning of the resources and benefits of a community. According to this second mode of division, each of these three is directly related to the overall genus of justice as a species and subjective part, as a part "of which the whole is predicated essentially" while each is "less the whole."[114] The *ratio justitiae* (i.e., the right regulation of external conduct in favor of that which is due to some other) is predicated univocally and is equally verified in each of the three instances and exhausted in no one of them. On the basis of this division, and with legal justice being taken in a strict sense (as bearing only upon the letter of the law), that species of justice which has as its objective the right regulation of external conduct to secure and promote the well-being of the community is fittingly named from its superior member, *epieikeia*. In other terms, as much as *epieikeia* remains directive of legal justice in the strict sense, one can principally predicate the *ratio justitiae* of it. Justice, therefore, is divided equally among commutative, distributive, and social justice. This last species of justice takes its name from its principal and directive component, *epieikeia*.

It is obvious that this coordination of *epieikeia* with particular and with legal justice is superior to Thomas's attempts in the *Scriptum super Sententias*. In addition, Thomas's coordination on the basis of a type of whole-part analogy surpasses Albert's attempts at relating these different dimensions of justice. Although this model would have been familiar to Albert (for example, it figured in early thirteenth-century accounts of the *articuli fidei*), he himself did not choose to employ it—to the consequent detriment of the precision of his coordination of *epieikeia* with other species of justice. Nevertheless, it is precisely Albert's insight that the *ratio justitiae* could be abstracted from a connection with one certain type of matter that seems to have provided Thomas with the key to his coordination of the members of the genus of justice. Not that Thomas relaxes his insistence from the *Scriptum super Sententias* that the formal aspect must always be connected with a material aspect; for him the purely abstract *ratio justitiae* that Albert proposes is unsatisfactory. The *ratio justitiae* must always be connected with some external conduct in relation to an other. Where he takes a page from Albert's book is in his view that the *ratio justitiae* need not be confined to one sort of other, namely, the individual other of particular justice. This development represents a significant advance upon and corrective of his view in the *Scriptum super Sententias*, where the restriction of the *ratio justitiae* to one sort of matter resulted in his placing legal justice (and therefore *epieikeia*) outside of the genus of justice properly so called.

To round off our study of Thomas Aquinas's doctrine of *epieikeia* we should consider two texts that could be cited as objections to our claim that the preceding considerations represent Aquinas's position. These texts have considerably exercised the speculative and synthetic genius of commentators down through the centuries after Thomas. The first of these texts is *Summa theologiae* II-II.147.4,[115] which should be compared for this purpose with the corresponding text from the *Scriptum super Sententias* we cited previously. Once again the issue is the obligation to observe positive (ecclesiastical) law in the matter of fasts. The terms in which the question is posed and answered should be carefully noted. The question concerns an omission or nonobservance of a precept; it is not a question of the service of a justice more intense and compelling than that which the letter of the law prescribes. The reason adduced for the nonobservance of the precept is its difficulty, some obstacle that would render its observance onerous. Thus, it is not a question of such observance going counter to that equality of justice which is the specific aim of the lawgiver. Because the equality of justice with which the lawgiver is concerned is the good of the community, whereas the motive for nonobservance of a precept such as that mentioned here is merely private benefit, the good of the community can in no direct way be secured or enhanced by indulgence shown an individual. Moreover, this text seems to envision a dynamic of operation different from that of *epieikeia*. For it asserts that, when cases of this sort arise and when the difficulty of observance in the face of some obstacle is manifest, then a subject may omit observance of the law, as it were, *per modum actus*. But in all cases where a doubt arises concerning the obligation of observance vis-à-vis some obstacle, recourse must be had to a legitimate superior for an authoritative interpretation and/or dispensation of the obligation. Although this situation could conceivably be one in which *epieikeia could* function in its distinctive mode, what is clear is that this text is not in fact describing *epieikeia* in operation. For *epieikeia* regards the service of the common good and has as its act not an omission but a fulfillment of the justice that is the intention of all law, when this or that prescription of the law may be deficient to deal with a certain situation. Although *epieikeia* may *per accidens* involve an omission (not returning a pledged sword to a maniac), it is formally a positive act realizing social justice in the concrete.

The second text that must be considered is I-II.96.6.[116] Here the issue is more difficult to decide because the terms of explanation and the examples that it employs are almost identical with those of II-II.120.1 and of *Sententia libri Ethicorum* V, 16. Moreover, this text from the *prima secundae* precedes II-II.120.1. The situation envisioned in it is a deficiency of law by reason of its generality. Because of this deficiency it can happen that the observance of the written law would be detrimental to the common good, rather than being in furtherance of that good as law should be. The text envisages action, which, although in breach of the letter of the law, complies with the intention of the lawgiver to promote the well-being of the social whole. Up to this point, the situation clearly corresponds exactly to that in which *epieikeia* would function. What gives pause, however, is Thomas's insistence in this text on recourse to the lawgiver for an interpretation of his intention and/or dispensation from the prescription of the written law in *all* such cases—saving those of strict emergency and dire necessity. As we saw, when he is treating the virtue of *epieikeia* Thomas makes no mention of such recourse; nor is there any indication that *epieikeia* was restricted to operating only in cases of strict emergency and dire necessity. The similarity of the moral situations being considered and indeed the verbal similarities between I-II.96.6 and II-II.120.1 have led many commentators to include such recourse to legitimate authority among the necessary constituents of the virtue of *epieikeia*. The alternatives would be at best a hesitation in Thomas's moral theory, at worst a flat contradiction.

If we attend to the architecture of Thomas's account of right human activity, however, a way out of this impasse opens. In the earlier article, Thomas is discussing law under the aspect of an *external* principle of human conduct; in the *secunda secundae*, by contrast, he turns to a consideration of the *internal* principles of right human conduct, the virtues. But a formal reason for this discrepancy can be adduced as well. For Thomas, law has as its proper effect the leading of its subjects to virtue.[117] Law would be unnecessary if all members of the commonwealth were virtuous.[118]

But, since some members lack such cultivation of character and others are even *de facto* vicious, law is necessary for the well-being of the community.[119] The earlier article (I-II.96.6) is to be interpreted in terms of this general necessity for the authority of law; thus, it does not envisage the act of a virtuous person, but rather precisely the lack of virtue. When an internal attunement to the common good as intended by the legislator is lacking, then there is need of some external principle of action in those situations where the written law is defective, i.e., an authoritative interpretation by the lawgiver to whom one must have recourse. The article on *epieikeia* moves in a different context; the same situation of the defect of written law is considered, but here it is the virtuous person who confronts this situation. Such a person is well supplied with the inner resources with which to act rightly even without the guidance afforded by the letter of the law. For the common good, of which law is the instrument, is what the virtuous person lives and breathes, so to speak. It is something interior to him or her by reason of a certain adaptation of the will, a certain proportioning of the intellectual appetite, to the rights of the community. Furthermore, there is no room for doubt when one is discussing the operation of *epieikeia*. The epieikeiac person proceeds on the basis of both a practical certitude in the reason about the just thing to be done and an affective gravity or inclination to effecting that just thing by his conduct. Thus, whereas Thomas's earlier account requires recourse to the lawgiver because the subject has no feel for the common good as the legislator intends it,[120] his specific discussion of *epieikeia* does not enumerate such recourse among the acts ingredient in *epieikeia* because such recourse would be superfluous. The person possessed of the virtue of *epieikeia* has a certain sense of the just thing to be done—without requiring further information or external guidance.

*   *   *

In a recent review of *The Abuse of Casuistry. A History of Moral Reasoning*,[121] the Jesuit moralist William Spohn assigns a favorable context to the heretofore opprobrium-laden term casuistry.[122] "The venerable tradition of casuistry," Spohn writes, "locates moral meaning in particular cases of action with their specific intentions and circumstances rather than in universal theory or abstract principles."[123] Spohn raises the possibility that some form of casuistry "where the typical cases ground the principles" may offer a way out of the impasse created by the debate between proponents of absolute moral norms and proportionalists concerning the appropriate means to realize the splendor of moral truth. This appeal to the particular context of action as a way of determining the moral good in concrete circumstances places both great significance and high expectations on the role that paradigmatic examples of good and evil serve toward providing reliable moral direction. In other quarters, certain authors even distinguish virtue-centered ethics and its emphasis on defining qualities of character from those systems of ethics that center on the *doing* of the good deed.[124]

In the view of Aquinas, "the intention of every agent acting in accord with virtue is that he or she follow the rule of reason."[125] This rule of reason is measured ultimately by the eternal law, the supreme pattern for all human conduct that represents how God knows the world to be. As a virtue of character, *epieikeia* embodies the inner principles of good conduct with respect to general or social justice. The one, then, who possesses this virtue is stably inclined to effecting the just thing by his or her personal conduct. In matters of such importance, no allowance should be made either for a breach between virtuous *habitus* and concrete action or for the dislocation of a moral principle from its application in concrete cases.

The virtue of *epieikeia*, whether it operates in exceptional cases or in the ordinary course of pursuing the good human life, ensures that every man and woman can accomplish the counsels of evangelical goodness and generosity. The Christian who acts in this way, namely, always seeking more perfectly to fulfill the *regula rationis divinae*, displays a special filial attitude toward God. The epieikeiac person possesses true piety, one that manifests itself in a heightened reverence for accomplishing the Father's plan of salvation. This grace comes only from Christ, who came down from heaven not to do his own will, but the will of the Father who sent him.[126] As a certain participation in Christ's once and for all perfect accomplishment of the Father's justice, the Christian believer who possesses the virtue of *epieikeia* likewise displays the meekness of those whom the Lord promises will inherit the earth.[127] For Thomas Aquinas then, the virtue of *epieikeia* aims at the perfection of evangelical justice and can never provide a casuistic excuse for compromising or adapting what remains the naturally just.

NOTES

1. For one classical study, see Edouard Hamel, S. J., "L'usage de l'epikie," *Studia Moralia* 3 (1965): 48–81. Some revisionist thinkers have appealed to *epieikeia*. For example, see Josef Fuchs, "'Epikeia' circa legem moralem naturalem?" *Periodica* 69 (1980): 251–70. More recently, in a review of Charles Yeats, ed., *Veritatis splendor—a response* (Canterbury: Canterbury

Press, 1994), Bernhard Häring refers to *epieikeia* in the course of commenting on the strongly negative reaction by Anglican bishop Alan Smithson to the encyclical's teaching on intrinsically evil acts. Häring remarks: "Here the Anglicans have raised a major objection, not only for Anglicans but also for Orthodox with their emphasis on *oikonomía* which surpasses even the traditional Anglican and Catholic stress on the virtue of *epikeía*. Where *epikeía* concerns cases which can be judged as not intended to be included under the law—not only human law but also natural law—*oikonomía* involves the whole household of the Church with the purpose of honouring God as the all-compassionate householder whose love heals" (*The Tablet* vol. 248, 17 September 1994: 1166–7). But Häring unfortunately does not elaborate on the connection that he sees between these two very diverse theological concepts.

2. *Nicomachean Ethics* Bk 5, chap. 10 (1137b29–32) as cited in Joseph Dunne, *Back to the Rough Ground: 'Phronesis' and 'Techne' in Modern Philosophy and in Aristotle* (Notre Dame, Ind.: University of Notre Dame Press, 1993), p. 283.

3. For a representative treatment of the issues that this framework evoked, see the thesis written at The Catholic University of America in the late 1940s by Lawrence Joseph Riley, "The history, nature and use of epikeia in moral theology," *Studies in Sacred Theology*, 2nd series, no. 17 (Washington, D.C.: Catholic University of America Press, 1948). For a more recent evaluation of the place of *epieikeia* in canon law, see Eugenio Corecco, "Valore dell'atto 'contra legem,'" *Jus Canonicum* 15 (1975): 237–57. Philosophers of law continue to recognize that existing legal rules do not always fit cases that come before the law. In his essay, "Problems of the Philosophy of Law," H. L. A. Hart discusses the different arguments that legal theorists advance for justifying the application of indeterminate rules to clear cases, observing that "very often the decision to include a new case in the scope of a rule or to exclude it is guided by the sense that this is the 'natural' continuation of a line of decisions or carries out the 'spirit' of a rule." For a complete discussion, see his *Essays in Jurisprudence and Philosophy* (Oxford: Clarendon Press, 1983), pp. 88–119, at 106–9.

4. See his article on "Épikie" in *Dictionnaire de théologie Catholique*, vol. 5.1: 358–61.

5. "Epikeia (ἐπιείκεια = aequitas) est benigna et aequa interpretatio non ipsius legis, sed mentis legislatoris." See his *Manuale theologiae moralis secundum principia S. Thomae Aquinatis*, vol. 1 (Freiburg-im-B.: Herder & Co., 1931), p. 154. In his treatment of the virtue of justice, the author returns to the notion and offers a similar definition: "Epikeia seu aequitas est congrua quaedam moderatio stricti juris" (See *Manuale theologiae moralis* vol. II, p. 480). Although *epiky* remains the only recognized, albeit obsolete, English equivalent for the Greek ἐπιείκεια, we shall use the more familiar *epieikeia*.

6. Wis 12:18.
7. IIMac 2:22; 10:4.
8. Ps 86:5; Bar 2:27; Dan 3:42.
9. See Phil 4:5.
10. (Fribourg-Paris: Éditions universitaires-du Cerf, 1991), pp. 544–8.

11. For example, see fragment #427 of Sophocles and fragment #1030 of Euripides as cited in Rene Antoine Gauthier & Jean Yves Jolif, *L'Ethique à Nicomaque. Introduction, Traduction et Commentaire*, tome II, 1ere partie (Paris: Editions Béatrice-Nauwelaerts, 1959), p. 432. For additional information on the classical meaning of *epieikeia*, see Francesco D'Agostino, *Epieikeia: il tema dell'equita nell'antichita greca* (Milan: A. Giuffre, 1973).

12. For example, see the texts in *Laws* Bk 9, 875; Bk 6, 757.

13. *Nicomachean Ethics* Bk 10, chap. 5 (1175b24); *Rhetoric* Bk 1, chap. 15 (1376a29); *Politics* Bk 2, chap. 7 (1267b5); Bk 5, chap. 9 (1309b8).

14. *Nicomachean Ethics* Bk 1, chap. 13 (1102a10); Bk 9, chap. 8 (1168a33); *Rhetoric* Bk 2, chap. 1 (1378a13).

15. *On Virtues and Vices* 8, 3 (1251b34).

16. *Rhetoric* Bk 1, chap. 13 (1374a26).

17. *Rhetoric* Bk 1, chap. 15 (1375a27).

18. *Magna Moralia* Bk 2, chap. 1 (1198b24ff.).

19. 1137b23ff.

20. *Nicomachean Ethics* Bk 6, chap. 11 (1143a19ff.).

21. For an account of the introduction of Aristotle's ethical writings into the West, see F. Van Steenberghen, *La Philosophie au XIIIe siecle* (Paris: Béatrice-Nauwelaerts, 1966), pp. 81–100, 100–142; see also R. A. Gauthier, "Praefatio" in *Ethica Nicomachea*, L. Minio-Paluello ed., *Aristoteles Latinus* 26, 1 (Leiden: E. J. Brill, 1974).

22. An impression of the reverence in which Cicero and Seneca were held may be gained from the Prologue of the *Moralium dogma philosophorum*: ". . . solo animi augurio primum illum esse latinae eloquentiae auctorem, Tullum, mihi innotuit; post quem ille moralitatis eruditor elegantissimus Seneca cum quibusdam aliis . . . se agebat" (*PL* 171: 1007A). On the subject of the influence of Cicero and Seneca in this period, see G. Influence, A. Brunet, and P. Tremblay, *La renaissance du XIIe siècle. Les écoles et l'enseignement* (Paris, 1933), pp. 46, 68, and especially pp. 147 and 155f.

23. We can isolate ten major moments in the process: (1) In the period from 1160 to 1200, an anonymous translation from the Greek of books Two and Three of Aristotle's *Nicomachean Ethics*, which came to be known as the *Ethica Vetus*, made its appearance. (2) At some time prior to 1210 (in the judgment of M. Grabmann, *I divieti ecclesiastici di Aristotele sotto Innocenzo III e Gregorio IX* [Rome, 1941], pp. 8f.), this text was supplemented by a rendering of Book One of the same work, which came to be known as the *Ethica Nova*. (3) These works quickly became objects of academic exposition at the nascent University of Paris. In August 1215, Cardinal Robert Courçon, who in his capacity as papal legate had been charged with a reorganization of the Paris curriculum, introduced the following provision into the University Statutes: "Non legant in festivis diebus nisi philosophos et rhetoricas, et quadruvalia, et barbarismum, et *ethicam* . . . ." (4) There is evidence that the *Ethica Vetus* and the *Ethica Nova* were soon supplemented by a partial translation of books Seven and Eight of the *Nicomachean Ethics* from the Greek by an anonymous translator. This partial translation is represented by Ms. Borghese 108 in the Vatican Library (see A. Pelzer, "Les Versions latines de ouvrages de Morale

conserves sous le nom d'Aristote en usage au XIIIe siècle," *Revue neo-scolastique de philosophie* 23 (1921): 329–35. (5) The period before 1240 also witnessed an endeavor to translate books Two through Nine (apart from the *Ethica Vetus* version). Fragments of this translation have been discovered in Ms. Hofer Typ233H at Harvard. On this basis it may be inferred that the *Nicomachean Ethics* was substantially available prior to the comprehensive project of the English bishop Robert Grosseteste (c.1175–1253). However, the rarity of manuscript evidence appears to support the view that this pre-Grosseteste version did not enjoy a wide currency. (6) To varying dates within the period from 1200 to 1240 belong the three commentaries on the *Nicomachean Ethics* (the first in the Latin West) which Dom Odo Lottin has brought to light (see his "Psychologie et morale a la Faculté des Arts de Paris aux approches de 1250," in *Problèmes de Psychologie*, tome 1, *Psychologie et Morale aux XIIe et XIIIe siècles* [Louvain, 1942], pp. 505f). The first of these is confined to the *Ethica Vetus* and probably dates from early in the period in question. While the second is similarly limited to the text of the *Ethica Vetus*, its citations from Averroes support a date after 1230, when Averroes's commentaries had been translated and had begun to be disseminated. The third of these commentaries includes the *Ethica Nova* in its scope and is probably roughly contemporary with the second. (7) The progress of the *Nicomachean Ethics* as a text for academic study during the period from 1230 to 1240 is testified to by Grabmann's discovery of Barcelona's manuscript (Ripoll 109), which is a sort of clew for the arts comprehensive examination at Paris composed by an anonymous (but compassionate) professor. Five columns of 242 lines are devoted to required examination material drawn from both the *Ethica Vetus* and the *Ethica Nova*, compared to much briefer space devoted to material from the *Physics* and the *Metaphysics* (the teaching of which was still officially interdicted at Paris). (8) The first complete translation of the *Nicomachean Ethics* is that produced from the Arabic by Herman the German at Toledo in 1240. To his efforts as well is owed a translation of Averroes's Middle (really a paraphrase) Commentary on the *Ethics*. Herman completed his translation in June 1240. (9) The first complete translation of the *Nicomachean Ethics* from the Greek was produced during the years from 1240 to 1243 by Robert Grosseteste. With some emendations from earlier versions, Grosseteste's translation prevailed as the vehicle by which the *Nicomachean Ethics* became known, was studied, and was commented upon before the sixteenth-century Humanist revival. (10) The other possible source from which the Latin West might have learned of Aristotle's notion of *epieikeia*, namely the *Magna Moralia*, was a latecomer. It was translated in 1258 by Bartholomew of Messina under the command and during the reign of Manfred of Sicily.

24. The progress of the knowledge of the *Nicomachean Ethics* after this date has been traced in a limited way by O. Lottin; see his "Saint Albert le Grand et l'Ethique a Nicomaque" in *Psychologie et Morale aux XIIe et XIIIe siècles*, tome 6 (Gembloux: J. Duculot, 1960), pp. 315–31.

25. There is a separate tributary to the channel of the development of the notion of *epieikeia* by the theologians of the medieval period. It flows from the discussion of *aequitas* by the medieval canonists. The latter, with Roman law as their operational model, conceive of *aequitas* after the fashion of a principle of jurisprudence rather than as a virtue as in the case of *epieikeia*. For a discussion of canonical equity, see Ladislas Orsy, S. J., "The Interpretation of Laws: New Variations on an Old Theme." In *The Art of Interpretation. Selected Studies on the Interpretation of Canon Law* (Washington, D.C.: Canon Law Society of America, 1982), especially pp. 61–63 and Pier Giovanni Caron, *"Aequitas" romana, "misericordia" patristica ed "epicheia" aristotelica nella dottrina dell'"aequitas" canonica (dalle origini al rinascimento)* (Milan: A. Giuffre, 1971).

26. For the dating of this work, see W. Kübel, *Alberti Magni Super Ethica Commentum et Quaestiones* in *Alberti Magni Opera Omnia*, tome 14, pars 1 (Munster: Aschendorff, 1968–1972), especially "Prolegomena," p. VI. Unless otherwise noted, all citations will be from this edition of Albert's commentary on the *Nicomachean Ethics* (hereafter *Super Eth.*). Citations will be according to following format: book no., lecture no., sectional no., page and marginal line nos. from Kubel's edition.

27. *Super Eth.* V, ii, #367 (p. 311, ll. 73–75).

28. ". . . ista rectitudo potest considerari dupliciter: aut secundum quod est determinata ad materiam, aut secundum quod est abstracta. Si autem secundum quod est determinata ad materiam damni et lucri, sic est iustitia proprie dicta, cui opponitur avaritia. Si autem secundum quod est abstracta, hoc dupliciter: vel considerabitur ipsa essentia rectitudinis secundum se, quae est aequalitas, et sic erit secundus modus, secundum quem aliquis iustus dicitur aequalis et iniustus inaequalis; aut secundum respectum ad aliud, secundum quod est regulans, quod est lex, et sic erit iustitia legalis" (*Super Eth.* V, ii, #367 [p. 311, ll. 75–86]). Albert admits one exception to this simple identification of general justice (as a right ordering of inferior powers) with legal justice. For he notes that in this matter of general justice "the moderns speak more subtly"—and, one might add, more theologically. Because it effects in us a right order in which the lower powers are made subject to reason and reason to God, that justice whereby sinners are justified also can be termed general justice (See *Super Eth.* V, ii, #376 [p. 320, ll. 11–13]). But this general theological justice is more properly a state than a *habitus* and is therefore not a virtue. Moreover, although right order belongs to both as a *ratio formalis*, they differ because the standards against which right order is measured are different in each instance. General justice, as the theologians understand it, is measured against the divine exemplar of justice; the general justice of which the ancients speak as philosophers is measured by arithmetical and geometrical ratios. (See *Super Eth.* V, ii, #376 [p. 320, ll. 17–26]. For a parallel instance in which Albert considers general justice to be twofold, see H. Kuhle, C. Feckes, B. Geyer, and W. Kubel, eds., *Alberti Magni De Bono* in *Alberti Magni Opera Omnia*, tome 28 [Munster: Aschendorff, 1951]: Tractatus V, Quaestio IV, art. 2, #567 [p. 301, ll. 21–41]).

29. Albert supplements this definition with another, more formal one, including both the proper matter and the *ratio formalis* of the virtue of justice. As its proper matter justice deals with the communication or distribution of goods on the basis of either arithmetical or geometrical ratios; goods of this sort would be such as those involved in commercial exchanges. The formal

aspect of justice consists in a *right order* in communicating such goods according to arithmetical or geometrical ratios: "... iusta autem sunt bona, quae in communitatem deducuntur secundum proportionem geometricam vel arithmeticam communicata vel distributa, huiusmodi bona, quae scilicet veniunt in emptiones et venditiones, erunt materia propria iustitae. Forma autem ipsius erit rectitudo communicando ad alterum secundum proportionem geometricam vel arithmeticam" (*Super Eth.* V. iii, #375 [p. 319, ll. 15–19]). The distinction of the material and formal aspects of justice leads to a further distinction of the virtue of justice itself. When the formal aspect of justice is linked with the proper matter of justice, one has special justice or justice properly so called. If the formal aspect be considered apart from its determined proper matter, it can be taken as simply a sort of universal right order of all powers inferior to itself, so as to be extended to all the acts of the other virtues to the extent that they are referred to a social life. In this case, the justice in question is legal justice, which regulates the acts of the virtuous man in conformity with the law. Legal justice is special as much as it shares the *ratio formalis* of justice; it is general in regard to its subject matter (See *Super Eth.* V, iii, #375 [p. 319, ll. 22–37]).

30. *Super Eth.* V, ii, #373 (p. 316, ll. 42–44).
31. *Super Eth.* V, xv, #447 (p. 380, ll. 12–15).
32. *Super Eth.* V, xv, #448 (p. 380, l. 80, p. 381, l. 5).
33. "Et ideo non potuit esse, quod lex prosequeretur omnes casus, sed quantum fieri potuit, sub universali edicto eos conclusit; tamen propter multos varios eventus non potuit esse, quod illud applicaretur ad omnes" (*Super Eth.* V, xv, #448 [p. 381, ll. 3–7]) Cf. *Super Eth.* V, xv, #446 (p. 379, ll. 6–7).
34. "... sed ubi lex deficit in particularibus casibus, quae universaliter promulgata est ad plura respiciens ... epieikes quis operatur rectum per seipsum et supplet defectum legis ..." (*Super Eth.* V, xv, #446 [p. 379, ll. 14–17]).
35. See *Super Eth.* V, xv, #446 (p. 379, ll. 10–12).
36. "Et ideo haec est diffinitio et natura epieikes, ut sit directio legis in illis in quibus lex deficit propter universale" (*Super Eth.* V, xv, #450 [p. 383, ll. 25–26]).
37. See *Super Eth.* V, xv, #450 (p. 383, ll. 70–71).
38. See *Super Eth.* V, xv, #450 (p. 382, ll. 1–3).
39. See *supra* note 28; see *infra* note 35.
40. "Dicendum, quod epeikes dicitur minorativus, inquantum poenas positas a lege mitigat et minuit, secundum quod sibi videtur expedire ad finem legis" (*Super Eth.* V, xv,., #449 [p. 381, ll. 48–51]).
41. *Super Eth.* V, xv, #446 (p. 379, ll. 16–17).
42. "... epieikes quis operatur rectum per seipsum et supplet defectum legis, ut lex praecipit pignus esse reddendum; si ergo aliquis impignoravit gladium et efficiatur furiosus et repetat gladium reportans debitum, epieikastos non reddet sibi, providens, ne illo gladio aliquem interficiat, et dimittet regimen legis et diriget per seipsum" (*Super Eth.* V, xv, #446 [p. 379, ll. 17–22]).

43. "Ambitus autem legis extendit se ad opera, quae sunt imperata per legem, et ad intentionem legis, quam consequi vult per huiusmodi opera quae imperat, quod est salus rei publicae" (*Super Eth.* V, xv, #447 [p. 380, ll. 12–15]).

44. See *Super Eth.* V, xv, #447 (p. 380, ll. 8–9).

45. ". . . iustitia potest considerari . . . secundum communem suam rationem, secundum quod abstrahit ab omnibus determinatis iustis, et sic epieikes erit iustum et in genere iusti . . ." (*Super Eth.* V, xv, #450 [p. 382, ll. 38–41]).

46. ". . . epieikia est in genere iustitiae, ut genus non dicatur commune per praedicationem, sed secundum ambitum. Ambitus autem iustitiae legalis, de qua loquimur, extendit se ad omnia quae ambit lex. Ambitus autem legis extendit se ad opera, quae sunt imperata per legem, et ad intentionem legis, quam consequi vult per huiusmodi opera quae imperat, quod est salus rei publicae" (*Super Eth.* V, xv, #447 [p. 380, ll. 8–15]).

47. See note 37.

48. "Quantum igitur ad ipsa opera imperata epieikia non est sub ambitu iustitiae legalis, sed tantum quantum ad intentionem, quia finem legis consequitur per aliquos actus, ubi actus imperati a lege non possunt consequi finem legis, et ideo supplet defectum legis et dirigit ipsam" (*Super Eth.* V, xv, #447 [p. 380, ll. 15–20]).

49. See *Super Eth.* V, xv, #447 (p. 380, ll. 29–31).

50. ". . . illud quod mensurat per simplicitatem naturae, quae est in ipso, oportet, quod habeat indeflexibilem rectitudinem, sed quod dirigit quntum ad esse, opertet, quod habeat rectitudinem, quae possit inflecti ad unumquodque particularium, ad quod applicari debet rectitudo universalis . . ." (*Super Eth.* V, xv, #450 [p. 383, ll. 32–37]).

51. "Cum igitur operabilia sint indeterminata, non sufficit eis mensura communis, nisi inveniatur alia mensura propria, per quam rectitudo communis applicetur ad singula, et huiusmodi est sententia [= *gnōmḗ*], quae variatur secundum omnes diversos casus, secundum quam mensurat epieikes" (*Super Eth.* V, xv, #450 [p. 383, ll. 32–37]).

52. "Alio modo est directivum aliquid alterius secundum esse, quod est ex applicatione formae ad materiam secundum omnes partes, et huiusmodi directivum regulatur supplendo ea quae desunt universali naturae, dum applicat ipsam ad omnia particularia; et hoc oportet necessario esse magis concretum quam id quod per ipsum dirigitur, et sic posterius . . . et hoc modo epieikia est directiva legalis iusti, quia ubi finem legalis non potest aliquis consequi per actum imperatum a lege, epieikia procedit alia via ad consequendum finem legis, et sic imitatur ipsam in intentione, non tamen in actione" (*Super Eth.* V, xv, #446 [p. 379, ll. 49–56, ll. 56–61]).

53. "Patris autem ad filium, domini ad servum et ipsius ad seipsum nulla ponitur lex, et ideo in illis modis non est vera iustitia, sed tantum per similitudinem dicta" (*Super Eth.* V, ii, #367 [p. 312, ll. 5–8]).

54. ". . . epieikia est universale per imitationem veri universalis" (*Super Eth.* V, xv, #446 [p. 379, ll. 67–68]).

55. "Unde oportet, quod [epieikia] sit magis particulatum quam lex, dum intentionem legis, scilicet salutem rei publicae, in singulos casus applicat,

quod lex propter sui universalitatem facere non potest" (*Super Eth.* V, xv, #446 [p. 379, ll. 61–64]). For the context of this sentence, see note 46.

56. Considerable orthographic variation marks the use of this word during this period. In Aquinas's works alone, the following spellings occur: *epieikeia, epiikia, epieicia, epiceia.* In what follows the editions cited are: M. F. Moos, ed., *S. Thomae Aquinatis Scriptum super Sententiis Magistri Petri Lombardi,* tomus III (Paris: P. Lethielleux, 1933). The page number appended in parenthesis after the text citation is that of this edition. Hereafter cited as *III Sent. Sancti Thomae Aquinatis Sententia libri Ethicorum (Sancti Thomae Aquinatis Opera Omnia,* tomus XLVII), vol. II (Rome: Santa Sabina, 1969). Hereafter cited as *SLE;* the page and line numbers appended to the citations in parentheses are those of this edition. The *Summa theologiae* (hereafter *ST*) will be cited according to the standard text of the Leonine edition.

57. See no. 28884e in Roberto Busa, S. J., et al., eds., *Index Thomisticus,* section II, vol. 8 (Stuttgart-Bad Canstatt: F. Fromman Verlag Guenther Holzboog, 1974), pp. 300–301.

58. In "Le Père Mandonnet OP., Historien de l'Église," in *Les hommes et les œuvres de l'Université. Cent ans de recherche scientifique à l'Université de Fribourg Suisse* (Fribourg: Éditions universitaires, 1991), Marie-Humbert Vicaire thus describes the preferred method of Pierre Mandonnet for studying Aquinas: "lire sur le thème choisi les exposés successifs avec les autres maîtres. Ce n'est plus une parole figée comme une orthodoxie qu'il [Mandonnet] atteint de la sorte, mais la pensée vivante du maître réagissant selon les circonstances, se corrigeant, s'approfondissant" (p. 13). For a basic chronology of Aquinas's works, see I. T. Eschmann, "A Catalogue of St. Thomas' Works," in E. Gilson, ed., *The Christian Philosophy of St. Thomas Aquinas* (New York, N.Y.: Random House, 1969), pp. 384f., 386ff., and 404f and, especially, Jean-Pierre Torrell, *Initiation à saint Thomas d'Aquin. Sa personne et son oeuvre* (Paris-Fribourg: Cerf-Éditions universitaires, 1993).

59. See Jean-Pierre Torrell, O. P., "Thomas D'Aquin," in *Dictionnaire de Spiritualite,* tome 15 (1991): 725. For further information on the composition and publication of this work, see J. A. Weisheipl, O. P., *Friar Thomas d'Aquino: His Life, Thought and Work* (Washington, D.C.: The Catholic University of America Press, 1983), pp. 67–76 and 358–9.

60. *III Sent.*, d. 23, q. 1, a. 3, q^{ula} 3 sol. (p. 707).
61. *III Sent.*, d. 23, q. 1, a. 3, q^{ula} 3 sol. (p. 707).
62. *III Sent.*, d. 33, q. 1, a. 1, q^{ula} 1 sol. (p. 1018f.).
63. ". . . tripliciter assignantur partes prudentiae et aliis virtutibus. Uno enim modo assigantur ei partes quasi integrales, cum scilicet partes virtutis alicujus ponuntur aliqua quae extinguntur ad virtutem, in quibus perfectio virtutis consistit. Et hae partes, proprie loquendo non nominant per se virtutes, sed conditiones unius virtutis integrantes ipsam. Alio modo, per modum partium subjectivarum. Et sic partes illae nominant quidem virtutes et ad invicem distinctas, sed non quidem a toto cujus partes assignantur, quia illud de eis praedicatur. Tertio modo, per modum totius potentialis, inquantum scilicet aliquae virtutes participant aliquid de modo qui principaliter et perfecte invenitur in aliquae virtute" (*III Sent.*, d. 33, q. 3, a. 1, q^{ula} 1 sol. [p. 1073]).

64. ". . . rectitudo . . . in communicationibus ad alterum" (*III Sent.*, d. 33, q. 1, a. 2, q^{ula} 3 sol. [p. 1022]). Compare this definition with that of Albert cited in note 24.

65. "Propria ergo materia justitiae sunt operationes exteriores secundum quod ordinantur ad alterum." Although other virtues have as a remote objective the moderation of exterior conduct *insofar as it flows from those interior passions* that form their proper objective, justice bears upon external conduct insofar as it engages one in interaction with another: "Et haec quidem adæquatio est quando ei redditur quod et quantum ei debetur; et haec adæquatio proprius modus justitiae est" (*III Sent.*, d. 33, q. 3, a. 4, q^{ula} 1 sol. [p. 1096]; see also q. 1, a. 3, q^{ula} 2 sol. [p. 1037]).

66. *III Sent.*, d. 33, q. 3, a. 4, q^{ula} 1 sol. (p. 1036f.).

67. "Unde ubicumque invenitur ista adæquatio complete, et justitia quae est virtus specialis et omnes virtutes in quibus salvatur, sunt partes subjectivae justitiae" (*III Sent.*, d. 33, q. 3, a. 4, q^{ula} 1 sol. [p. 1096]); ". . . distributiva et commutativa quae sunt partes subjectivae justitiae specialis" (*III Sent.*, d. 33, a. 4, q^{ula} 5 sol. [p. 1101]). On the subjective parts of justice other than these, see q^{ula} 3 sol. (p. 1099).

68. "Ubi autem ista adequatio non secundum totum salvatur, sed secundum aliquid, reducitur ad justitiam ut pars potentialis, aliquid de modo ejus participans" (*III Sent.*, d. 33, a. 4, q^{ula} 1 sol. [p. 1096]).

69. ". . . justitia quaedam est generalis, quaedam autem specialis. Specialis quidem est secundum quod habet materiam determinatam communicationes quae ad alteram sunt secundum rationem debiti; et sic ponitur hic una de quattuor cardinalibus virtutibus. Alio modo dicitur generalis . . . prout est idem quod omnis virtus ratione differens, prout actum virtutis quis ordinat ad bonum commune, secundum imperium legis . . . ." (*III Sent.*, d. 33, q. 1, a. 2, q^{ula} 3 ad 3 [p. 1023]). "Quaedam vero hoc circa quod est virtus, non principaliter, sed secundario ordinant ad alterum; sicut quando fortitudo actum exteriorem circa quem secundario est, ordinat ad alterum ut ad bonum gratiae, et sic induit quodammodo formam justitiae et sic omnis virtus potest reduci ad justitiam: unde justitia legalis dicitur idem quod omnis virtus . . . ." (*III Sent.*, q. 3, a. 4, q^{ula} 1 sol. [p. 1097]). "Legale autem et principale justum non dividunt justitiam; sed illud ex quo obligatio debiti et justitiae, quia vel est jus naturale vel positivum" (*III Sent.*, q. 3, a. 4, q^{ula} 5 sol. [p. 1101]).

70. Thomas never explicitly states that *epieikeia* is a virtue, except when he affirms that it is equivalent to that conformity to the intention of the lawgiver that lies at the heart of all virtues (see *III Sent.*, q. 3, a. 4, q^{ula} 5 ad 5 [p. 1102]).

71. ". . . epieikia, per quam homo, praetermissa lege, legislatoris intentionem sequitur" *III Sent.*, d. 37, a. 4c (p. 1247).

72. ". . .epieikia adjungitur legali justitiae et circa eadem est . . . ." (*III Sent.*, d. 33, q. 3, a. 3, q^{ula} 5 ad 5 [p. 1102]).

73. ". . . epieikia . . . differt a justitia legali in hoc quod non servat intentionem legis in his ad quae forma legis se non extendit" (*III Sent.*, d. 33, q. 3, a. 3, q^{ula} 5 sol. [p. 1101]). In this text, one finds the usual *intentio legis*

instead of Thomas's more usual *intentio legislatoris* (see note 73), and the former is opposed both to the latter (which *epieikeia* follows) and to the *forma legis*. In this usage Thomas differs from Albert, for whom the *intentio legis* is the end intended to be achieved by law. Thomas's usage seems to oppose it as the meaning of the legal text to its purely written form.

74. ". . . epieikia . . . non ex eodem dirigat [ex quo justitia legalis]; quia legalis dirigit ex scripto legis, sed epieikia ex intentione legislatoris . . ." (*III Sent.*, d. 33, q. 3, a. 3, q^{ula} 5 ad 5 [p. 1102]).

75. ". . . et sic clementia magis est circa actiones; et sic est pars justitiae epieikia, quia epieikes est diminitivus poenarum, ut dicit Philosophus. . ." (*III Sent.*, d. 33, q. 3, a. 2, q^{ula} 1 ad 2 [p. 1083]).

76. ". . . et quamvis [epieikeia] sit excellentior quam justitia legalis, non tamen potest dici cardinalis" (*III Sent.*, d. 33, q. 3, a. 3 q^{ula} 5 ad 5 [p. 1102]).

77. ". . . est in supplementum legalis justitiae, et etiam quodammodo praesupponit illam" (*III Sent.*, d. 33, q. 3, a. 3 q^{ula} 5 ad 5 [p. 1102]).

78. ". . . est idem omni virtuti aliqualiter, sicut et legalis justitia" (*III Sent.*, d. 33, q. 3, a. 3, q^{ula} 5 ad 5 [p. 1102]). For a later development of this point, see *Summa theologiae* II-II 58, 6.

79. ". . . ad *gnomen* petinet rectum judicium de illis in quibus lex deficit quae specialem habent difficultatem in quibus epieikia dirigit . . ." (*III Sent.*, d. 33, q. 3, a. 1, q^{ula} 3 ad 3 [p. 1076]).

80. *IV Sent.*, d. 15, q. 3, a. 1, q^{ula} 4 ad 3 (p. 708). The context is a discussion of the situations in which the ecclesiastical precept of fasting might not bind. Thomas, however, does not use the word *epieikeia* in this context.

81. On Thomas's procedure in commenting upon Aristotle, see M. D. Chenu, *Toward Understanding St. Thomas* (Chicago, Ill.: H. Regnery, 1964), pp. 206–8.

82. *ST* I-II.90.1c.

83. *ST* I-II.90.2c.

84. *ST* I-II.90.1c.

85. *ST* I-II.95.2c.

86. *ST* I-II.95.2c and 91.3.

87. *ST* II-II.120.1c; see also *SLE* V, 16 (p. 323, ll. 124ff.).

88. *SLE* V, 16, (p. 323, 11, 96ff.).

89. *SLE*, 11, (100ff.).

90. *SLE*, 11, (109ff.); see also *ST* II-II, 120, 1.

91. *SLE* V, 16 (p. 323, 11, 92ff.).

92. "Quia enim materia humanorum operabilium est indeterminata, inde est quod eorum regula, quae est lex, oportet quod sit indeterminata, quasi non semper eodem modo se habens" (*SLE* V, 16 [p. 324, ll. 169ff.]).

93. In the *Summa theologiae* II-II.120.1c, Thomas explicitly states that *epieikeia* is a virtue.

94. "Quem tamen in aliquibus casibus servare est contra æqualitatem justitiæ et contra commune bonum quod lex intendit. . . . In his ergo et similibus casibus malum est sequi legem positam; bonum autem est, prætermissis verbis legis, sequi id quod poscit justitiae ratio et communis utilitas" (*ST* II-II.120.1c).

95. ". . . justitiae proprium est inter alias virtutes ut ordinet hominem in his quae sunt ad alterum. Importat enim aequalitatem quandam, ut ipsum nomen demonstrat: dicuntur enim vulgariter ea quae adaequantur justari. Aequalitas autem ad alterum est" (*ST* II-II.57.1c).
96. *ST* II-II.120.1ad2.
97. *ST* II-II.120.1 ad3.
98. This is implied both by *epieikeia* being termed a virtue and by Thomas's discussion in II-II.120.2.
99. ". . . iste habitus qui dicitur epiikia est quaedam species justitiae et non est aliquis alius habitus a justitia legali, sicut et de eius objectum dictum est" (*SLE* V, 16 [p. 325, ll. 200ff.]).
100. This may be the force of the reportorial "dicit" with which he prefaces the statement cited in note 93. Moreover, as will be argued, legal justice taken in one sense could be viewed as encompassing *epieikeia*.
101. In the *Summa theologiae*, justice is termed "general" when it has for its concern the good of the community as opposed to goods of members of that community; see *ST* II-II, 58, 5c. This represents a difference from the meaning he assigns to it in the *Scriptum super Sententias* where its generality derives from the fact that it directs the external activities of all the other virtues.
102. ". . . quia scilicet per eam [justitia legalis] homo concordat legi ordinanti actus omnium virtutum in bonum commune" (*ST* II-II.58.5c).
103. *ST* II-II.58.6c.
104. *ST* II-II.120.2ad1.
105. *SLE* V, 16 (p. 323, 11, 62ff.).
106. *ST* II-II.120.2ad1.
107. *ST* II-II.48, art. unicus.
108. T. C. O'Brien, "Epieikeia," appendix 2 of *Virtues of Justice in the Human Community, Summa theologiae*, vol. 41 (New York, N.Y.: McGraw Hill, 1972), pp. 322f.
109. Origen, *Fragments* 18 on Luke 1:40; see Henri Crouzel, *Origène. Homélies sur Luc* (Paris, 1962), p. 51.
110. With the corresponding vices and subvirtues, this comprises questions 80 through 119 of *secunda secundae*.
111. ". . . epieikeia non adjungitur justitiae particulari, sed legali." In the context of this text, "adjungitur" is the equivalent of "is a potential part of."
112. ". . . epieikeia non est pars legalis justitiae, sed est pars justitiae communiter dictae, contra justitiam legalem divisa sicut excedens ipsam."
113. *ST* II-II.80, art. unicus.
114. *ST* II-II.120.2c.
115. ". . . statuta communia proponuntur secundum quod multitudini conveniunt. Et ideo legislator in eis statuendis attendit id quod communiter et in pluribus accidit. Si quid autem ex speciali causa in aliquo inveniatur quod observantiae statuti repugnet, non intendit talem legislator ad statuti observantiam obligare . . . Nam si causa sit evidens, per seipsum licite potest homo statuti observantiam praeterire . . . si non posset de facile recursus ad

superiorem haberi. Si vero causa sit dubia, debet aliquis ad superiorem recurrere qui habet potestatem in talibus dispensandi."

116. "Contingit autem multoties quod aliquid observari communi saluti est utile ut in pluribus, quod tamen in aliquibus casibus est maxime nocivum. Quia igitur legislator non potest omnes singulares casus intueri, proponit legem secundum ea quae in pluribus accidunt, ferens intentionem suam ad communem utilitatem. Unde si emergat casus in quo observatio talis legis sit damnosa communi saluti, non est observanda . . . Sed tamen hoc est considerandum, quod si observatio legis secundum verbum non habeat subitum periculum, cui oporteat statim occurri, non pertinet ad quemlibet ut interpretetur quid sit utile civitati et quid inutile; sed hoc solum pertinet ad principes, qui propter hujusmodi casus habent auctoritatem in legibus dispensandi. Si vero sit subitum periculum, non patiens tantam moram ut ad superiorem recurri possit, ipsa necessitas dispensationem habet annexam: quia necessitas non subditur legi."

117. *ST* I-II.92.1.

118. *ST* I-II.95.1ad1.

119. *ST* I-II.95.1c.

120. This does not preclude the possibility that recourse to the legitimate superior might be included as acts of other virtues, e.g., observance or obedience; it merely concludes that such recourse is not proper to *epieikeia* itself. For further information, see T. C. O'Brien, "Epieikeia," p. 323.

121. A study published by Albert Jonsen and Stephen Toulmin, (Berkeley, Calif.: University of California Press, 1988). See my review in *The Thomist* 54 (1990): 151–4.

122. William C. Spohn, S. J., "Notes on Moral Theology: 1992. Casuistry: An Alternative Approach," *Theological Studies* 54 (1993): 109–11.

123. Spohn, "Notes on Moral Theology," p. 95.

124. For example, Joseph J. Kotva, Jr., "An Appeal for a Christian Virtue Ethic," *Thought* 67 (1992): 158–79, argues along these lines.

125. *ST* I-II.73.1c.

126. See Jn 6:38.

127. See Mt 5:5.

Index

Addiction 6, 41n65
African American 1, 11, 13, 37
Anger 22, 23, 28, 47, 50, 51, 53–67,
  69–77, 81n44, 82nn53,54,
  83nn60,62, 84nn71,74,77,
  85nn88,89,90, 85nn93–5,98,
  87nn108,110, 88nn124–128,130,
  94, 95, 100, 101, 104, 113, 115,
  118–121, 133n121, 156
    causes of 55, 57, 63, 64, 67, 109
Appetite 14, 29, 30, 39n24, 42n72,
  51–55, 57–59, 61–63, 75, 79n21,
  88n130, 128n62, 184, 188, 193
Appetitus 39n24, 43n98, 79n16,
  80nn29,33,35, 113, 130nn83,88,
  131nn93,98
Apprehension 7, 9, 58
Aristotle 14, 41nn50,51,58, 44n99,
  45n120, 55, 56, 79n15, 82n53,
  104–105, 107, 111, 128nn61,63,
  129n68, 135, 140–148, 150, 155,
  156, 165nn16,17,20, 166nn26–28,
  171–177, 179–181, 183, 185, 187,
  195n2, 196nn21,23
Augustine 110, 114, 137, 162,
  165n7, 175
Authority 69, 76, 96, 97, 99, 100,
  111, 126n36, 192

Beatitude 135, 148, 151, 156, 161,
  163

Body 15, 18, 19, 24, 53, 62, 68, 75,
  92–96, 98, 102–104, 106–112, 114–
  116, 118–121, 124n14, 125nn24,
  32,33, 126nn34–36,38, 127n53,
  129nn73,75, 130nn78,86, 162
    in pain 20, 59, 96–98, 103
    in passion 90, 109
    of Christ, 116, 120, 121, 162
    unity with soul 16, 19, 79n21,
      94, 95, 106–110, 119, 120
    see also Embodiment

Character 3, 4, 6, 24, 52, 79n21, 90,
  94, 108, 109, 111, 115, 116,
  125n23, 134, 140–147, 164,
  166nn33–36,38,42–46, 170, 171,
  173–175, 188, 189, 192, 194
    defects of, 57, 72, 105, 157,
      184, 193
Charity 2, 7, 8, 55, 119, 134–137,
  148, 149, 151–164, 167n78
Children 5, 11, 25, 44n105, 55, 67,
  82n49, 89, 91, 92, 94–96, 98, 101,
  102, 105, 111, 122nn5,6, 123n11,
  124n17, 125nn22,26, 126n39, 148
Choice 4, 7, 10, 11, 13, 14, 16, 20,
  21, 25, 27, 28, 33, 39n17, 72, 94,
  106, 107, 110, 116, 156, 170
Christ 116, 117, 120, 121, 132n104,
  136, 151, 152, 156, 158–164, 181,
  194

Class 4, 23–28, 30–32, 37n2, 42nn76,77, 48, 179
  Working class 4, 23, 25–28, 32, 37, 42
Classism 27, 28, 56
Common good 8, 147, 176, 179, 180, 186–189, 191–193
Community 8–10, 12, 18, 47, 55–57, 59, 62, 84n80, 86n91, 118, 120, 121, 133n122, 137, 146, 152, 156–159, 177–180, 182, 185, 187–193, 204nn101,108
Conscience 37n3, 78nn3,5, 134
Consumerism 7, 136, 137, 139, 140, 163
Culture 5, 19, 26, 32, 33, 35, 89, 163
  Capitalist 5, 26
  Dominant 66, 77, 135, 136, 139
  Therapeutic, 6

Delight 54, 72, 118–120, 149, 153
Discipleship 156, 158, 160, 161, 164
Domination 26, 31, 37n2, 139, 140

Embodiment 89, 91, 100, 102, 103, 106, 108, 189
Emotion 14, 15, 27, 28, 41n50, 42n75, 126n41. *See also*, Feeling, Passion
Equality 60, 67, 75, 76, 87n101, 113, 176, 186, 191
Eucharist 120, 121, 153, 159–162, 168n98
Eudaimonia 142, 145, 147, 150, 151, 166n30
Excellence 55–58, 60–69, 71, 72, 76, 113, 118, 143–146, 161, 166n37, 173, 174, 183, 184

Feeling 13, 15, 39n21, 49, 60, 63, 66, 71, 77, 93, 103, 109, 114. *See also*, Emotion, Passion
Forgiveness 57, 85n86, 103, 116, 120, 121, 132n119, 133nn121,122, 135, 149, 153, 160, 164

Gnōmē 10, 184, 188, 203n79. *See also*, Justice, Prudence,
God 5, 7–9, 11, 22, 29, 30, 37nn4,5, 45n123, 55, 64, 82n49, 86n91, 90, 92, 93, 96, 97, 104, 106, 108, 115–117, 120, 121, 124n17, 125n28, 128n62, 132nn101,104, 134–140, 148–164, 166n49, 170, 176, 194, 194n1, 198n28
  as delight 7, 8, 18, 107, 119, 120, 135, 149
  as final end 7, 9, 16, 30, 90, 106, 107, 148, 150, 151, 154, 158
  as creator (source) 7, 90, 106, 115, 116, 152, 158
  attraction to 7, 9, 90, 129n70, 135, 150
  image of 29, 34
  Word of 97, 120
Grace 13, 134, 149, 151–155, 157, 160, 163, 164, 172, 189, 194

Habit 4–8, 10, 12–16, 18–29, 32, 33, 35, 36n1, 39nn17,23, 40n25, 41n57, 51, 90, 104, 107, 108, 116, 152
Habitus 39nn18,23, 40n25, 42nn62,63,67,73, 44nn103,112, 107, 108, 129n69, 153, 154, 161, 167n69, 172, 176, 177, 182, 187, 194, 198n28, 204n99
Hatred 54, 55, 59, 64, 67, 68, 73, 74, 100, 121

Hope 4, 26, 27, 31, 54–56, 58, 63, 72, 73, 82n54, 108, 112, 116, 117, 130n86, 131nn89,101, 132n102, 149, 155

Incarnation 159, 161
Individualism 43n92, 137, 139, 140, 163

Joy 8, 54, 113, 121, 136, 137, 140, 141, 148, 154, 156, 157, 164
Justice 11, 12, 40n43, 48, 50, 59, 60, 62, 69, 75, 76, 97, 113, 118, 119, 121, 133n121, 135, 136, 138–140, 152, 155, 160, 164, 167n78, 170–184, 186–192, 194, 195n5. *See also, Gnōmē*, Prudence

Liberation 1–4, 29, 31, 33–36, 37n2, 44n107, 77, 98, 105

Materialism 139

Natural Law 8, 12, 13, 29, 30, 38n7, 40n31, 195n1
Nature, Human 1, 3–5, 7–9, 12, 13, 18, 20–22, 25, 29–36, 37n4, 38nn7,8,9,14, 39nn18,23,24, 43n82, 44nn99,111,113, 45nn124,125, 65, 71, 81nn44,49, 86n92, 127n49, 138, 153, 160
   composite 109
   contrary to 1, 5, 16
   corporeal 52, 107, 113
   fallen 29, 30, 35, 152, 153
   (first) nature 1, 21, 29, 31, 32, 35, 36, 45n118, 46n125, 107, 108, 117
   perfection through virtue 13, 15, 16, 22, 30, 145, 160
   second nature 1, 3, 4, 25, 29, 31–36, 39, 42n67, 44n114, 46n125
   social 121, 137, 142

Oppressed 2, 4, 11, 13, 15, 26, 27, 29, 31–36, 36n1, 37n2, 39n17, 43n94, 48, 72, 75, 77, 78, 88n130
Oppression, 1–4, 7, 9, 11, 13, 17, 19, 23–29, 31–36, 36n1, 37n2, 39n17, 43n94, 45nn113,114, 139
Oppressor 1, 9, 25, 36n1, 72, 75, 88nn120,130
Original Sin 29, 30, 44n106, 45n118, 152, 153

Pain 10, 14, 15, 18–20, 43n75, 59, 60, 63, 69, 70, 72–74, 93, 94, 96–98, 101–103, 109–111, 113–116, 118, 119, 124n16, 125nn24,32,33, 126nn34–36,38, 127n53, 130n78, 132n111
Parents 6, 11, 34, 64, 88n91, 89, 92, 94–97, 100, 105, 108, 109, 111, 116–118, 120, 121, 124n14, 125n22, 132nn109,119, 133n121
Passion 7, 14, 15, 18, 19, 22, 51, 53–55, 57, 69, 71, 87n117, 90, 107–114, 116–119, 121, 129n71, 130nn77,87, 202n65. *See also*, Emotion, Feeling
Power 6, 9, 27, 32, 39n23, 40n25, 49, 51, 54, 55, 60–67, 77, 97, 99, 104, 106, 108–114, 116–118, 121, 128n60, 139, 144, 152, 153, 182
   coercive, 15, 63, 96, 104, 111, 113, 126nn36,42
   disparity of 96, 99, 104, 111, 113

Power—*continued*
  over (*See also* Dominate), 26, 43n92, 62, 79n13, 55, 82n54, 84n80, 69, 75, 77, 90, 97, 126n37, 139
  to heal, 9, 65–67, 90, 104
  to liberate, 77, 87n109, 105, 116–118
  to overcome, 9, 70, 105
Prudence 7–11, 13, 16, 17, 20, 21, 147, 184. *See also, Gnōmē*, Justice

Racism 27, 56, 64, 66, 69–71, 74, 75, 77, 85n89, 87n117
Rational 27, 42n72, 67, 96, 106, 114, 117, 184
Rationality 40n43, 87n101, 114, 115, 119
Reason 10, 11, 14–16, 29, 31, 38, 39n24, 40n35, 49, 58, 59, 62, 75, 86n92, 87n101, 185, 194, 198n28
  contrary to 14
  loss of 19, 20, 114
  particular 51, 52
  practical 8, 10, 20, 21, 184, 185,
  universal 58, 62, 88n130
Reconciliation 7, 116, 119–121, 153, 154, 160
Resistance 4, 6, 12, 15, 29, 31, 33, 41, 44, 53, 55, 74, 113, 121

Sacrament 160–162
Self 12, 29, 37n4, 45n114, 50–57, 63, 69, 72, 76, 78n8, 79n21, 87n109, 89, 93–95, 97, 99, 103–106, 108, 112–120, 130n87, 134, 136, 138–140, 142, 143, 147, 159, 162, 163, 165nn1,7–9
  -control 29, 139
  -deception 72, 137

  -destruction (annihilation) 69, 90, 95, 100–102, 105, 114, 116, 127n49, 153
  -determination 48
  divided 4, 26, 69, 100, 101, 119
  love of 57, 63, 67–69, 75, 83n60, 85n88, 139
  social 4, 121, 137, 138
  validate (heal) 26, 71, 80, 116, 121, 163
  -violation, 105
  -will 100, 101, 124n16
  -worth (-esteem, -regard) 35, 56, 61, 120, 126n42
Sexism 2, 27, 37n4, 45n123, 56, 66, 69–71, 74, 75, 77, 87n117
Sin 19, 21, 29, 30, 42nn65,70, 84n92, 151–154, 159, 160
  Original 44n106, 45n118, 152, 153
Slight 5, 55–59, 61, 63–66, 69, 71, 72, 75–77, 113
Sorrow 14, 20, 54–59, 61–63, 67, 69–71, 76, 82n54, 109–114, 116–119, 121, 131n88
Soul 18, 62, 92, 94, 95, 99, 101, 104, 110–112, 120, 123n13, 124nn16–21, 125n25, 128nn62,64, 145, 162
  disunity with body, 94, 112, 114, 115, 119
  unity with body 16, 79n21, 106–110, 119, 120, 128nn62,64
Spirit 10, 38, 94, 99, 106, 107, 110, 118, 119, 139, 151–154, 162
Suffering 25, 26, 31, 56, 89, 90, 102, 110, 117, 124n15
Synderesis 8, 29

Teleology 10

Vengeance 58, 59, 61–63, 72–75, 77, 81n48, 84n74, 121
Vice 2, 4, 6, 15–27, 29, 30, 33, 41n58, 45n115, 176
Violence 28, 65, 91, 93, 94, 98–100, 113, 118, 123n12, 124nn21,22, 126nn39,42, 127nn47,48, 139, 157
Virtue 2, 4–10, 9–11, 12–18, 20–22, 30, 32, 33, 37n6, 38n7, 39n24, 41n57, 45n113, 62, 64, 67, 77, 81n48, 86n91, 87n101, 90, 105, 116, 117, 129n71, 135, 140–149, 154, 156, 157, 163, 166nn33,37, 170–172, 175–177, 181–184, 186–189, 192–194, 195nn1,5, 198nn25,28,29, 202nn65,70, 203n93, 204n98, 205n124
Virtuous 7–10, 12–15, 20, 23, 33, 36, 37n5, 41nn54,55, 79n21, 90, 125n23, 134, 143–146, 156, 163, 170, 178, 180–182, 184, 187, 188, 192–194, 199n29

www.ingramcontent.com/pod-product-compliance
Lightning Source LLC
Chambersburg PA
CBHW020837160426
43192CB00007B/690